FRUIT

PRESENT AND FUTURE

VOLUME II

1973

THE ROYAL HORTICULTURAL SOCIETY
VINCENT SQUARE
LONDON SW1P 2PE

SBN 90062 957 6

Editor: Elspeth Napier
Honorary Assistant Editor: Brian Self
Editorial Committee: The R.H.S. Fruit Group

Made and printed in Great Britain by
William Clowes & Sons, Limited, London, Beccles and Colchester

Contents

Profile: J. M. S. Potter

F. R. TUBBS
formerly Director, East Malling Research Station

MR J. M. S. Potter, o.b.e., v.m.h., retired as Director of the National Fruit Trials, Faversham, Kent, in 1972. He is remembered with gratitude and respect by all skilled fruit gardeners, especially the older ones of a now passing generation, by outstanding experts at home and overseas, by the Royal Horticultural Society itself and particularly the members of the Fruit Group, by the commercial fruit industry as a whole and by all the advisers and scientists who play their part in its continuing success.

"*Si monumentum requiris circumspice!*" This tribute to Wren could equally well have been the epitome of tribute to Potter as he said farewell to his formal responsibility for an organization whose acres now house trials and collections of world-wide reputation and importance. These collections arose out of the success he achieved in his devoted study and comparison of the cultivars of hardy fruits. The account of the history of the Trials in this volume should be read thoughtfully by all who fear that the role of the individual in the constant battle for the continuing good of mankind is being overwhelmed, rather than supported, by the machinery of government. So with him, we respect all those with vision who, as officials or as fruit growers and fruit lovers, helped him lay the foundations for the Trials and supported their successful progress. We also respect those who assisted him in such later developments as the Plant Variety Rights Act and, in what was his special interest, the rapid and successful development of national (and later international) registers of the names, synonymy and identity of varieties of hardy fruits. Appropriately, the first of these, *The National Apple Register of the United Kingdom*, based as it is on the National Fruit Trials organization, was published last year by the Ministry of Agriculture. It is, of course, the direct fruit of his work and of his support of the labours of that excellent editor on his staff, Miss M. W. G. Smith, and it has received a world-wide welcome.

To see him as the man of achievement alone would be to lose sight of the man himself: generous of his work to a fault, utterly enthusiastic, and prepared to sacrifice much for the betterment and achievement of his ideal—the better knowledge and improvement of our fruit varieties. Honoured by the Queen with the o.b.e. for his services to the nation, and accorded by the Society that treasured mark of high regard, the v.m.h., may he and his ever-hospitable helpmate and support, Mrs Grace Potter, long continue in our midst, in happiness to lend their continuing support to fruit—the Fruit Group, the National Fruit Trials, and the fruit industry in all its aspects.

The Development of Apple Orchards in England

F. A. ROACH

formerly A.D.A.S. National Fruit Specialist

A STUDY of the development of apple production in this country as recorded in the literature since the early part of the sixteenth century shows a pattern much of which has been paralleled during more recent years.

The early developments in apple growing here were doubtless influenced by the Roman occupation. The Romans in their own country had developed the art of grafting and budding in order to perpetuate the special kinds of tree fruits which the Greeks had collected from various countries of the east. This knowledge of grafting was introduced to England and in most of the first books on fruit-growing printed here, considerable attention was given to the art of grafting and the raising of rootstocks (Fig. 2).

Up to the sixteenth century and for the greater part of the seventeenth century apple trees were normally grown on seedling rootstocks as standards. Fitzherbert writing in 1525 had recommended, "for all maner of appels, the crab tree stock is beste". Lawson in 1618, advised sowing the seeds of apples *in situ* where the orchard was to be, and the later selection of one of the seedlings to be grafted without transplanting. Austen, a leading nurseryman at Oxford, in 1651 wrote, "I account crab-trees better than sweeter Apple trees to graft on, because they are usually free from the Canker and will become a very large Tree and I conceive will last longer than stocks of sweeter Apple trees". Austen advised planting trees at 24 to 30 feet apart on ordinary soils and up to 32 to 48 feet apart on good soils where land was not limited. He suggested that where the trees were planted wide, "Much profit may be made of ground under and about the Trees. You may plant Gooseberries, Rasberries, Currants, Strawberries, Roses, Flowers and all sorts of Garden-stuffe, commodious as well for sale as for housekeeping." Such underplanting was still the practice on many holdings up till recent years and is still used by some growers to bring in early returns.

For many centuries the use of seedlings for establishing orchards was common practice in the west country where the fruit was mainly used for production of cider and this practice existed until fairly recent years. The seedlings raised were often left to grow without grafting and in this way many of the named cider cultivars, some still growing today, originated. It was largely because of the absence of water transport at a time when roads were often impassable, especially in the winter, that

2

TEXT FIGURE. Illustrations from Crescentius Basle (1548), reproduced by courtesy of the Trustees of the British Museum.

apple growers in the west country had to use their apples for local consumption, mostly as cider.

For many centuries, Kent had been important for the production of both fruits and vegetables sent to London markets and other parts of the country, making use of barge transport up the Thames and transport by sea to northern towns.

Apart from Kent the London markets were mainly supplied from market gardens on the outskirts of the urban areas, chiefly in Middlesex and it was here that the greatest changes in the commercial development of apple orchards took place.

Use of dwarf trees

The first reference to any form of dwarf apple tree in English literature was in the celebrated *Herbal* written by Gerard and first published in 1597. In this he mentioned "a dwarfe kind of sweet apple called the Paradise apple which beareth apples very timely without grafting". There was no mention here of this type of apple being used as a rootstock, but, in 1629, Parkinson described the Paradise apple as growing

"not much higher than a man may reach . . . the fruit is a faire yellow apple and reasonably great but very light and spongy or loose and of a bitterish sweet taste and nothing pleasant . . . it (the tree) will have many bunches or tuberous swellings in many places . . . the roots sendeth forth many shoots and suckers whereby it may be much increased.

" . . . being a dwarfe Tree whatsoever fruit shall be grafted on it, will keep the graft low, like unto itselfe and yet beare fruit reasonable well. And this is a pretty way to have Pippins, Pomewaters or any other sorte of Apple (as I have had myself and also seene with others) growing low that if any will, they may make a hedge row of these low fruits, planted in an Orchard all along by a walke side."

Although Parkinson mentioned the possibilities of growing dwarf apple trees in this way, it appears that it was left to the French to perfect this method of culture which was well established in France in the seventeenth century and probably earlier than this. As so often happened at this time, new horticultural techniques were introduced by monks and priests many of whom were keen horticulturists. One such was Le Gendre, Curé of Henoville whose book, *The Manner of Ordering Fruit Trees*, was translated into English by John Evelyn, the famous diarist, and published in England in 1660. Le Gendre gave a full account of dwarf tree growing including methods of producing apples and pears in this way.

"The best Plant to graffe such apple trees upon as you would have to grow against a wall, in Pallisades or Hedges, and such as you desire to keep low for dwarf trees is that of the Paradise (a kind of Codling) apple tree, which grows but little into wood, bears quickly and much fruit. These kindes of plants are brought up of spriggs, or cuttings put into the ground. The Sweeting (Doulcain) is another kind of apple tree, which comes very near to that of the Paradise apple, and which likewise is grown from a sprigge; but the Plant is not too good for this purpose because it grows too much into wood and cannot be kept low, as a dwarf or shrub.

Free-stocks (such as are raised from the Kernels of Pears and Apples) are not so proper for their use, because they, by nature, shoot up too fast: and if you cut off any branch to stop their growth and keep them low, they put forth divers others with more force and so till they arrive at their full growth to produce nothing but wood and very little fruit."

Le Gendre suggested planting apples on Paradise stocks 9 feet apart on a square plant or 6 feet apart in a single row, compared with 18 to 24 feet apart for trees on seedling rootstocks. It seems from these planting distances and the description of the Paradise apple given by Parkinson and Le Gendre, that this rootstock was very similar to our own M.9 and that the Doulcain of Le Gendre was the Doucin, or M.2. As years passed, however, there was much confusion as to the identity of the different vegetatively propagated rootstocks and the term Paradise was applied by nurserymen to a number of stocks of very varying vigour. It was left to workers at East Malling many years later to sort out many of the rootstocks in use in the early days of the present century and the work of Hatton and others has benefited fruit-growers throughout the world.

However it becomes obvious from the literature in the seventeenth century, that there was considerable interest in this new form of growing apples on small trees. One enthusiast, J. Worlidge, writing in 1691 of cider and other apples said:

"To dispose of the trees to your best advantage . . . plant your tall Standard-Trees in such places where you intend to make use of the land for Grazing, that they may be above the reach of Cattel. But in such places where you can dispense with the Cattel and use the Land only for the Sythe or Spade, there it is best to plant dwarf or low grafted Trees for several Reasons—

1. You may plant more of them on the like quantity of Land, because the Shadow of the one Tree doth not reach the ground of the other, as that of the tall Trees doth.

2. The low Trees sooner attain to be Fruit-bearing Trees, and grow fairer than the tall; the Sap in them wasting in its long passage, which in the shorter Trees expends itself soon in the Branches.

3. The lower and broad spreading Tree is the greater bearer, by

reason the blossoms in the Spring are not so obvious to the bitter blasts, nor the Fruit in the Autumn to the fierce and destructive Winds.

4. Fruits are more easily gathered from a low than a tall Tree, beating or shaking down Fruit from such Trees, being to be rejected by all.

5. Any Fruit on a low well-spread Tree, is better and fairer than that on a tall Tree, by the same reason that the Tree is fairer, that is, that the Sap is not so much wasted in the low and humble Tree, as in the tall and lofty.

This way of planting dwarf-Trees is but lately in use, deriving its original from France. Let not any think it a disparagement to our Nation, to imitate the excellencies of any other, nor think that our Forefathers were so wise, as to know all things; every Race of Mankind, and every Age endeavouring to improve the Actions of the former, do assuredly discover something better than what was before or at least bring into practice that which before they concealed."

The argument put forward by Worlidge in favour of dwarf trees shows remarkable similarity with views expressed of recent years. The point made that shading of one tree by another was avoided shows that Worlidge appreciated the need for full exposure to sunlight as had the Romans about 2,000 years ago. In developing the use of the Quincunx system for planting their apple orchards Roman fruit-growers, including Virgil, took care to plant the trees sufficiently far apart to avoid their shading each other excessively. It is only now that this need for good exposure to light is being appreciated by some growers planting intensive orchards.

Commercial use of intensive planting

The first English growers to make use of the new rootstocks and ideas introduced from France in the seventeenth century, were the owners of market gardens on the outskirts of London. They would obviously be interested in any method of production which would enable them to grow maximum crops on the rather limited areas of land they had available rather in the same way that the Dutch fruit-growers in the postwar plantings obtained maximum output by using closely planted spindlebushes.

Professor Bradley, writing in 1726, said:

"For dwarf apples I believe every one will allow that those grafted upon Paradise stocks are best. I mean for keeping in a small compass and bearing abundance of Fruit with very little Pruning. Paradise stocks are raised by cutting or suckers. They are brought originally from France but now they are to be met with in almost every nursery about London.

I have had the opportunity of observing this year the gardens of Messrs Warners at Rotherhith. These Gentlemen, who are Brothers and near neighbours, have gardens curiously designed for the propagating of Fruit, and each of them excellently skill'd in the manner of Pruning, and in that Philosophy which is necessary to bring Trees to good bearing. Could everyone have the Liberty of seeing their gardens, in my opinion, they could not have a better Example for the management of Dwarf-trees of Apples and Pears in England. One of these Gentlemen, in this bad year, in one part of his Garden, not much more than half an acre, has more Fruit than any Garden, among the many I have seen, can boast of in three acres, yet we may see at the same time a promising Prospect of Blossoms for the Furniture of next Summer."

Throughout the eighteenth and nineteenth centuries writers on fruitgrowing gave details of the management of dwarf apple trees worked on Paradise rootstocks, generally recommending a planting distance of 12 feet. But although dwarf trees continued to be used for gardens and in market gardens, crab apple or cider apple seedlings were still mainly used for the standard trees generally planted for apple production on a farm scale. The practice did however develop of using trees on dwarfing, or other vigour controlling, vegetatively propagated rootstocks, as temporary filler trees between the standard trees of dessert and cooking apples.

From time to time enthusiasts have advocated very intensively planted apple orchards, with trees spaced as closely as 3 feet apart in rows 6 feet apart. It is perhaps not without significance that in the last century two protagonists for such orchards were also nurserymen selling trees: Rivers in the earlier and Bunyard in the latter part of the century. It is also of interest to note that following any trend to over-intensification apple growers usually seem to have discovered the problems caused by excessive growth and shading and the trend has then usually been reversed and wider planting has been advocated. Let us hope that today, with our greater knowledge and facilities, our apple growers will be able to avoid some of the pitfalls of the past. Perhaps we can take to heart the five points put forward by Worlidge nearly 300 years ago.

The National Fruit Trials (1922–1972): A Brief History*

AFTER the first world war commercial fruit growing was in rather a disorganized state with orchards consisting of a mixture of cultivars, some good, some bad, some indifferent. The standard cultivars of the time had not really been systematically studied, and new ones were being introduced in a haphazard manner so that growers were finding their orchards uneconomic.

Some of the major fruit growers, and others concerned with the fruit industry, decided that the cultivar situation must be rationalized so that growers could be given sound, unbiased advice and that only the best cultivars, giving a supply of fruit spread over the whole season, would be grown. For this, a central testing organization was essential, where new cultivars could be grown and studied on a sufficiently large scale, together with well-known standard ones, and the results made available to growers who would thus, by waiting a few years, be able to plant new cultivars of known performance instead of adopting the wasteful method of trying them out for themselves.

So in October 1922, after a year or two of exploratory talks, the Ministry of Agriculture and the Royal Horticultural Society took the first step towards establishing the Commercial Fruit Trials, believed to be the first in the world, when the newly formed committee met in London to discuss the setting up of the trials at the Royal Horticultural Society's Garden at Wisley. The members of this first committee (5 of whom were nominated by the Ministry and 5 by the Society with a chairman mutually agreed) were: Chairman Dr W. Bateson FRS, Secretary Mr F. J. Chittenden; Professor B. T. P. Barker, Mr E. A. Bunyard, Mr W. Cuthbertson, Mr (later Sir) John Fryer, Mr G. W. Leak, Mr (later Sir) William Lobjoit, Mr C. G. A. Nix, Mr C. G. Smith and Dr H. V. Taylor.

The present committee, under the chairmanship of Mr Edward Vinson, is representative of the Agricultural Research Council, the Department of Agriculture for Scotland, the Horticultural Advisory Council, the Horticultural Trades Association, the National Farmers' Union (representing growers), the Northern Ireland Horticultural Association, the Northern Ireland Ministry of Agriculture, the Royal Horticultural Society, the wholesale industry and the Agricultural Development and Advisory Service. Throughout its 50 years, the National Fruit Trials has been able to call on the interest and help of the most knowledgeable men in the fruit world, including Sir Daniel Hall,

* Reproduced by permission of the Ministry of Agriculture, from a booklet of the same title, published in 1972.

Sir Thomas Neame, Sir Ronald Hatton, Dr F. R. Tubbs, Mr M. B. Crane, Mr Spencer Mount, Mr Paget Norbury and many others. During the whole of this period there were only two directors, Mr A. N. Rawes and Mr J. M. S. Potter, who took over from him in 1936 and was responsible for the transfer to Brogdale. He in turn was succeeded by Mr P. H. Harding in 1972.

Aims

From the first it was envisaged that all the hardy fruits commonly grown out of doors in Britain would be tested at Wisley, the more promising to be sent to sub-stations in all the main fruit-growing areas. They were to be merit trials only; trials of spraying, pruning, soil, manuring, rootstocks and other aspects of fruit culture were not envisaged, though at a later date a frost protection trial was set up for a few years, and a trial of dwarfing rootstocks for cherries was planted in 1968. Besides testing and reporting on new cultivars, one of the original objects of the scheme was to compare trial cultivars with "known varieties, so that accurate descriptions may be made, synonyms determined and the nomenclature of fruits made more exact". For this, collections of fruits were to be grown as a living reference library and the importance of maintaining comprehensive collections, quite apart from their application to the trials, was early recognized and reiterated many times through the years.

Organization

The trials were originally the joint responsibility of the Ministry of Agriculture and the Royal Horticultural Society, the Society providing the land, collections, buildings, labour and expertise, and the Ministry a grant which diminished as the trials began to show some financial return and ceased in 1943. The owners of cultivars accepted for trial have never been asked to contribute towards the cost; the Society always refused to charge, maintaining that it was desirable to encourage all having promising cultivars to enter them, and that in any case no charge commensurate with the cost of testing could be levied. Another clause of the original scheme which has always been honoured is the undertaking that no trees, buds or grafts of a cultivar submitted for trial will be allowed to leave the central station or sub-stations without the permission of the owner.

In the very early years the main source of trial cultivars was the Society's Fruit and Vegetable Committee which recommended for trial the best of the cultivars submitted to them at the fortnightly shows, mainly by amateurs and nurserymen. The top fruit industry, in contrast to the soft fruit industry, owes a great deal to the amateur and the nurseryman. Our most widely planted apple, 'Cox's Orange Pippin', and the best-known cooker, 'Bramley's Seedling', were raised by amateurs, and the famous pear 'Conference' was raised by the nurseryman Francis Rivers. Nowadays, the National Fruit Trials receives very few top fruit cultivars from amateurs or nurserymen. By far the largest number come, as soft fruits have long done, from plant breeders at East Malling Research Station, the John Innes Institute, Long Ashton Research Station, the Scottish Horticultural Research Institute and research stations in many foreign countries, including Belgium, Canada, Denmark, France, Germany, Italy, Japan, the Netherlands, New Zealand, Sweden, Switzerland, the U.S.A. and the U.S.S.R.

Change and resettlement

With the inevitable disruptions caused by the second world war, the Fruit Trials continued along the path laid down for them until, in 1946, after a review of existing and future research in fruit by the Agricultural Research Council, the Trials were put on a different footing, being brought under the umbrella of the National Agricultural Advisory Service, then being set up. As Wisley could provide no more land for expansion, a search started for a more suitable home in a fruit-growing area. Apart from its size limitations, the site at Wisley was bedevilled by late spring frosts which ruined the crop and therefore the records two seasons out of three. It was also unsuitable for cherries, which had to be grown at Borden in Kent. After a long search Brogdale Farm just south of Faversham was acquired and the move from Wisley started in 1952.

When Brogdale Farm was taken over the land had to be thoroughly prepared before planting started in 1953. Over the years a packhouse and cold store, grain driers and silage pits were built, and a brick-built barn was transformed by stages into a pleasant office block with library and conference room. The cattle yard is filled with bullocks for fattening through the winter to provide dung, and on the land where the soil is not deep enough for fruit-growing, forage crops are grown. By 1960 the transfer from Wisley, involving the repropagation of thousands of trees, was complete and the work of the trials took on more or less its present familiar pattern of cycles of screening trials with a few special trials of rootstocks and clones. To begin with, main trials, consisting of the best from the screening trials, were planted, but were later found to be unnecessary and discontinued.

The National Fruit Trials is responsible for co-ordinating extended trials of the more promising cultivars ranging from strawberries to apples. When these extended trials started in 1925, they were established mainly at county agricultural institutes throughout the country from Durham to Cornwall. Nowadays they are confined to the Ministry's Experimental Horticulture Stations at Efford (Hampshire), Luddington (Warwickshire), Rosewarne (Cornwall) and Stockbridge House (Yorkshire).

Wider range of work

Side by side with the trials other work goes on. The importance of pollen compatibility in tree fruits is recognized, and cross and self compatibility tests of promising cultivars of apples, pears and plums are carried out in controlled conditions. In conjunction with this, comprehensive records of the flowering periods of all fruits are taken and the effects of temperature on the flowering dates of apples are also being studied. The systematic botany department is working on a system of classification for the various fruits grown on the station. This involves the careful description and detailed comparative measurement of plants and fruit and the segregation of the characters, not only vegetative but also chemical, into groups so that the various cultivars can be identified.

The National Fruit Trials is national registration authority for all hardy fruits, and international registration authority for apples. The department dealing with this is charged with rationalizing nomenclature and producing national registers of each fruit and an international register for apples. Mr J. M. S. Potter, Director from 1936 to 1972, is chairman of an international working committee which controls this work.

On the station is an official Meteorological Office weather station, where all the usual weather records are kept and which can provide information to local growers.

The station has basic photographic equipment and several members of staff trained in its use, while the MAFF Photographic Branch also provides professional help. The colour slide library, covering all fruits, consists at present of more than 4,000 slides. Colour slides are taken of most trial cultivars, the more promising being photographed in some detail. Fruits in the national apple and plum collections are photographed in colour and black-and-white and photography is also used as a quick method of recording. The slides are also used to illustrate lectures and for research work.

Collections

For both registration and systematic botany, the large collections, the living "reference libraries" which the original terms of reference insisted on, are indispensable. They also serve as gene banks for plant breeders and as a workshop for plant pathologists and entomologists. They are regularly inspected to see whether, with new methods of cultivation, some of the older cultivars may be worthy of trial. Thus the apples 'Ashmead's Kernel' and 'Saint Edmund's Pippin', and the pears 'Triomphe de Vienne' and 'Beurré Alexandre Lucas', to mention only a few, have been included in trials. The importance of virus-free or virus-tested material is recognized and trees of all EMLA clones are established to determine whether the treatment has induced any variation or mutation.

Besides the more usual hardy fruits, collections of peaches and nectarines and grape vines were planted to see if any were suitable for growing in the open in this country, but they all exemplify one of the most important functions of the National Fruit Trials—to advise the grower what NOT to plant. After years of observation, it was evident that they would never flourish in the conditions provided at Brogdale and the peaches and nectarines were grubbed out, the vines being retained for the time being.

Working together

Close co-operation with the research stations has long been a feature of the trials, and also, since the first raspberries were sent for canning tests to Chipping Campden in 1929, with various research organizations concerned with processing and storage. Since the Nuclear Stock Association and the Plant Variety Rights Office were set up they have been closely associated with the National Fruit Trials; soft fruit cultivars are recommended to the Nuclear Stock Association on their performance in the trials, and apples, pears, plums and cherries to the Nuclear Stock Association (Tree Fruits). A Plant Variety Rights officer is permanently stationed at Brogdale to examine all fruits submitted for rights to establish distinctness, stability and uniformity. Cultivars from the state-aided research stations undergo a merit trial first, but those coming from elsewhere go through the Plant Variety Rights distinctness test only.

Making a name for ourselves

Although breeding was not originally envisaged, and in fact never seems to have been discussed, some apple and pear crosses were made casually at Wisley in about 1947 and the trees retained as a matter of interest. By a quirk of nature, which seems to favour the production of good cultivars by chance, at least one apple, 'Pixie', and one pear, 'Onward', have proved good enough to name and have been given the Award of Merit by the Royal Horticultural Society as cultivars for the private garden. So the National Fruit Trials, while not pretending to be a fruit-breeding station, has made a tangible contribution to the industry, as well as its wider and more considerable achievements in the field of testing and reporting.

Some figures

Since planting started in 1923, hundreds of cultivars have gone through the trials, but the number that have become established commercially as a result of the trials is very small indeed, on an average only about 3%, a fact that underlines how necessary the trials are. The following table shows the approximate total number of cultivars that have undergone trial since 1923, the number at present on trial and the number at present in the collections, but excluding the nursery.

| Fruit | On trial | | In collections (1972) |
	Total since 1923	At present (1972)	
Apple	447	177 (10 trials)	1900
Cherry	91	62 (6 trials)	250
Pear	79	20 (2 trials)	470
Plum and Damson	94	30 (2 trials)	400
Quince	—	—	8
Black and Hybrid Berry	4	—	30
Currant, Black	100	22 (2 trials)	80
Red, White and Pink	14	—	120
Elderberry	—	—	3
Gooseberry	65	—	220
Hazelnut	—	—	40
Raspberry	106	12 (1 trial)	—
Strawberry	149	24 (2 trials)	—
Vine	—	—	30

Publications

The National Fruit Trials publishes reports on the individual trials as each is completed. Articles on a variety of fruit topics have appeared in Experimental Horticulture, the Progress Report of the Experimental Husbandry Farms and Experimental Horticulture Stations, Agriculture and a number of non-Ministry publications. The first book, the *National Apple Register of the United Kingdom*, the result of 15 years' work at Wisley and Brogdale, appeared in January 1972.

SELECT LIST OF PUBLICATIONS (1951–1972)

POTTER, J. M. S. 1951. Report of the National Fruit Trials 1921–1950. *J. Roy. hort. Soc.*, Vol. 76, pp. 240–252, 280–293.
POTTER, J. M. S. 1960. The National Fruit Trials. *J. Roy. hort. Soc.*, Vol. 85, pp. 174–184.
POTTER, J. M. S. 1963. The National Fruit Trials. (Amos Memorial Lecture). *Rep. E. Malling Res. Stn 1962 (1963)*, pp. 40–50.
SMITH, MURIEL W. G. 1963. The nomenclature and registration of fruit varieties. *Fruit var. hort. Dig.*, Vol. 18, pp. 34–36.
GOODING, H. J. 1966. The National Apple Collection: A classification problem. *Expl Hort.*, Vol. 15, pp. 38–46.
POTTER, J. M. S. 1970. *The National Fruit Trials: an Introduction* (revised ed.), Min. Agric. Fish. Food, Faversham.
POTTER, J. M. S. 1970. The National Fruit Trials and the amateur fruit grower. *J. Roy. hort. Soc.*, Vol. 95, pp. 116–117, 203–214.
POTTER, J. M.S. 1971. *Report on the fourth apple cultivar screening trial.* Min. Agric., Lond.
SMITH, MURIEL W. G. 1971. *National Apple Register of the United Kingdom.* Min. Agric., London, 652 pp.
SMITH, MURIEL W. G. 1972. The registration of fruit cultivars. *Expl Hort.*, Vol. 23 (in press).

Fruit Registration

MURIEL W. G. SMITH

National Fruit Trials, Faversham

ALL crops need a stable system of nomenclature and registers are essential to pinpoint the correct name of each cultivar, particularly with crops such as fruit where most species comprise large numbers of cultivars. The apple is our most important fruit crop, and in spite of several earlier attempts to rationalize its nomenclature, it remained in a somewhat confused state, until early in 1972, after many years of work, the Ministry of Agriculture, Fisheries and Food published the *National Apple Register of the United Kingdom*. This book contains entries for 6,000 distinct cultivars which together run to 22,000 names; such an abundance of names obviously led to confusion in the past. Probably a majority of the cultivars recorded have one name and no more, which points to an overplus of synonyms for the remainder. A similar problem arises with pears and the other top fruits which, being long-lived and cosmopolitan, are very prone to gather to themselves synonyms, translations, mis-spellings and other variations of their names.

Fruit is usually sold under its cultivar name, so it is important that the name should be correct, both from the point of view of the housewife buying a few pounds of apples and the grower buying trees. The main commercial cultivars, however many other names they may have, are on the whole known by only one, or a recognizable variant of it, but this may not be the case with many less well known cultivars and those which are of interest and importance historically and for breeding. Here we see cultivars with several names in common use or several cultivars with the same name, so here also we see the absolute necessity of knowing exactly what cultivar is under discussion. Has 'Dumelow's Seedling' some useful character that the breeder would like to pass on? Then it is best that he uses the name 'Dumelow's Seedling' and not 'Wellington', a synonym by which it is probably better known, as he might find himself using another 'Wellington', a present-day American cultivar, and quite distinct from our favourite old mincemeat apple. Or perhaps 'Geheimrat Doktor Oldenburg' and 'Duchess of Oldenburg' each have some desirable quality not shared by the other. If the abbreviated name 'Oldenburg' is used, as it is in Germany for 'Geheimrat Doktor Oldenburg', confusion would result, so the full name in each case must be used.

This also underlines the desirability of giving new cultivars names that will not be confused with any already in existence, or even those which have apparently disappeared. However, in this particular case those who named 'Geheimrat Doktor Oldenburg' can scarcely be blamed, as in Germany the cultivar we call 'Duchess of Oldenburg' is known by the name 'Charlamowsky', and the name used in Russia, its country of origin, is 'Borovinka', while the French call it 'Borovitsky'. Whether it would ever be possible to bring about the worldwide adoption of the same name for a cultivar of this sort is very doubtful—the habit of more than a century is not so easily broken—but for new cultivars the outlook for international co-operation seems brighter. Someone consulting the apple register will find that all these names refer to the same cultivar and when the international register is published, the different names will be identified by country. The entry in the National Apple Register is under 'Duchess of Oldenburg' and this itself posed a problem that is bound to occur when compiling a national register which includes foreign cultivars—whether to record it under the name used in the country of origin or the familiar one of the country whose register is being produced. With an international register it goes without saying that the former would be used.

Similarity in names is an obvious cause of confusion, and the habit of raisers, and even introducers, of prefixing a cultivar name with their own, though understandable, is a source of exasperation and leads to indexing problems. The natural tendency is to shorten names, generally by using the first word only—'Cox' instead of 'Cox's Orange Pippin', 'Golden' instead of 'Golden Delicious'. 'Laxton' generally means 'Laxton's Superb' when buying apples at the greengrocer's, but it could stand for one of a dozen different cultivars of Laxton's raising when possible parents are under consideration. 'Stark' ought to mean the old Ohio apple of that name, but it could also mean almost anything if divorced from the distinguishing element of the name, as the American nurseryman Stark has introduced, or acquired the rights of, hundreds of cultivars of all kinds of fruits and has prefixed his name to many of them. This points to the importance of using the full names of existing cultivars and of choosing one-word names for future ones, as recommended in the International Code of Nomenclature for Cultivated Plants.

The registration of new cultivar names is the best means of ensuring that no name is shared by more than one cultivar and that no cultivar has more than one name. This should be possible with new introductions although existing names cannot be changed, but before the uniqueness of a given name can be determined, one must know what has gone before. Registers of existing cultivars, and even some defunct ones, must therefore be compiled and this involves discovering and clarifying, by reference to both growing plants and written information, the correct names of all the known cultivars of the various hardy fruits and publishing these names, backed by references, information on their history and descriptions of the cultivars concerned. These registers are historical documents, foundations on which new information can be built, and in order to build firm foundations to ensure order in the future and to clarify the present, much historical research has to be done. The International Society for Horticultural Science is responsible for organizing horticultural registration and for such wide-ranging crops as apples, pears, plums and other hardy fruits it was felt that it was too much to expect one individual to be responsible for compiling an international register unaided. They therefore decided that national registers should first be produced and then collated to form international registers. These should help us to avoid the sort of complications mentioned earlier in the case of 'Duchess of Oldenburg'.

When in 1953 the National Fruit Trials was asked to undertake registration of fruit crops for the United Kingdom, we had no real precedent to work from. We had already done something similar for our own collections in an effort to identify the cultivars correctly, but without any idea of a wider use. A national register was a much larger exercise and the best method had to be worked out. After some false starts, a method for the apple register very like the present one was evolved, a section of the register produced in draft and examined by a working group of ISHS members from a dozen different countries, who made some further recommendations. These were incorporated and the result accepted as the method for drawing up all the national registers of apples, thus making their ultimate amalgamation into the international apple register less complicated. It is expected that registers for other fruits will follow much the same lines with variations in the descriptions to take account of characters of particular importance to the fruit concerned.

The 6,000 cultivars in the register are all known to have been grown in the United Kingdom between 1853 and the present day and except for the latest introductions, to have had their names at least recorded in the literature, generally with some historical details and something in the way of a description. A complete entry in the register consists of the accepted name of the cultivar, which is nearly always that under which it was first described or published*; a list of synonyms and other forms of the name; a list of its references; a note on its status (whether, and where, being grown at present or when it was last known to be growing); parentage (though this is rarely known for the older cultivars) and other information about its provenance (name of raiser, place of raising, etc.); all relevant dates (raising, first fruit, introduction); particulars of trials and awards, and a description.

The National Fruit Trials collection of about 1,540 named apple cultivars provided material for many of these descriptions, but if no living fruit is available, the description must be compiled from the published descriptions available to us. The register is not a pomology,

---

* From 1959, the name, to be valid, must have been published with a description or reference to a previously published description, but for anything published prior to 1959 this is not necessary.

and the descriptions have been kept to the minimum—size, shape, colour and texture of skin and flesh, flavour and season. Words being somewhat inadequate, apples should never be identified from written descriptions alone, and the descriptions in the register are certainly not meant for that purpose, but merely to give the inquirer a general idea of the fruit.

To get all this information our sources are various. With cultivars sent to us for trial or observation, we use the information supplied by the senders, but for the rest we start by referring to all the British pomological literature, journals, catalogues, etc. published since 1853 available to us, working systematically through each one. Each name is recorded on a separate slip of paper together with all the relevant facts from each source consulted. We then further check all the slips by consulting the older British books dating back beyond 1853 and a number of foreign pomologies for further information about the many foreign cultivars grown in this country and also our native ones as grown abroad. Foreign pomologies and older books which are used solely for checking cultivars which figure in the post-1853 literature, are of course rich sources of synonyms and variants on the original name.

For the national apple register we used about fifty books, each one of which had to be consulted for every entry although many names might appear in only one or two of them. Consultation of the older books or the foreign ones might bring to light a distinct cultivar with a name the same as, or very similar to, that of a candidate for registration and the two would have to be distinguished. When all possible information has been recorded, the slips of paper have to be carefully studied for discrepancies in that information taken from the various sources. These can arise at every step of the way, from the spelling of the name to the final item in the fruit description. Here there is plenty of scope for confusion and disagreement, particularly in descriptions which sometimes vary considerably from author to author. Even if they do not contradict one another, it is sometimes difficult to compare them as authors do not necessarily describe the same features. One will describe the skin in great detail but forget to mention the flavour, another will describe the shape but not the flesh, and sometimes even the season is left out, so that although a composite picture can be drawn up, one has to take it on trust that all the authors have the same cultivar in mind and not several different ones of the same name.

Published descriptions also suffer from the comparative vagueness of the terminology. Qualitative terms are used without a standard or, which is even more confusing, the same standard for two different terms or vice versa. We found this particularly in the matter of fruit size. When the actual measurements are given it does not matter what term is used (small, medium, large) as we have provided our own standards, but some authors (and Hogg comes to mind) often give the size in both words and actual measurements but with no consistency in the application of a given word to a given measurement, so that when the size is only described with no measurements given, one is at a loss to know whether "medium" means, say, 3, 2¾, 2½ or 2 inches (the extremes of Hogg's use of the term "medium" but also described by him as "large" and "small"). The terms for the parts of the fruit can vary and it has happened that apex and base have been confused. With plums this is understandable from their shape, and to some extent with apples, which can stand on either end, but it is an unusual pear that can stand on its stalk end, so should pears be regarded as having a base and apex? Hogg has certainly referred to the stalk end as the apex, which is sensible, even though with apples he uses the terms the other way round. Perhaps it is best to refer to stalk and calyx ends for all fruits.

Other difficulties arise when certain characters are just not mentioned. If, for instance, no mention is made of russet, it could well be that it has just been forgotten, or it might mean that there is no russet to mention. In the register, in order to save space, we have on the whole not mentioned characters that are absent, though as a general rule, in a pomology, we would deprecate this practice. Flavour is a difficult character to describe, apart from sweet and acid, but a few terms have come to be accepted over the years as indicative of high quality, such as "rich" and "aromatic". But one thing we do not set out to do is to pass judgment on the quality of a fruit, though in the pomologies consulted this has generally been done. Sometimes, in fact, the only indication for flavour is an adjective indicating the opinion of the author such as "pleasant", "excellent", which does not give the sort of information we need to draw up our descriptions; these aim to be strictly factual.

Some of the causes of disagreement between published accounts can be traced to the language difficulty or to faulty transcription from old pomologies and this is why we like to go back to original sources where possible. Though mistakes in the names themselves may be the result of simple misreading of handwritten labels, they can also be due to wild guesses on the part of someone unfamiliar with the language. One may find two names looking very much alike, or having some element in common, and not knowing the language someone jumps to the conclusion that they mean the same thing and thus another false synonym is perpetuated. An extreme example of this is 'Grimes Golden' given as a synonym of 'Graham' (Royal Jubilee) in one modern pomology.

Something that strikes anyone looking even casually into the register is not only the multiplicity of names but also the similarity of many of them. There are whole groups of names, all referring to the same cultivar, which vary from one another so slightly as to be obviously variations of the same name, many of them so similar that it seems unnecessary to print them all, but the reason we do so is, we think, sound and stems largely from this language difficulty. In the first place, the slight difference may be crucial, or it may be of no importance—for instance, the apples 'Davey' and 'Davy' are different, but 'Willy Sharp' and 'Willie Sharp' are the same. While compiling the register we have kept in mind the user with little or no knowledge of English or for that matter any other European language. The examples just given are proper names, and we should ourselves hesitate to say categorically without further investigation that one of them must be a misprint and that they represent the same cultivar, and we would be right to hesitate. However, with other words, we know perfectly well that, for example, 'Newer Fail' is a misprint for 'Never Fail', but a Hungarian, for instance, or a Japanese, would not know this and would be wrong to assume it, just as we would be wrong to make such assumptions about Hungarian and Japanese words. People must be able to find in the Register the exact spelling they are looking for or some doubt is bound to remain.

The difficulties and frustrations of compiling a register have perhaps been given undue emphasis, but there is also a lighter side to the work. The histories given are just the bare bones, but they stand for many pleasant little stories such as are to be found in Simmonds' *A Horticultural Who was Who*. There is certainly more to the history of 'Blenheim Orange', 'Bramley's Seedling' and 'Granny Smith' than appears in the register. The names themselves are worth a separate study and many were apparently bestowed without any thought of their impact. Who could believe that 'Pig's Nose' or 'Spanish Onion', even though descriptive of the shape, made an attractive name for an apple, or 'Chalk' for a pear, or 'Tragedy' for a plum? Working back through the literature to find the original name can be fascinating, frustrating and puzzling. Some cultivars, generally the international elite, have dozens of other names ('Court Pendu Plat' has 165) and the reasons for this proliferation are generally obvious—translation, transliteration, misunderstanding, lost labels and plain straightforward substitution, but some synonyms are more interesting to trace. There is an apple called 'Puffin', also called 'Puffin Sweet' and, presumably because it cropped heavily, it acquired the synonym 'Come Bear and Tear'. Someone must have referred to 'Puffin Sweet' or 'Come Bear and Tear', and from this came 'Sweet Orcome', then 'Sweet Orcombe'. Another rather similar process helped us to confirm the synonymy of some of the apples in our collection.

Two of them, called 'Tare de Ghinda' and 'Windauer Hartapfel' are identical. 'Tare de Ghinda' is Romanian and originated at Ghinda near Bistrita. It has two synonyms, 'Winter Dauerapfel' and 'Hartapfel'. It does not take much imagination to run these two together to make 'Windauer Hartapfel'. Although we could find no published information about 'Windauer Hartapfel' we felt justified in accepting that it was genuinely synonymous with 'Tare de Ghinda' and not meant to be something else. Another confirmatory detail, though not enough by itself, is that "tare" and "hart" both mean hard or firm in Romanian and German respectively.

Somewhat similar is the case of 'Reinette Simirenko'. This was growing in the garden of Platon Fedorovich Simirenko, an enthusiastic amateur gardener, in the Ukraine towards the end of the last century, but his son, the pomologist Lev Platonovich (1855–1920) did not know its origin, whether a chance seedling in his father's garden or a cultivar obtained from elsewhere. Pursuing the matter further, we found that the Romanian pomology regarded it as synonymous with what they call the English cultivar (actually American) 'Wood's Greening', introduced in 1820. In our collection 'Reinette Simirenko' has proved to be the same as 'Renetta Walder', received from Italy with no historical information, though the German element in the name might indicate that it is grown in the Tyrol. This gives us the connection through the name Wood—Wald in German. So the Romanian assertion that the apparently Russian 'Reinette Simirenko' and the American 'Wood's Greening' are the same has very strong backing from an Italian rendering of a German name for an American apple. Unfortunately, we lack 'Wood's Greening' itself under that name to make the trio complete.

Now that we have started to tackle registration seriously the future naming of new cultivars should be relatively straightforward. But beyond ensuring that a name has not been used before and otherwise conforms with the International Code of Nomenclature for Cultivated Plants it will still be necessary to see that synonyms do not arise. Even now new cultivars may acquire a synonym simply because insufficient thought was given to the name in the first place and it has been found for some reason unacceptable. Recent examples are 'Thurston August', renamed 'Discovery', 'Royal Epicure', renamed 'Epicurean', and 'Mutsu', renamed 'Crispin'. It is, therefore, important to encourage people to take great care when they choose a name so that it meets all requirements and does not need to be changed.

Under Plant Variety Rights, new cultivars of species covered by a scheme must be named, and the name must be distinct and agree with the International Code and with certain regulations of the Plant Variety Rights Office. It seems possible, therefore, that with reasonable vigilance the chaos of the past will not be repeated.

REFERENCES

GILMOUR, J. S. L. *et al.*, eds. 1969. *International Code of Nomenclature for Cultivated Plants*. International Bureau for Plant Taxonomy and Nomenclature, Utrecht, Netherlands.

HOGG, R. 1884. *The Fruit Manual*. 5th edition. Journal of Horticulture Office, London.

BORDEIANU, T. *et al.*, eds. 1964. *Pomologia Republicii Populare Romine*, Vol. II, Bucarest, Romania.

SIMIRENKO, L. P. 1961. *Pomologiya*, Vol. I, Kiev, U.S.S.R.

SIMMONDS, A. 1945. *A Horticultural Who was Who*. Royal Horticultural Society, London.

SMITH, M. W. G. 1971. *National Apple Register of the United Kingdom*. Min. Agric., London.

OTHER PUBLICATIONS OF INTEREST

BROWN, A. G. 1952. The Confusion of Varietal Names. *R.H.S. Fruit Year Book 1953*, No. 6, pp. 44–49.

DUNKERLEY, C. L. 1954. Some Notable Early Nineteenth-Century English Fruit books. *R.H.S. Fruit Year Book 1955*, No. 8, pp. 11–19.

DUNKERLEY, C. L. 1957. Some Notable Nineteenth-Century English Fruit Books. *R.H.S. Fruit Year Book 1958*, No. 10, pp. 70–75.

MILES, H. W. 1966. A Short Guide to the Literature on Fruit Culture in Britain. *Fruit Present and Future*, R.H.S. London. pp. 219–245.

WAY, R. D. 1971. Apple Cultivars. *Search Agriculture (New York State Agricultural Experiment Station)*, Vol. 1, No. 2.

Fruit Growing in the Small Garden

H. BAKER

Fruit Officer, R.H.S. Garden, Wisley

REGRETTABLY, perhaps, the average size of gardens today is less than it was before the last war and so the emphasis must be on the word "small". The reason is all too obvious, the increase in population means that the same amount of land has to be divided amongst more people. Not everyone wants a large garden, some have not the time, being too busy with other pursuits. Others may feel unable to cope with a large orchard—"whilst the spirit is willing, the flesh is weak". Nevertheless, having a small garden does not mean one is not able to to grow fruit. Indeed, the same range can be grown as in a large garden, though not in as great a quantity.

How is this done? By adopting a policy of "containment", a word borrowed from the realm of commercial fruit growing where the problem is exactly the same, i.e. growing the same amount of fruit or preferably more on less land. Containment means containing the closely planted fruits within a given area without the plants becoming unproductive and over crowded. Containment of tree fruits is achieved by the use of a number of cultural factors, the important ones being choice of rootstock, tree form, pruning technique, manurial treatment and last but not least the choice of cultivar. The same factors more or less apply to soft fruits, although choice of rootstock does not.

CHOICE OF ROOTSTOCK

This, above all other factors, is the most important, for it is the rootstock more than anything else which determines the eventual size of the tree.

What rootstocks are available which will create small trees? Taking each fruit separately they are:

Apple
M.9. The most dwarfing rootstock available at present to the amateur and commercial grower. It makes a tree of ultimate height and spread from 7 to 10 feet depending on soil, cultivar and cultural treatment. The trees are precocious and the dessert fruits usually more highly coloured and of larger size in their early years than apples from trees on the more vigorous stocks, though sometimes their storage quality is not as good. Whilst the root system is extensive, the roots are brittle and, therefore, the anchorage is poor. It is recommended that the trees are staked or supported in some way.

Undoubtedly M.9 should be the first choice for the small garden, but where the soils are light and dry, and the rainfall low then a semi-dwarfing stock may be more suitable. The difficulty arises when the soil conditions prove to be better than at first thought and consequently the tree is more vigorous than desired and, therefore, the problem of containment more difficult. It is, perhaps, better to plant M.9 where practicable and improve the soil or at least ameliorate the soil's influence by feeding and other good cultural treatment.

M.26, M.7 and MM.106. Semi-dwarfing rootstocks in ascending order of vigour. M.26 makes a bush tree between 10 to 15 feet height and spread. Trees on M.7 and MM.106 grow to between 12 and 18 feet though on very good soils there is not much difference between all three. M.26 has a brittle root system and is susceptible to collar rot (*Phytophthora cactorum*). In trials MM.106 has proved to have a better cropping record than M.7.

Pear

The choice lies between Quince A and Quince C. Of the two Quince C is more dwarfing but unfortunately it is infected by a complex of viruses. Therefore Quince A is mainly used, until a virus-free selection of Quince C becomes available.

Quince A is semi-vigorous and makes a tree of between 10 and 15 feet height and spread, though much depends upon the cultivar. Some pears are narrow, tall and upright in habit whereas others are more spreading.

Plum, Peach, Nectarine and Apricot

There is no very dwarfing rootstock, although there are several which produce small to medium-sized trees. Only a few are compatible with all plum, peach and apricot cultivars. The common plum rootstock, for example, produces medium-sized trees and is excellent for gages but shows definite incompatibility with several cultivars of plum including 'Czar', 'Marjorie's Seedling' and with damsons and peaches.

The only suitable rootstock compatible with all is the semi-dwarfing St Julien A. On poor to medium soils this produces a bush or half standard requiring a spacing of 10 to 12 feet though on good soils up to 18 feet might be necessary.

Cherry

The sweet cherry is the one exception to the range of fruit which can be grown in the small garden. The difficulty is there is no dwarfing or semi-dwarfing rootstock available at present. All are vigorous and make bush or standard trees which can grow up to 60 feet high.

It is possible, however, to grow the sweet cherry in fan trained form against a wall and keep it reasonably contained by summer pruning. In the open it is better to grow the sour Morello cherry which is inherently dwarf even on the vigorous stocks upon which it is grafted.

DWARFING ROOTSTOCKS FOR THE FUTURE

It is pleasing to note that thanks to the work of our research stations there will be available to the grower, in the not too distant future, dwarfing rootstocks for the pear, plum and cherry and an even more dwarfing rootstock than M.9 for the apple. For pears there is the new heat-treated Quince C. For plums there are a number of rootstocks, including E.340/4.6 which in trials at East Malling Research Station has produced trees which, at 5 years old, are considerably smaller than the control trees on St Julien A. For cherries work is proceeding on *Prunus* species, interspecific hybrids, selected mazzards (*Prunus avium*) and genetic dwarf cherry rootstocks, many of which have proved to be very much more dwarfing than the widely used sweet cherry stock F.12/1. The present hindrance to their production is that some are difficult to propagate vegetatively. Soon to be released to nurserymen by East Malling Research Station for propagation under the EMLA scheme is the very dwarfing apple rootstock M.27. Trees on this stock, when mature, should be no more than 6 to 8 feet high, and could be eminently suitable for the tiny suburban garden, provided that the soil is good.

CHOICE OF TREE FORM

Choice for the small garden, as far as apples and pears are concerned, will be limited to either the dwarf open centre bush, the spindle bush or one of the restricted tree forms which are summer pruned. The restricted tree forms most commonly planted are the cordon, the dwarf pyramid, the espalier and the fan.

The dwarf open centre bush is the simplest to maintain of those mentioned and along with the spindle bush is the most productive. A bush tree on M.9 well grown should yield an average of not less than 40 lb fruit, possibly more, each season. It will require more space than the cordon or dwarf pyramid and, therefore, not as many cultivars can be grown to a given area.

Cordons are ideal for the small garden as they are planted closely, $2\frac{1}{2}$ to 3 feet in the row, by not less than 6 feet between the rows. Obviously many cultivars can be grown though they do not yield as heavily, giving an average of 10 lb to 12 lb of fruit per cordon. A fence support system is, of course, required.

The dwarf pyramid is another useful form. It is closely planted, not less than $3\frac{1}{2}$ by 7 feet, and again a lot of cultivars can be grown in a small area. It does, however, require summer pruning every year and if this is neglected, trees can get out of hand.

The espalier and fan can be grown on a wall, or to mark a boundary or to edge a path. When well grown these two forms are most pleasing to the eye. One can expect about 20 to 30 lb of fruit from either.

The spindle bush, of which there are many variants, basically consists of a vertical central stem upon which are borne the cropping laterals. The spindle is supported by a stake, 8 to 8½ feet long, and tying down the young laterals in the early years is often an essential part of the training. Whilst the spindle can be just as productive as the dwarf open centre bush, aesthetically it is not pleasing because of the presence of the long stake and the tying down materials. The pruning, done in the winter, is on a renewal basis and, whilst not difficult to the skilled fruit gardener, it does require a careful interpretation of the rules, otherwise tree growth can become crowded and unproductive.

The choice for plums and gages, in the context of this article, are the pyramid and the fan. The plum pyramid is a relatively new innovation, devised at East Malling Research Station, and which can be seen in the Model Fruit Gardens at the R.H.S. Garden, Wisley. Grafted on to St Julien A and summer pruned it makes a small to moderately sized, compact tree with a strong framework. Experience of this form is so far limited, but it does appear to have the advantage of regular cropping and minimal branch breakages. These are important points especially when compared with a half standard which is inclined to produce heavy crops in some years, with consequent branch breakages, and hardly any fruit at all in others.

The fan is a useful tree form for wall trained gages and high quality dessert plums requiring a southerly aspect.

Peaches, nectarines and apricots also need a warm, sheltered situation and are, therefore, best grown in fan trained form, though in favoured areas certain peach cultivars can be grown in the open.

CHOICE OF PRUNING TECHNIQUE

Closely planted fruit trees unpruned in a small garden are liable to degenerate into an unproductive tangled jungle. The important questions are how to prune and when to prune?

All restricted forms, i.e. the cordon, dwarf pyramid, espalier and the fan have to be pruned in summer and the usual system advocated is the "Modified Lorette" detailed in some fruit books, including our own *The Fruit Garden Displayed*.

Summer pruning checks vigour. The removal of leaves in the summer reduces the supply of carbohydrates to the roots and thus slows down growth. With this training method fruit buds are produced at the base of the pruned shoots, and these develop into fruiting spurs.

Conversely, winter pruning stimulates growth. Very hard pruning causes most of the buds that remain to grow out as shoots instead of developing into fruit buds. Tree growth is strong but the crops can sometimes be small. The aim in winter pruning should be to maintain a correct balance between fruitfulness and growth.

The open centre bush and the spindle bush are pruned in the winter, though where growth has for one reason or another proved to be excessive then some form of summer pruning could be adopted to advantage.

Certain bush fruits for example gooseberry, red and white currant, benefit from summer pruning, not only does this contain their size it also lets in light and air thus helping in the development of fruit buds as well as in the ripening of the fruit.

The pruning system usually advocated for both bush and cordon involves pruning back the current season's laterals to 5 leaves beginning in the third week of June. The leaders are not pruned unless it is also necessary to inhibit their growth.

FERTILIZER PROGRAMME

There are four major elements, nitrogen, phosphorus, potassium, magnesium, as well as trace elements necessary for healthy growth and fruitfulness. It is the use, or misuse, of the first element, nitrogen, which is relevant to this policy of containment. Nitrogen is necessary to maintain growth and obtain optimum fruit size, but an excessive amount results in too much growth at the expense of fruitfulness. Growth then becomes rank and soft and by its nature is susceptible to disease. Tree fruits in particular are lacking in colour, have poor keeping qualities and are liable to early breakdown and storage rots.

A recommended annual manurial programme during the winter months to cover most fruits is as follows:

Sulphate of potash—48% K_2O (potash), $\frac{3}{4}$ oz per sq. yd.

Superphosphate—18% P_2O_5 (phosphorus), 2 oz per sq. yd, every 2 to 3 years.

Sulphate of ammonia (alternatively nitrochalk if the soil is very acid) —21% N (nitrogen), 1 oz per sq. yd, in early April.

Culinary apples, pears and plums should be given more nitrogen than the above. Trees growing and cropping normally in grassed down orchards may need extra nitrogen to offset the competition from the grass for this nutrient. A recommended rate for such trees is between $1\frac{1}{2}$ and 2 oz per sq. yd of sulphate of ammonia or nitrochalk.

Black currants also should be given extra nitrogen to encourage plenty of young growth upon which most of the fruits are carried. This is best accomplished by a heavy mulch of well rotted farmyard manure or compost.

CHOICE OF CULTIVAR

Despite the influence of the rootstock some cultivars are inherently vigorous whereas others are inherently more compact. Triploids, in particular, are often very vigorous and they are, in any case, poor pollinators. Examples are the apples 'Bramley's Seedling', 'Crispin', 'Gravenstein', 'Blenheim Orange', and the pears 'Pitmaston Duchess', 'Merton Pride' and 'Doyenné Boussoch'.

Bush and cane fruits also vary considerably in ultimate size. Avoid, for example, vigorous cultivars such as the black currant 'Boskoop Giant', the raspberry 'Norfolk Giant', the gooseberry 'Whinham's Industry', the blackberry 'Himalaya Giant' and plant instead the less ebullient.

The following is a selection of fruits which have been noted in the fruit collection at Wisley as being of compact habit or at least of manageable proportions.

Apples

Culinary	Grenadier	August–September
	Royal Jubilee	October–December
	Hector MacDonald	October–February
	Lane's Prince Albert	December–March
	Rev. W. Wilks	September–November
Dual purpose	Charles Ross	October–December
Dessert	Epicure	mid Aug.–mid Sept.
	Worcester Pearmain	early Sept.–early Oct.
	Lord Lambourne	late Sept.–mid Nov.
	Sunset	October–December
	Margil	October–January
	Sturmer Pippin	January–April
	May Queen (Fig. 6)	January–March
Cherry	Morello	
Pears	Jargonelle (Fig. 7)	August
	Williams' Bon Chrétien	September
	Louise Bonne of Jersey	October
	Winter Nelis	November–January
	Josephine de Malines	December–January
	Olivier de Serres	February–April
Plums	Early Laxton	mid July
Damsons	Frogmore	early Sept.
	Bradley's King	mid Sept.
	Prune (Shropshire Damson)	Sept.–Oct.
Black currants	Blacksmith	mid-season
	Baldwin	late

Red currant	Red Lake	mid-season
Gooseberries	Golden Drop (yellow)	mid-season
	Lord Derby (red)	late
Raspberries	Malling Jewel	mid-season
	September	autumn
Blackberry	Oregon Thornless	
Loganberry	Clone LY.59	
	Clone L.654 (thornless)	

Finally, mention should be made of the existence of "spur" or "compact" forms of apples. These are sports or mutations of certain apple cultivars, the important ones being of 'Golden Delicious' and 'Red Delicious'. They are naturally dwarf due to the characteristic of producing laterals which are much shorter than normal. They also spur heavily. On M.9 they make very small trees because of the double dwarfing effect of the stock and the scion. 'Wellspur' and 'Starkrimson' are sports of 'Red Delicious'. 'Yellospur', 'Starkspur' and 'Morspur' (Fig. 5) are sports of 'Golden Delicious'.

FIG. 1—J. M. S. Potter, Chairman of the Fruit Group.

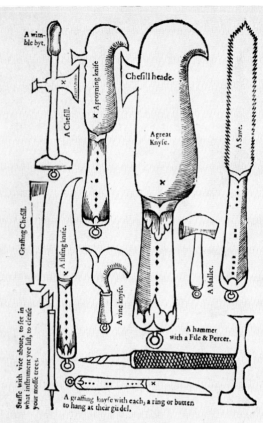

The following labels appear on the tools illustration:

A wimble byt.

A Chefill.

A proyning knife.

Chefill heade.

A great Knyfe.

A Saw.

Graffing Chefill.

A liding knife.

A vine knyfe.

A Mallet.

A hammer with a File & Percer.

Staffe with vice aboue, to fet in what inftrument yee lift, to clenfe your moffie trees.

A graffing knyfe with each, a ring or butten to hang at their gidel.

The Development of Apple Orchards in England, pp. 2–7

Fig. 2—Illustrations from *Book of the Arte and maner how to Plant and Graffe all sorts of Trees*, Leonard Mascall (1575)

(*left*) tools for use in graffing fruit trees; (*below*) method of grafting fruit trees.

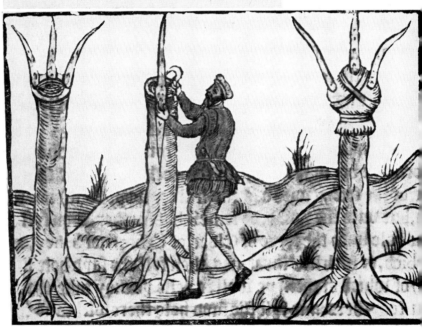

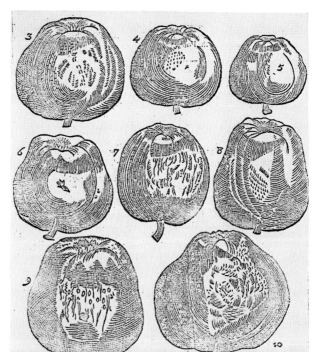

3—*right*: illustrations
apple cultivars from
rkinson's *Paradisi in*
e (1629). 3=Pome-
ter. 4=Golden Pippin.
= The Pearmaine.
The Queene Apple.
Genneting. 9=
ntish Codlin. 10=
rdfield Quining.

. 4—*below*: mural
m the ruins of
mpeii, now in the
tional Museum,
ples.

The Development of Apple Orchards in England, pp. 2–7

Fruit Growing in the Small Garden, pp. 22–28

Photos: H. Baker

FIG. 5—*above left*: apple 'Morspur', on M.9, planted in 1969. FIG. 6—*above right*: apple 'May Queen' on M.7, planted 1947. FIG. 7—*below*: pear 'Jargonelle' on Quince A, planted in 1963.

Promising New Cultivars of Hardy Fruit

J. M. S. POTTER

Former Director, National Fruit Trials

THIS is really a continuation of the article in the last issue of *Fruit Present and Future*, and sets out to describe cultivars which have shown promise since that time. Before dealing with the subject, however, it might be of interest to make a review of the changes that have or are taking place in the field of fruit growing where the amateur is concerned. Perhaps one of the main changes is the relatively small number of fruit nurserymen compared with 30 or 40 years ago. But even more important is the vast reduction in the number of fruit cultivars which the modern nurseryman lists. An examination of a modern catalogue will indicate that most of the cultivars listed have some commercial merit and that those which could be described as only suitable for the amateur are few.

The reason for this change is relatively simple. In view of rising costs the fruit nurseryman just cannot afford to maintain stocks of a large number of cultivars for which there may be a very limited demand, and he must concentrate on the more popular cultivars which he knows will sell.

The other major change that is taking place is the impact of the work of the scientific breeder, particularly in the field of new apples, sweet cherries, strawberries and black currants. Large scale breeding of apples and to a lesser extent pears, raspberries and black currants is being undertaken at East Malling Research Station. It is of interest to note that a new late flowering black currant has been raised there which will not be so subject to damage by late spring frosts, one of the problems of the regular cropping with this fruit. Plums and strawberries are in the Long Ashton programme but this station's breeding projects are still quite young, while the John Innes Institute is concerned with strawberries and sweet cherries, including self-fertile cherries, which will make it possible for the amateur to grow a single tree of this fruit. New strawberries, raspberries and black currants will also be forthcoming from the Scottish Horticultural Research Institute so there should be no shortage of new and improved cultivars in the future.

Characters such as improved yield, combined with size, are being aimed at in the breeding programme, while appearance, storage life and susceptibility to pests and diseases are other important factors which are not being overlooked. It is often said that the breeder tends to neglect flavour, but this is not so; there is no reason to suppose that an apple for example, having all the characters already mentioned, should not lose anything in edibility and in fact there is no reason why improved flavour cannot also be obtained.

Pests and diseases are difficult to control in the small garden, but apples have already been bred which are resistant to scab and it should not be long before new material is also resistant to mildew. In the meantime the following new cultivars are worthy of note.

APPLE

'Discovery'. This is a very attractive apple, ripening about mid-August and keeping in reasonable condition for several weeks after gathering. The flavour for an early apple is reasonable, but the trees are a little slow in coming into bearing, although once cropping begins it is regular and reasonably heavy. Introduced by Matthews Fruit Trees Ltd., Thurston, Bury St Edmunds, being originally named 'Thurston August' and renamed 'Discovery'. Parentage may be 'Worcester Pearmain' × 'Beauty of Bath'.

The tree is moderately vigorous, rather spreading and somewhat inclined to tip bearing. Flowering about the same time as 'Cox's Orange Pippin'. The fruit is medium, $2\frac{5}{8} \times 2$ inches, round, flat, regular, pale greenish yellow, half to three-quarters flushed with bright red. Flesh is creamy white, firm, juicy with a pleasant flavour. Stalk level with base, or slightly protruding. Season, mid-August to mid-September.

'Merton Knave'. This is a rather small, but very attractive bright red apple of good quality, which is probably derived from the parent 'Epicure' and is free cropping. Its season is the end of August to September. Raised at the John Innes Institute by crossing 'Laxton's Early Crimson' with 'Epicure'.

It is moderately vigorous, making a round headed tree not unlike 'Laxton's Early Crimson'. It flowers approximately two days after 'Cox's Orange Pippin'. The fruit is small $2\frac{1}{8} \times 2$ inches, round, fairly regular, greenish yellow almost completely covered with bright scarlet red. The flesh is creamy white, the flavour pleasant and slightly aromatic. Stalk medium. Season late August/September.

'King Russet'. This is a russet form of 'King of the Pippins' and has most of the characters of the parent, although the flavour tends to be a little more "nutty" in character. Introduced by K. A. Robbins (Rookery Farm) Ltd., Bordon, Hants.

The tree is upright to slightly spreading very much like 'King of the Pippins', and flowering is about the same time as 'Cox's Orange Pippin'. The fruit is medium, $2\frac{1}{2} \times 2\frac{1}{4}$ inches, round conical, fairly regular, greenish yellow, practically covered with a solid golden brown russet. The flesh is creamy yellow, rather dry, nutty with a good flavour. Stalk short. Season, September/November.

'**Summered**'. A very free cropping apple with a bright red colour and a reasonably good shelf life for a midseason cultivar. Raised and introduced by the Canadian Department of Agriculture, Summerland, B.C., from an open pollinated seedling with a seedling from 'McIntosh' and 'Golden Delicious'. An apple rather of the 'McIntosh' type.

The tree is vigorous, upright to slightly spreading, spurring freely and flowers approximately six to seven days before 'Cox's Orange Pippin'. The fruit is medium, $2\frac{1}{2}$ to $2\frac{3}{8} \times 2\frac{1}{2}$ inches, round conical, fairly regular, pale yellow green, half to three-quarters striped and flushed with a deep, bright red. The flesh is white, firm with a pleasant flavour and gives off a slight aroma. The stalk extends beyond base. Season, September to November.

'**Pixie**' (Fig. 8). The fruit will often keep until March in natural store and has a very good shelf life for its particular season. Cropping is regular and the flavour good. It should be an ideal garden apple for late use. Raised at the National Fruit Trials. Parentage unknown.

The tree is moderately vigorous, fairly spreading, spurring freely and it flowers three days after 'Cox's Orange Pippin'. The fruit is medium small, $2\frac{1}{4} \times 2$ inches, greenish yellow with an occasional slight red flush or similar coloured stripes. The flesh is creamy, firm, juicy, sweet, subacid, of good flavour. Stalk protruding beyond cavity. Season till beginning of March.

A.1379. A very promising late keeping apple, cropping regularly with fruit of an attractive orange red with a slight amount of russeting, and with a pleasant flavour. This apple is soon to be named and released. Raised at East Malling Research Station by crossing 'Cox's Orange Pippin' with 'Jonathan'.

Tree is moderately vigorous, about the same as 'Cox's Orange Pippin', cropping regularly both on spurs and on the one year old wood. It flowers at approximately the same time as 'Cox's Orange Pippin'. The fruit is medium to medium large, $2\frac{1}{2}$ to $2\frac{3}{4} \times 2\frac{1}{2}$ inches, conical, fairly regular, greenish yellow, half to three-quarters flushed and striped with orange red, with small patches of russet. The flesh is greenish white, firm, moderately juicy with a moderately good flavour. Stalk protruding beyond base of cavity. Season, December/February.

N.F.T.1. One of the attractive features of this new apple is its late flowering character, blossoming about the same time as 'Edward VII'. Cropping is regular, producing a large bright green fruit of the 'Edward' type, which will keep in natural store until March or April. Could be a useful apple for gardens subject to late spring frosts. Raised at the National Fruit Trials by crossing 'Edward VII' with 'Crawley Beauty', and is shortly to be named and released.

The tree is vigorous, upright, spurring quite freely and not unlike 'Edward' in habit. The fruit is large, $3\frac{1}{2} \times 3\frac{1}{4}$ inches, round oblong, slightly uneven, bright green, changing to slight yellow with an occasional light brown-orange flush. The flesh is white, tinged green, firm, acid. Stalk extending beyond base. Season, till March or April. Flowering about the same time as 'Edward VII'.

PEAR

E.M.18 (Fig. 9). A very free and regular cropping pear, producing a fruit not unlike a small 'Williams', and which has a good flavour. The tree is relatively weak on Quince A, making it suitable for the small garden. As 'Williams' is one of its parents, it could be assumed that the fruit would be suitable for preserving. Raised at East Malling Research Station by crossing 'Beurré Superfin' with 'Williams' Bon Chrétien'.

The tree is medium in vigour, slightly spreading and spurring freely. Fruit is medium small, bergamot to conical, pale yellow, sometimes a quarter flushed pale orange red with a little russet around the stalk. The texture is melting, juicy with a good flavour. Stalk is medium. Season, beginning of September. Flowering approximately three days after 'Conference'.

PLUM

'Edwards' (Fig. 10). This is a large fruited plum of American origin, not unlike 'Belle de Louvain', but of better quality than that variety. Raised by Mr Edwards, California, U.S.A.

The tree is moderately vigorous, upright spreading, forming a rather round headed tree, cropping regularly. The fruit is large, oval, distinctly tapering to stalk, pale reddish purple becoming blue-black, with a thick and tough skin. The flesh is pale creamy yellow, sometimes tinged purple, firm, a little fibrous, very juicy, sweet but a little acid, more for dual purpose. Stone clinging. Season, early to mid-September. Blossoming about the same time as 'Czar' and 'Purple Pershore'.

CHERRY

'Stella'. This is the first self-fertile sweet cherry to be named and will now permit the amateur to plant a single tree without having to ensure planting another suitable cultivar to ensure cross pollination. 'Stella' is late midseason, black, of good size and has a reasonable flavour when fully ripe. Parentage 'Lambert' × JI self-fertile seedling 3/45. Raised at Summerland, B.C., Canada.

Tree moderately vigorous, upright spreading, coming into bearing early. Fruit, large, to very large, heart shaped, regular, mahogany, almost black when fully ripe, shiny. Flesh dark purplish red, very juicy. Quality fair to good. Stone small. Season about the same as 'Bradbourne Black'.

RASPBERRIES

'Glen Clova'. An early raspberry which ripens one or two days after 'Malling Promise' and which crops very heavily. The berry is of medium size, round, firm, somewhat acid and quite well displayed on the cane. It has the unusual feature of often producing two laterals from a node which no doubt accounts for some of its heavy cropping potential. Raised at the Scottish Horticultural Research Institute.

The canes are numerous, moderately tall, fairly erect. Laterals are well dispersed and fairly stiff. Fruit is of medium size, round conical with the drupelets closely packed to give a firm berry. Colour is pale red, and the flavour slightly acid.

'Malling Orion'. A midseason variety which has outyielded 'Malling Jewel' in a cropping trial and the moderately large fruit has quite a good flavour.

The cane is tall, strong and numerous, and the fruiting laterals medium, semi-erect, but those on the lower part of the cane are almost lost amongst the dense spawn. Fruit is medium large to large, short conical to roundish, compact, firm, of good flavour and the colour is medium dark red. Plugs easily.

'Malling Admiral' (Fig. 11). A late cultivar whose season is approximately the same as that of 'Norfolk Giant'. It has a very large berry of bright colour, but the long laterals tend to get broken, and it is one which would benefit from protection. Raised at East Malling Research Station.

The cane is very tall, vigorous and numerous and the fruiting laterals very long particularly towards the base of the cane. Fruit is large, long conical, compact, slightly soft but not tending to crumble, rather acid, dark medium red and shiny. Plugs moderately easily.

'Phyllis King'. This raspberry has cropped about the same as 'Malling Orion', and it produces a large, attractive fruit which is well displayed. The habit of the whole cultivar is not unlike that of 'Malling Jewel'. The one main fault with this raspberry is that it tends to be difficult to plug particularly after rain. Raised by Mr R. J. L. King, Amersham, Berks.

The cane is tall, strong, semi-erect and the fruiting laterals well dispersed and of medium length. The fruit is very large, distinctly conical, firm. The plug leaves a rather large cavity which gives the fruit a slightly loose feel. Colour bright red with a slight gloss. Flesh firm, slightly acid, sometimes difficult to plug.

STRAWBERRIES

'Merton Dawn' (Fig. 12). A new strawberry not unlike 'Cambridge Favourite' which is one of its parents. Has cropped more heavily than the parent and has the similar pale orange red type of berry. Raised at the John Innes Institute.

The plant is vigorous, spreading and the berries do not extend beyond the leaf canopy, but are reasonably well exposed. The fruit is large to medium large, round conical, pale orange red with a pale orange flesh. The berry is firm, the flavour is moderate and it husks fairly easily. It is a midseason to late midseason strawberry, continuing ripening for a few days after 'Favourite'.

'Marmion'. Where the problem of red core is important this new strawberry is well worth considering as it shows a fairly high degree of field resistance to this disease. It is a good cropper, although the orange-red berry tends to be a little bit on the soft side. Raised at the Scottish Horticultural Research Institute, Auchincruive.

The plant is moderately vigorous, upright to spreading, and as the trusses are comparatively short it means that some of the berries tend to be partly hidden by their leaf canopy. The fruit is medium large, conical to round conical, orange red with a pale orange flesh and a moderate flavour. Calyx is particularly easy to husk. Midseason.

'Montrose'. This is a late midseason strawberry which has cropped more heavily than 'Cambridge Favourite' in a trial, but produces quite a good proportion of large berries which have quite a good flavour. Raised at the Scottish Horticultural Research Institute, Auchincruive.

The plant is moderately vigorous, upright to spreading and the fruits extend to the edge of the leaves and are well displayed. The fruit is large to medium large, round conical, orange-red turning scarlet. Flavour good, a little acid. The calyx is clasping and not very easily husked. Season late midseason.

'Domanil'. A Belgian strawberry which shows some promise as a late midseason cultivar. It produces a very high proportion of large fruits, but the berry tends to be a little dull in appearance owing to its being highly pubescent. Raised at the Belgian Plant Breeding Station, Gembloux.

The plant is vigorous, tall and fairly dense, and the fruits extend to the edge of the leaves but some tend to be partly hidden. The fruit is large, round conical to a little pointed, orange-red and downy. Flesh firm, but rather acid. Husking fairly easily. Season late midseason, picking for some days after 'Cambridge Favourite'.

Practically all these cultivars have been introduced since the first *Fruit Present and Future* was published and there is little doubt that in view of the present programme an even greater number will be included in the next issue.

The Pollination of Fruit Trees

R. R. WILLIAMS

University of Bristol, Long Ashton Research Station

SUCCESSFUL pollination is essential for a good fruit set in most tree fruits and it is, therefore, one of the most decisive processes determining cropping. Effective pollination often necessitates transfer of pollen from another cultivar, and this can be greatly influenced by weather and the levels of insect activity at the time of flowering.

Recognition of the important role of pollen goes back at least to classical times. Maheshwari (1950) notes an account by Herodotus of his travels in the east during the fifth century B.C. in which reference is made to the Arabs and Assyrians holding special ceremonies during which a priest would touch the female inflorescences of dates with male flowers in order to ensure a good supply of fruits.

One of the earliest references to fruit tree pollination in our horticultural literature was cited in the *R.H.S. Apples and Pears Conference Report* (1935). This referred to a report in the *R.H.S. Transactions*, 1822 by the Rev. George Swayne pointing out that cross-pollination was necessary in the pear 'Gansell's Bergamot'. From 1902 onwards F. J. Chittenden carried out a series of experiments concerning the need for cross-pollination, later to be published in the *R.H.S. Journal* (1912). Further studies into the pollination requirements of specific cultivars followed at Wisley and the John Innes Horticultural Institute. These investigations and others carried out abroad, confirmed that the major factors in fruit tree pollination were the availability of viable pollen, a vector, pollen tube compatibility with the flowers receiving pollen, and similar flowering dates. A survey published by the Horticultural Education Association (1961) summarizes information available at that time while many additional references are quoted by Knight (1963). Today centres such as the National Fruit Trials at Brogdale screen recently introduced cultivars for pollination characteristics.

Practical recommendations for pollination remained virtually unchanged for a considerable period after the R.H.S. Fruit Conference in 1934, but more recently a re-examination of this aspect of fruit culture has begun. This has been stimulated by changes in other aspects of orchard management which could have an impact on fruit set. For instance there has been a widespread trend towards the planting of fewer cultivars, which could reduce the opportunities for cross pollination: and the hedgerow system of planting has led to the concentration of the pollinators in separate rows, which reduces the likelihood of pollen transfer. Earlier, Crane and Lawrence (1929) were able to state that a 5% set could be regarded as a forerunner of a good crop but, with changes in pruning and expectations of higher yields, a 15–20% set may be realistic today. Furthermore there is also a commonly held belief that pollinating insects may be less abundant than in the past, though this is very difficult to prove.

Does inadequate pollination limit cropping? Considerations such as those given above has helped to bring about a fresh appraisal of the adequacy of pollen transfer in orchards and the role of other factors which may modify the fruiting response to pollination.

Although the plant processes initiated by pollen transfer and culminating in fruit set were accurately described, their study had been limited by the demanding microscopic techniques involved. Investigations into the happenings which follow pollen transfer received a great impetus with the development of a fluorescent microscopy technique which made it relatively easy to follow the processes of pollen germination, stigma penetration and subsequent tube growth in the pollinated flower (Currier, 1957). The examination of large numbers of flowers from fruit trees in various orchard situations revealed two interesting pollination features. Firstly, the level of compatible pollen transfer was often low enough to suggest that cropping may be limited, and, secondly, even when compatible pollen had been deposited on the stigmas, the transfer often took place too late in the blossoming period for fertilization to be possible. Some cultivars were found to require compatible pollination within a day or so of flower opening if pollen tube growth was to be completed before the female organs of the flower started to age. These observations suggested that inadequate cropping of fruit trees in Britain could be associated, not just with insufficient transfer of compatible pollen, but with a failure to achieve transfer soon enough after the flower opens.

In some situations it is found that ovules—the female organs which when fertilized develop into seeds—had developed abnormally, resulting in flowers showing partial or complete sterility. Such flowers, externally identical with healthy blossom, are particularly common in seasons when there have been cold spells just before flowering. 'Cox's Orange Pippin' and 'Doyenné du Comice', two of our most important cultivars, are invariably the worst affected. The presence of a high proportion of sterile blossom implies a need for a corresponding increase in the proportion of flowers pollinated, otherwise fruit set may be insufficient for a good crop.

Attempts were made to verify these conclusions by studying yield response to supplementary pollination. Open flowers with unruptured healthy anthers were picked and brought indoors where the petals were removed and the flowers mounted in perforated petri dishes. The dishes were left overnight in a room sufficiently warm to ensure complete anther dehiscence without the flowers becoming brittle. The dishes of dried flowers were then taken into orchards and each dried donor flower was brushed onto the stigmas of a selected, fully receptive, young flower of a compatible cultivar. Donor flowers which gave profuse quantities of pollen being used for two pollinations. A single blossom was pollinated in approximately every fourth cluster throughout each treated unit and great care was taken to ensure that all the hand pollinations were effective and potentially capable of fertilizing blossoms. The results indicated that in some orchards pollination was already at a luxury level so that supplementary pollination did not improve fruit set appreciably. However, in many orchards, supplementary pollination increased the yield significantly and the average crop of all the orchards showed a 29% increase. Similar results were obtained in 1968 and 1969 (Williams 1970). In 1972 hand pollinations again indicated that many orchards would have benefited from more generous pollination (Figs. 13, 14).

IMPROVING POLLINATION AND FRUIT SET

Other factors besides inadequate pollination can cause yields below those normally expected. However, if other obvious factors such as pests and diseases are not thought to be limiting a check should be made to determine whether the trees will respond to supplementary hand pollination.* Where results indicate a deficiency in pollination the fruit-grower has a number of remedial measures which can be considered.

There are measures already established as part of good fruit growing practice which can improve pollination and fruit set. The retention of additional flowering wood on the main crop cultivar when pruning may achieve the desired level of cropping, for dense blossom is a more powerful attractant to pollinating insects than sparse blossom. It should be remembered that the extra blossom, with any resultant increase in cropping, places an additional stress on the tree and this may need to be compensated by an increased availability of nutrients. Although starved fruit trees often blossom abundantly the flowers can be very weak and difficult to set. Increasing the quantity and variety of blossom available as a pollen source can also have a beneficial effect on pollen transfer. Here also the retention of more flowering wood when pruning is helpful. The transference of this pollen by insects is improved if the pollen source is mixed more intimately with the main crop trees by cutting branches at blossom time and distributing them in containers of water. Incidentally this practice makes a virtue of late pruning! A more permanent improvement in pollinator dispersal can be obtained by introducing grafts into main crop trees. It is advisable that the chosen pollinators should have fruit of a different colour and harvesting period to the main cultivar.

* Details of the technique and an account of related orchard experiments are to be found in the booklet "Towards Regulated Cropping", available from Long Ashton Research Station.

One of the quickest ways of improving pollen transfer is to introduce hive bees. With the increasing cost of hiring bees it is worth ensuring that the colonies are strong and contain plenty of brood at the time of introduction into the orchard. It is also advantageous to provide shelter for the hives and so encourage bee activity when weather conditions are marginal.

POLLINATING TECHNIQUES FOR THE FUTURE

Many commercial fruit growers are beginning to appreciate the possible benefits which might follow if the provision of pollinators in orchards could be avoided. Main crop cultivars such as 'Cox' and 'Comice' are readily sold but the demand for the pollinators is often appreciably less. Furthermore, the elimination of pollinator trees from an orchard would facilitate more specialized management of the desired cultivar and simplify harvesting.

There are several experimental approaches which may provide the fruit grower with an opportunity to exploit the advantages of a single cultivar plantation and also afford an improved control over cropping. Some of these techniques would obviate the need for cross-pollination entirely. Thus it has been shown experimentally that 'Cox's' can be induced to produce parthenocarpic (seedless) fruits by spraying the flowers with growth promoting substances. In other investigations attempts are being made to overcome self-sterility by spray treatments and to induce a self-fertile mutant (sport) of cultivars such as 'Cox' by artificial irradiation.

The technique of artificial hand pollination mentioned previously is too labour demanding to have a wide application in commercial orchards although it is a useful technique for the amateur grower. Various methods of mechanical application have been developed abroad ranging from small hand-held puff guns to large tractor-drawn machines and even aeroplane dusting. The extraction and storage of fruit tree pollen is not difficult and, given the development of plantations specifically for flower production, pollen could be made available to British growers. Experiments may prove that the amounts required for effective fully mechanized application are too large to be commercially acceptable but some form of hand-held aerosol pollen gun might be a popular development for the enthusiastic amateur.

Improvements on the traditional method of natural pollination may not necessarily be so revolutionary as a fully mechanized system of artificial pollination. The use of pollen dispensers fitted to the exit of hives has been used on a limited scale in other parts of the world and its potential in British orchards is being examined. By ensuring that bees leaving the hive already carry compatible pollen their cross-pollinating effectiveness may be appreciably increased. Nevertheless, the distribution of the dispenser pollen is dependent on the behaviour pattern of the bees and the weather, providing only a minor improvement in control over pollination.

A further innovation is the use of ornamental species of *Malus* as pollinators. This offers no increased opportunity to regulate fruit set beyond that already available in the traditional system but it does facilitate the planting of large blocks of a single market cultivar. The *Malus* selected for trials are more floriferous than commercial cultivars and can be allowed to develop denser canopies, so that the proportion of pollinator to cropping canopy can be reduced without necessarily lowering the pollinator efficiency.

At present a number of alternative ways of achieving fruit set in apples and pears are being explored and it is too soon to say whether any one method, or combination of methods, will seriously challenge the traditional practice which has been used in Britain since commercial orcharding began. It is certain however, that the urgent need to achieve a more regular cropping pattern will ensure that any promising approach to pollination will be closely scrutinized by the fruit growing industry.

REFERENCES

CHITTENDEN, F. J. 1912. Contributions from the Wisley Laboratory XII. Pollination in orchards. *J. Roy. hort. Soc.*, Vol. 37, pp. 350–361.

CRANE, M. B. and LAWRENCE, W. J. C. 1929. Genetical and cytological aspects of incompatibility and sterility in cultivated plants. *J. Pomol.*, Vol. 7, pp. 276–301.

CURRIER, H. B. 1957. Callose substances in plant cells. *Amer. J. Bot.*, Vol. 44, pp. 478–488.

HORTICULTURAL EDUCATION ASSOCIATION. 1961. The pollination of fruit crops. 68 pp. Reprinted from *Scient. Hort.*, Vol. 14, pp. 126–150; Vol. 15, pp. 82–122.

KNIGHT, R. L. 1963. Abstract bibliography of fruit breeding and genetics to 1960, *Malus* and *Pyrus*. *Tech. Commun. Commonw. Bur. hort. plant. Crops*, Vol. 29. 535 pp.

MAHESHWARI, P. 1950. *An introduction to the embryology of Angiosperms*. McGraw-Hill Book Co., New York. pp. 1–27.

ROYAL HORTICULTURAL SOCIETY. 1935. Pollination in apples, pears and plums. *Rep. Conf. Apple and Pear*, R.H.S. 1934. pp. 38–46.

WILLIAMS, R. R. 1970. The effect of supplementary pollination on yield. In *Towards regulated cropping* (R. R. Williams and D. Wilson, ed.), Grower Books, London. pp. 7–10.

Bees in the Garden and Orchard

T. J. K. SHOWLER

Bee Research Association, Gerrards Cross

A GREAT many writers have explained the mechanism of pollen transfer in fruit crops, distinguishing between pollination "pollen transfer" and fertilization "fusion of the male and female cells". The Horticultural Education Association produced in 1961* a clear summary of the then extant literature on "Pollination of fruit crops", with tables on pollen compatibility for several kinds of fruit, diagrams of orchard layouts, and lists of flowering times. A digest of this material appears in the latest edition of the Royal Horticultural Society's *The Fruit Garden Displayed*; but with the notable exception of the relevant chapters of John B. Free's monumental *Insect Pollination of Crops* (1972), there are no other readily available reviews on the subject written for the gardener and orchardist.

It is clear from my experience both as an orchardist and as a bee-keeper that there is a widespread desire to know more about bees in the garden and orchard, and some discussion is therefore desirable of bees themselves and not the pollination/fertilization mechanism.

Looking back over the decade covered by the R.H.S. Fruit Year Books, 1947–1958, it can be said that, so long as wartime food rationing continued the honeybee was regarded as an important source of supplementary food—honey—but with the easing of controls over fruit imports bee keeping rapidly declined in importance and popular esteem. As the value of bees in providing a source of food declined, their importance became more widely recognized as an improver of seed and fruit crop yields within the context of otherwise weed-free and insect-free agricultural practice. Today the higher and lower social bees, honey and bumble, and the non-social bees, are receiving increasing attention as their role as pollinators is more clearly demonstrated. The change in the use of bees from direct to indirect agents in food production is very recent, and this may explain why the R.H.S. Fruit Year Books and their companion volume *Fruit, Present and Future* (1966)—which covered a great many subjects pertinent to fruit growing by amateurs and professionals—paid little or no attention to bees or to the benefit to be obtained by the artificial provision of adequate pollinating insects. The only reference to honeybees that I can recall is that made by Gavin Brown in his examination of "The factors affecting fruit production in plums" (*R.H.S. Fruit Year Book* 1950).

* *Scientific Horticulture*, Vol. 14.

Bees are, in simple terms, modified hairy vegetarian wasps, and their devotion to a nectar/pollen diet makes them important pollinators. Nectar-gathering bees cannot help but get pollen on the body hairs, and even if much of this pollen is retained as food, some of it is inescapably transferred from flower to flower during pollen or nectar gathering. Most species of bees in the United Kingdom are solitary. The fertilized female overwinters, and on emergence in spring she makes a small nest containing a number of food pellets of nectar and pollen. On these pellets eggs are laid, which in turn hatch into larvae, and these, without direct maternal assistance or contact, consume the food provided, and in due course develop into pupae. The mother bee will die before the new generation of males and females has emerged. The males die after mating and the females seek out winter quarters, which they inhabit until the following spring. Some species of solitary bees may congregate in areas well suited to their nesting habits, either above or below ground, and so give rise to large communities.

Bumble bees have developed an organized social life. The fertilized females overwinter as solitary bees but in spring proceed to construct a nest and raise several broods of non-reproductive stunted daughter bees. These workers assist the mother and largely take over the work of feeding her and subsequent broods of young. In the late summer and early autumn, dependent on the species, males and reproductive females are produced, which leave the parental nest. The nest falls into decay and the mother bee and workers die; the males also die and only the young mated females overwinter.

The distributions of the 25 species of bumble bees of Britain and Ireland are at present being studied by professional and amateur recorders and collectors in the Bumble Bee Distribution Maps Scheme. Six species of bumble bees are "cuckoo bees", parasitic on other host species, the female making a takeover bid for an established nest.

The honeybee or hive bee has evolved a complex perennial colonial life. Each colony consists of one specialist egg-laying female, the queen, with 20,000 to 50,000 food-gathering females (the workers) and in summer a few hundred males (the drones). The workers construct the nest from wax produced in their wax glands; they defend the hive, using their barbed stings; they tend the queen and drones, and feed the larvae with food secreted from their own glandular system. A fresh generation of queens can be produced every year, but, in fact, the life span of the queen honeybee can extend over several years. It may be complicated by colonial reproduction or swarming, when she leaves her colony with a large number of workers and some drones, to found a new daughter colony. A new young queen replaces her in the original colony.

The gardener and orchardist will be helped by his ability to recognize which of the major groups of bees are present, in assessing the need to introduce colonies of honeybees or to establish conditions more favourable to bees. It is not easy to introduce solitary and bumble bees, although nesting tins and boxes have been devised for the purpose. Many studies have been made to try to make this practical on a farm or garden scale. Natural nesting can be encouraged on special sites set aside for the purpose—for example on land that is difficult to work, field corners, banks and hedgerows—which are useful nesting areas if left to revert to a fairly wild tussocky state.

Most gardeners are familiar with the solitary bees which nest in sandy soil, where they throw up small cones of fine soil, particularly noticeable on well made lawns and dry banks, and with those which make or use holes in buildings and posts. The latter can be induced to inhabit perforated bricks in special walls or garden buildings. On sites suitable for solitary bees, large numbers of individual nests may be made, and it is the bees' activity at the mouth of their nests which attracts attention to them. Bumble bee nests often remain unobserved until the number of occupants entering or leaving the nest betrays its location. Some bumble bees construct their nests in abandoned mouse nests at or just below the surface of the ground. Others will take over nesting boxes from small birds such as the tits. Bumble bees' nests are often mistaken for honeybee swarms by the uninitiated observer, but they are in fact very different, being a spherical accumulation of grass or vegetable waste containing a small chamber with a few coarse waxen receptacles. Some of these look rather like up-turned, open thimbles, and others like pods about the size of a small acorn. The open ones contain either dilute honey or feeding larvae and the sealed ones the pupal stages. Bumble bee nests can often be left undisturbed if in or near buildings, so that the bees can perform their pollinating function and fade quietly away. Bumble bees are unlikely to sting humans unless extremely provoked.

In contrast, the honeybee swarm is a cluster of thousands of bees, temporarily without any "nest". If any observer is present when the swarm arrives the air will be seen to be full of excited bees, which either settle in a tight pulsating mass, sometimes as large as a rugby football, or enter the building or tree of their choice. The layman is unlikely to have noticed the scout bees examining the potential nesting site in the days before the swarm's arrival. The swarm will arrive suddenly and may, if not taken, just as suddenly depart. A fresh swarm is very docile, but one that has been unable to locate a suitable home can get very peevish.

Populations of solitary and bumble bees rise and fall as local conditions favour or discourage them, and it is difficult to build up a population artificially. In contrast, the number of honeybee colonies can be increased at will and this therefore is their prime advantage as a booster of insect pollinator populations. Most suburban and orcharding areas contain some honeybee colonies, although in spring the numbers of their foraging bees may be too low in relation to the blossom to effect a worthwhile pollination, or their effectiveness may be restricted in seasons when the weather only permits a limited amount of pollination and fertilization. The honeybee colony in its modern portable hive can easily be introduced during the blossoming period of a crop and is just as easily removed.

It is often noted that the bumble bee will continue to collect nectar and pollen at lower temperatures than hive bees, but the work of Dr R. R. Williams at Long Ashton has shown that, for tree fruits at least, the pollen itself and the receiving organs are critically temperature-sensitive. Although the movement of pollen from flower to flower may have taken place, the transferred pollen may be unable to effect fertilization at lower temperatures. So the honeybee's preference for higher temperatures than the bumble bee may not be such a disadvantage.

The gardener or farmer may not wish to have honeybee colonies present on his ground all the year round. The enthusiastic bee keeper who regularly tends his bees would not wish to be restricted in the examination of his colonies by fear of the bees stinging people near the hives. Today in most suburban areas honeybee colonies are hidden away in unobtrusive sites, but with the increasing density of housing in urban areas, the choice of sites is becoming limited and honeybee populations may be on the decline there.

On fruit farms where there are few hedges, weeds or waste land, the bee keeper may find it difficult to keep his honeybees in good condition once the main fruit crops have flowered, when the grass below the trees is mown or a weed-free soil is maintained. Indeed it may be better for the bees if they are kept on sites outside the orchard, and introduced only for the blossoming period. Fruit growers in general are aware of the need to conserve their pollinating insects, and avoid spraying open blossom with insecticides. But, thereafter, the bees may be subject to slow starvation and decimation by routine spraying.

Advice on the use of bees in orchards and gardens can be obtained from a number of sources. Several local education authorities have bee-keeping officers, as do the three Scottish regional colleges. The Ministry of Agriculture has one advisory officer in England and one in Wales. There are national and county associations of bee keepers who will also advise on the introduction or supply of colonies. The Bee Farmers' Association is a specialist United Kingdom organization catering for the larger bee keepers, which provides a link between the bee keeper and the commercial fruit grower by offering a pollination service.

The Ministry of Agriculture has for many years published five bulletins on the techniques of bee keeping and the handling of bee products, and there are four free advisory leaflets particularly concerned with pollination:

No. 328 Use of bees in orchards (revised 1971)

No. 377 The pollination of apples and pears (1971)
No. 485 The pollination of plums (revised 1967)
No. 486 The pollination of cherries (1968)

The Bee Research Association (Hill House, Chalfont St Peter, Gerrards Cross, Bucks) has published a number of bibliographies, of which no. 4 is on "The pollination of fruit crops". Their book, *Pollination of Seed Crops*★ based on the journal *Apicultural Abstracts*, could usefully be followed by one on *Pollination of Fruit Crops*. The Association's leaflet "Save our Pollinating insects" has received a very wide general distribution.

Reading through the early editions of the Fruit Year Books, I have been struck by the enthusiasm, freshness, and the wide-ranging interests of their contributors. Regrettably, there has been a subsequent decline in the interest in fruit growing and also in bee keeping, and other leisure activities have become more popular. Now other changes are at work in society, and in many parts of the country there is a growing interest in all aspects of horticulture. Bee keeping is included in this newly aroused interest in creative outdoor arts and pursuits; it is benefiting too from our increased knowledge of the physiology and chemistry of the honeybee colony, and of new materials for bee keeping equipment. The growing appreciation of "other bees" is widening the bee keeper's and the fruit grower's horizons and responsibilities.

★ (1972) edited by Dr. E. Crane.

Prospects for Systemic Fungicides in Fruit Growing

A. H. M. KIRBY

Formerly Head of Plant Protective Chemistry Section, East Malling Research Station

THIRTY years ago success in controlling many weed species was obtained with chemicals (the hormone weed-killers) that entered the plant after spraying, moving into growing points and into roots. This aroused the hope that compounds might be found which, entering crop plants from the soil or through the foliage and moving within the plant, would provide control of deep-seated diseases such as wilts, and also of more superficial diseases such as scab and powdery mildew, more efficiently than the products then available. Unfortunately, the initial promise of antibacterial materials, such as the sulphonamides, failed to yield practical results and the only antibiotic in commercial use, streptomycin, is not acceptable in all countries because resistant strains of bacteria can so easily emerge.

In recent years much has been hoped for from the exploitation of substances that contribute to the natural resistance of plants to disease, or of cheaper substitutes for them, but so far no product has reached a commercial stage.

However, the well-tried procedure of trial and error, that has so far produced almost all the crop protection products on which we have come to rely, has brought about a striking change in the scene. In the past seven years, compounds falling into close on a dozen chemical groups have been stated to possess a useful degree of systemic action, and at least six products are already approved for use on edible crops in various countries.

BENZIMIDAZOLES

In France, thiabenzadole (the 2-(4-thiazolyl) derivative of benzimidazole) was found to be taken up by sugarbeet roots and translocated in sufficient quantity to protect the foliage against *Cercospora* leaf spot. This property has turned out to be of commercial significance: for example, the degree of control of this disease achieved by five sprays of captafol (Difolatan®) at 6 kg per ha could be achieved with only two sprays of thiabendazole as the 60% wettable powder at 730 g per ha. Increased yields and sugar content have also been claimed. Although thiabendazole is toxic to many fungi causing disease on fruit, it seems rarely to have advantage in disease control over benomyl (see below)

45

and indeed in some cases is much inferior (see section on storage diseases).

The analogous 2-furyl derivative of benzimidazole, called fuberidazole, has been in experimental use under the code number, Bay 33172; it has usually given inferior results. But the methyl ester of benzimidazole-carbamic acid, now usually referred to as MBC, is a fungitoxicant of exceptionally wide range. As was the case with the antibacterial sulphonamides, the biological activity of a derivative came to light first. The compound in this case was the 1-butylcarbamoyl derivative of MBC, initially offered as a wettable powder formulation under the code number EF 1991 and later marketed as Benlate®; the common name, benomyl, has been recommended on a world-wide basis for the derivative itself. Not surprisingly, other compounds giving rise to MBC have been developed (see below), and products based on MBC itself are now being offered for experimental use.

Like the other benzimidazole derivatives mentioned, and indeed all the systemic fungicides so far reported, benomyl is of no value for controlling diseases caused by Phycomycetes, such as potato blight or vine downy mildew, or by Pythium spp. (damping-off fungi). But the control of apple scab, especially on the fruit, is so outstanding that world-wide interest has been aroused. Nor is this performance limited to this disease; many leaf spot diseases, such as those on cherry and black currant, are controlled very successfully. It is true that thiabendazole is effective against most diseases that are controlled by benomyl, but it seems that something like double the rate is necessary and its use for foliar diseases on fruit it not likely to be widely recommended.

Benomyl has also been shown to give at least as good control of powdery mildew on a number of crops as is given by safe rates of binapacryl and dinocap. But whereas for control of apple scab the interval between applications can be extended up to 21 days, for apple mildew control the interval should not exceed ten days, especially during the period of high spore release (May–June). Although the rates recommended for apple scab control may give good control of powdery mildew, the cost compared with that of dinocap or binapacryl programmes is so great as to make the use of benomyl, and probably other products, very unattractive for mildew control throughout the season. However, spraying at three-week intervals from May onwards has been shown to prevent sporulation by young cankers on apple in the U.K. and this added advantage could justify the extra cost in areas where Nectria galligena is a serious problem.

In the U.S.A. on peach and nectarine, excellent scab control by benomyl has been reported, and on apricot this product gave promise for control of limb dieback (gummosis) where thiabendazole failed. Brown rot of stone fruits (Monilia spp.) is also better controlled by benomyl than by previously used fungicides, and this applies to the blossom blight due to fungi of this genus. It is possible that the increase in crops of the apple cultivar 'Cox's Orange Pippin', reported from East Malling and Long Ashton Research Stations (following use of benomyl for scab and mildew control) was in part due to protection of the blossom against fungal attack, but a growth-promoting effect on fruit set cannot be ruled out. Unfortunately, neither benomyl nor any other of the systemic fungicides so far tested has given any control of peach leaf curl.

On grapes, benomyl has been reported to control powdery mildew and to give exceptional control of black rot (*Guignardia bidwellii*). With no adverse effects on flavour or on fermentation, it is likely to become the fungicide of choice for botrytis control on grapes.

Before passing to other, unrelated systemic fungicides, mention must be made of several new experimental products, including three from Japan: NF 35, NF 44 and NF 48. The common name, thiophanate, has been proposed for NF 35 which is a diethyl ester; NF 44 is the dimethyl homologue and is referred to as thiophanate-methyl. NF 48 has a less complicated structure, but may be regarded as a stage through which NF 44 is converted to MBC, the stable breakdown product of benomyl. In general, much larger amounts of the thiophanate fungicides are required to achieve the same degree of control given by benomyl, probably because conversion to MBC (or in the case of NF 35 to the ethyl isomer of MBC) is slow and by no means complete in most cases. As is to be expected, the range of diseases controlled is essentially the same as that controlled by benomyl. From West Germany, there is BAS 320F, for which the common name, mecarbinzid, had been proposed; this differs from benomyl only in the replacement of the butyl group by a methylthioethyl group, and it is reasonable to assume that it also breaks down to MBC.

OTHER SYSTEMIC FUNGICIDES

Among other products that have been offered, several (such as ethirimol and tridemorph, specific for cereal mildews; dodemorph, for rose mildew; and Kitazin-P, for rice blast) are not of interest for control of outdoor fruit diseases. However, a compound containing a pyrimidine group, introduced as EL-273 and now known by the recommended common name, triarimol, is effective at exceptionally low concentrations against apple and pear scab, grape, cucurbit, cereal, black currant, gooseberry and peach powdery mildews, and black currant leaf spot at remarkably low rates. The control of apple scab is not so good on fruit as it is on foliage, the reverse of the position with benomyl, and the range of diseases controlled is smaller than that for benomyl; botrytis diseases, for example, are not reduced at economic rates of use. Unfortunately, this product has had to be withdrawn from the market as its safety to consumers is in doubt, but it remains one of the most interesting so far discovered.

Among newer products under trial for control of fruit diseases is CELA W 524, for which the common name, triforine, has been accepted. It is reported to give very good control on apple of powdery mildew, scab, cedar apple rust and (at least on 'Cox's Orange Pippin') of Gloeosporium storage rot. Recently, it has been found to be as effective as benomyl in preventing outbreaks of spider mites in apple orchards in New York State. From the same area a report has appeared that triforine gave by far the best control of brown rot on 'Stanley Prune' plums, superior to that given by benomyl, dichlozoline (see below), or triarimol. No results of trials on soft fruits have been seen.

Another new product, developed in Japan, is Sclex®; the common name, dichlozoline, appears to have been accepted in some countries. No claims for control of diseases on pip or soft fruits have been noted, but outstanding control of blossom blight (caused by Sclerotinia fructicola) was obtained in New York State on sweet cherry and peach, and of fruit rot, due to the same organism, on nectarine. Swiss trials have also shown very consistent control of blossom and twig blights (caused by S. laxa) on apricot and sweet cherry by this compound as well as by benomyl and the thiophanate group fungicides.

SPRAY DAMAGE

An extremely attractive feature of the non-systemic fungicide captan has been the excellent fruit finish which has been obtained following its season-long use on apple and pear. It is therefore a source of some anxiety that records of increased fruit russet and of an opalescent finish have appeared in reports of trials with benomyl at high volume in the U.K. and the U.S.A. It is possible that the use of low volumes, with usually more rapid drying of deposits, may sometimes avoid these undesirable side effects, but with the application of less chemical control could also be less reliable; in field trials at East Malling in 1971, russeting of 'Cox's Orange Pippin' was not reduced when only 50 gallons per acre were used in each application although the concentration of benomyl in the spray had been increased to 0·1% in order to achieve the same dose per acre.

STORAGE DISEASES

Another useful attribute of captan has been its value in reducing storage rots of apple, due mostly to Gloeosporium spp. Benomyl has been found to be very effective in reducing rotting by these and other fungi, including Botrytis and Penicillium spp. Of thiabendazole, it has been claimed that post-harvest use has reduced or virtually eliminated losses in pome fruit, bananas and citrus fruit during storage and shipping.

But much depends upon the identity of the disease causing the rotting. Both benomyl and thiabendazole inhibit germination of spores of *Gloeosporium album* but recent work at East Malling has shown that only benomyl will control rotting of apples due to *Nectria galligena*. Though both fungicides are effective for control of rots due to *Botrytis* and *Penicillium* spp., the rate of benomyl required is approximately half that needed of thiabendazole.

SOFT FRUIT

As the strawberry plant is non-woody and the vascular system cannot be very long in any cultivar, it is to be expected that compounds such as benomyl will be taken up by the roots in sufficient quantity to protect the foliage, but not the fruits, against disease. However, soil application is not likely to be economic for outdoor plants, except at the time of planting, when control of *Verticillium* wilt may be possible. At East Malling, soil drenches with benomyl have been shown to protect plants of 'Cambridge Vigour' planted in a chloropicrin-fumigated site after inoculation with *V. dahliae*. Spraying has proved very successful for the control of anthracnose (*Colletotrichum fragariae*), grey mould (*Botryris cinerea*) and powdery mildew. Fruit malformation has been reported to be less following use of benomyl than it was when dichlofluanid was used.

On black currant and gooseberry, excellent control of botrytis mould has been obtained with benomyl, and on black currant of leaf spot (*Pseudopeziza ribis*). As the powdery mildew (*Sphaerotheca mors-uvae*) that has afflicted black currant in recent years is also controlled by benomyl there is a real prospect that all three diseases on this crop can be controlled by one material. Recent work on black currant in Poland has shown that benomyl and the thiophanates controlled rust (*Cronartium ribicola*) as well as maneb. On raspberry, benomyl and thiabendazole controlled spur blight and also reduced rotting of fruits by *Botrytis* after picking.

ACARICIDAL ACTION

A claim that spider mites feeding on benomyl-treated plants do not multiply because their eggs fail to hatch has been partly confirmed by later work. Longevity of adult female mites is not impaired, but in glasshouse tests the fecundity of *Tetranychus urticae* Koch was reduced by 62%, and the fertility 82%, by benomyl at a normal concentration for spraying. Adult females of *Panonychus ulmi* (Koch), sprayed with benomyl in a Potter tower, showed a 35% reduction in fecundity, and 40% of the eggs were rendered sterile. In practice, these effects may not be sufficient to avoid the need for using specific acaricides. No other group of systemic fungicides has been reported to show this effect, but it is noteworthy that NF 44 and 48, both methyl esters, had a much bigger effect than NF 35 on the fertility of eggs of the glasshouse spider mite, *T. urticae.*

RESISTANT STRAINS

Attention has been drawn by Netherlands workers to the fact that most, if not all, the so-called systemic fungicides appear to inhibit one or more biosynthetic processes. MBC is reported to inhibit the synthesis of DNA rapidly and severely. With this degree of specificity of action, it is perhaps not surprising that strains of fungi should exist that tolerate benomyl. In fact, on one cucumber cultivar a resistant strain of powdery mildew grew poorly on unsprayed plants, but profusely on plants treated with benomyl. As resistance has also been observed in this crop to another systemic fungicide, dimethirimol, this pheno-menon cannot be ignored, especially as a strain of *Botrytis cinerea*, isolated from cyclamen, has been found to be resistant to benomyl, thiophanate-methyl, fuberidazole and, to a lesser extent, thiabendazole.

MODE OF ACTION

Strictly speaking, the control of fruit rots, either by pre-harvest sprays or post-harvest dips or sprays, is not due to systemic action of the fungicides used. This applies equally to the very successful control of rots of citrus fruits and bananas undoubtedly achieved. But there is evidence that rot control is assisted by the capacity of these new compounds to penetrate into the plant to an extent unknown with the previous materials, with the exception perhaps of dodine (Melprex®).

In fact, there is very little evidence of true systemic action by any of these so-called systemic fungicides in woody plants. Studies by various workers have shown that MBC is taken up passively by roots of plants treated with benomyl in pots or in nutrient solutions and travels through cell walls to the xylem vessels. It is then carried in the sap stream to those aerial parts of the plant that are provided with stomata. Thus it accumulates in leaves and not in petals or in fruits; in fruiting tomato plants, 98 % was found in the leaves. Moreover, in the leaves movement is from the veins toward the edges and not at all in the reverse direction, so that benomyl applied to the tip of a leaf does not affect the proximal part, nor does it move down the petiole. As a result, benomyl and, as far as is known at present, all the so-called systemic fungicides do not move from leaves present at the time of spraying into new leaves opening later. This means that one of the great hopes for disease control by such substances has not yet been realized. Only when, and if, fungitoxic substances (or their precursors) are found that will move in the living, as well as in the non-living, conducting elements will we have truly systemic agents.

Meanwhile, we must be content with the local, penetrant action of such products as benomyl, which is greater than that of dodine (the first organic fungicide to show penetrant and curative action against apple scab). Claims have been made for protection of rooted shoots or seedlings of apple against powdery mildew and of cherry seedlings against leaf spot by soil application, but even with benomyl this is a completely uneconomic procedure and only spraying is feasible on cropping trees. This is also true on bush fruits such as black currant or gooseberry.

The excellent penetrant power of benomyl (and/or MBC), coupled with the marked stability of MBC, does enhance the prospects of controlling apple and pear scab, and probably other diseases, by breaking the winter cycle of the fungi responsible. The value of organomercurials such as PMC for this purpose has been known for more than a decade, and urea can also give very good results. But clearly the use of mercury should be avoided if possible, and the promise offered by benomyl as a post-harvest spray on apple and pear may well revolutionize the approach to scab control. Work at East Malling Research Station has also shown that triarimol is very effective in this way, but that neither benomyl nor triarimol suppresses ascospore release when applied to mature perithecia in the spring.

CONCLUSIONS

The so-called systemic fungicides that have come into use during recent years constitute an important advance in our knowledge and are valuable new weapons in our armoury for disease control. Although they move upwards in non-living conducting tissues, and in non-woody plants can reach levels in foliage that are adequate for disease control, in woody plants and in fruit in storage or transit their remarkable effectiveness is due to a combination of local penetration and powerful fungitoxic action—protective, curative and even eradicant. The cost of these products, especially where frequent application is still necessary (as in control of powdery mildews), may restrict their appeal. The appearance of resistant strains of certain fungi is a cause for disquiet. There is as yet no sign of an adequate fungicide that would move downwards in the plant.

Root Diseases of Fruit

AUDREY V. BROOKS
Plant Pathologist, R.H.S. Garden, Wisley

D URING the course of a year many specimens of unhealthy plants are received by the Plant Pathology Department at Wisley, and about 11% of these are from various types of fruit. Every letter is cross-indexed according to the host plant and subject matter and as this procedure has been carried out for the last 40 years, much valuable and interesting information is contained in the files. From this we have a rough guide as to the incidence of certain diseases over the years and can determine which are now most troublesome in amateurs' gardens.

Numerous soil-borne diseases can attack plants including fruit crops but the root parasite which has been most troublesome during the last few years is *Armillariella mellea* (syn. *Armillaria mellea*), the honey fungus, or bootlace fungus as it is sometimes called. It has caused considerable losses in new gardens which have been laid out on the sites of old woodlands, but it has also killed a number of plants in old gardens where trees have been felled and the stumps have not been removed, or where dead plants have been left standing. The plants most susceptible to infection are probably apple, cherry and plum trees among top fruits and raspberry and gooseberry of the soft fruits. Both indoor and outdoor peaches and vines are occasionally affected and in fact honey fungus has been recorded on all types of fruit including strawberry.

The most obvious symptom caused by honey fungus is the fairly rapid death of a tree or bush. The first symptoms to appear, however, are discoloration of the foliage and dieback of the shoots, but these are often ignored or attributed to some other trouble. The fungus itself shows beneath the bark at the collar and on the roots, as thin white fan-shaped sheets of growth which, when fresh, smell strongly of mushrooms. The bark is often softened and blackened and growing from it may be found long black or brown root-like cords called rhizomorphs which are the origin of the name bootlace fungus. These grow at a rate of about three feet per year and may become ten feet or more in length providing they are still attached to sources of food materials.

If a plant affected by *A. mellea* is not removed or treated in any way, the fungus will live as a saprophyte on the dead tree stump for up to 30 years. From there it will spread through the soil by means of rhizomorphs. When the conical growing tips of these come into contact with the roots of living plants they are able to penetrate the tissues and grow through to the inner layers of the bark. As the fungus becomes parasitic on the plant tissues, the white mats of fungal growth form and eventually the root is killed. The fungus then spreads beneath the bark to other roots and the collar of the plant, and when most of the roots are dead, all the top growth dies back completely. In advanced stages of infection flattened rhizomorphs develop beneath the bark. These are often pale yellow or red in colour when first exposed, but soon become black or brown. In nature, the rhizomorphs are never white and should not, therefore, be confused with the thick white strands of fungal growth resembling lengths of cotton which are frequently found growing on the surface of woody debris or leaf mould in the soil; these white rhizomorphs of saprophytic fungi do not attack living plants.

In some seasons the fungus may produce toadstools in the late summer or autumn. They may emerge around the bases of affected trees, or in grass growing over dead roots. They can, however, arise from rhizomorphs in the soil well away from any apparent source of infection. The toadstools are produced in dense clumps and are very variable in size and colour, though at some stage of growth the cap or stalk is often honey coloured, hence the name of the fungus. A whitish ring is usually present on the stem just below the gills and this is one of the characteristics by which the toadstool is identified. Another is that the spores produced by the gills are white and they are often shed in such great numbers that they form a white coating on shorter toadstools or even on the stump or grass below. A third characteristic is that the gills run down the stem for some distance, and the cap, therefore, is not easily removed from the stalk.

The absence of toadstools is no indication that the fungus is not active in the soil and many plants may be killed before any toadstools appear. Their formation appears to be dependent on the climatic conditions and, in some seasons they appear in large numbers, whereas in another year no toadstools may form in the infected area. Most spores produced by the toadstools die soon after they are shed, but some may be wind-borne to newly exposed stumps or freshly cut logs. If conditions are favourable, a spore may germinate and attack the wood, thus starting a new source of contagion, but the likelihood of a new infection arising in this way is very remote.

It is sometimes stated that the honey fungus can only attack injured roots or those trees weakened through poor health. It has been found, however, that the roots of perfectly healthy trees growing in good conditions can become infected. Nevertheless, affected plants are likely to be killed more quickly by the fungus where adverse cultural conditions, such as waterlogging, drought or malnutrition prevail. Every effort should be made, therefore, to see that fruit crops are well cared for so as to prevent them from being killed so quickly following infection and also perhaps making them less susceptible to attack in the first place.

Once an outbreak has occurred in an orchard or garden it may prove impossible to eliminate the trouble completely. It should be possible, however, to reduce subsequent losses provided that plants killed by the fungus are dug up and burnt together with as many of the roots as possible and also any rhizomorphs which are found in the soil. Before replanting, the soil should be changed completely or sterilized in an attempt to kill any fungal growth which is living on small pieces of woody debris inadvertently left in the soil. If the former treatment is to be carried out, the soil from the affected area can be used in the vegetable garden and replaced with soil from there. Vegetables can be attacked by the honey fungus, but they are rarely in the soil long enough for infection to take place, with the exception of rhubarb which is often killed by the fungus.

In a small area, vacant of other plants, a thorough watering of the freshly forked soil with 2% formalin solution (1 pint 37–40% commercial formaldehyde to 6 gallons of water) may be worth trying. This should be applied at the rate of 5 gallons to the square yard. Formalin will kill living plants, but it is sometimes possible to make a barrier between living roots and the soil to be treated using sheets of thick polythene for the purpose. After the area has been treated with formalin, it should be covered with damp sacks or polythene for 24 hours. Following removal of the covering, the soil should be left vacant for at least three weeks if it is of a light type, or up to six weeks if it is heavy.

Until fairly recently there was no treatment which could be carried out to try to save a plant affected by honey fungus, and all diseased bushes and trees (with perhaps the exception of some large forest trees) eventually died within a year or so following infection. There is now, however, a proprietary product called Armillatox on the market which is being sold for the control of this root parasite. It is a phenolic emulsion which, in laboratory tests, has been found to kill the fungus. Some experiments with living material were carried out by a plant pathologist who has done a lot of research on *A. mellea*, who found that the product is not phytotoxic when used according to the manufacturer's instructions; thus where the material was used on living roots 1 to 4 cm in diameter, of healthy trees, no root injury was observed. (The emulsion must not be used on young fibrous roots.) He also found that the substance significantly reduced the total length of rhizomorphs, although not killing them outright, when these structures were grown on pieces of infected wood in soil in jam jars. The actual results of this experiment were variable depending upon the type of soil used (Redfern).

As yet no field experiments have been undertaken to prove scientifically that this proprietary product will give a good control of *A. mellea*, but it is hoped that such an investigation will be carried out very soon by a research worker. Nevertheless, this material has been tried during the last two years by many amateur gardeners on trees and shrubs of all types, which had previously been diagnosed by a specialist as having been affected by honey fungus, and in most cases the plants have made a good recovery. It is possible, therefore, that this proprietary product will save a fruit tree infected with honey fungus, but of course the sooner the disease is noticed and treated the greater is the chance of effecting a cure.

It was mentioned earlier that the honey fungus has appeared in gardens of new houses which have been built on sites of old woodlands. Where the plot has previously contained conifers, however, there is a risk that plants in the new garden will become affected by the fungus *Heterobasidion annosum* (syn. *Fomes annosus*). This fungus is very common and usually affects pine trees. It has been recorded on apple and peach (Moore) and specimens bearing the fungus taken from a dead pear tree were sent to Wisley a few years ago. This fungus also kills an infected plant, and fruiting bodies eventually develop at the base of the tree. They are not very conspicuous as they are usually obscured by grass, fallen leaves or even soil. These fructifications are irregular in shape and very variable in size, but always have a thin knobbly, reddish-brown upper surface and a whitish lower surface bearing very small pores through which the spores are discharged. These can only infect stumps or felled timber. The disease spreads from infected trees or stumps to healthy trees by root contact only and is incapable of free growth through the soil. The only control measure, therefore is to remove and burn any tree affected by the disease, and also any pine stumps which may be in the vicinity.

Another root disease which also kills trees is white root rot due to the fungus *Rosellinia necatrix*. It is found most commonly in the Isles of Scilly and south-west England. It attacks all types of fruit but is most troublesome on apple. An affected tree shows discoloration of foliage and dieback of branches, the symptoms becoming progressively worse until the tree is completely dead, usually within three years from infection. Infected roots bear a web of fine fungal threads (hyphae) which are at first white but later become grey-green, brown or black. No well-defined rhizomorphs are formed, but very fine hyphae do travel through the soil thus spreading the disease. Infection is confined to the roots and the fungus survives on these and woody debris in the soil. It is essential, therefore, to dig up and burn all infected trees together with all the roots. If the trouble is detected early enough, it is sometimes possible to save a young tree by lifting it in the autumn, trimming away the roots and replanting in uninfected soil.

The fungi *Verticillium albo-atrum* and *V. dahliae* cause verticillium wilts of fruit crops, but are only likely to be troublesome on raspberries and strawberries in a small garden. In raspberries, *V. dahliae* causes the disease known as blue stripe wilt. This name arose because an intense blue or purple stripe develops on diseased canes, starting at the base and extending upwards, chiefly along one side. Towards the end of June, the leaves of the striped side of an affected cane show yellow then brown strips between green bands of tissue adjacent to the veins, and gradually wither from the base upwards. The buds die on the diseased parts and some canes may die completely during the winter. Those which survive either remain stunted the following year and produce inedible fruit or wither before the fruit reaches maturity. This raspberry disease was apparently common in the 1930's and 1940's but now appears to be rare in gardens.

Although both species of *Verticillium* have been recorded on strawberry, *V. dahliae* is the most common on this host. Infection is followed by wilting of the older leaves which show blue-black streaks extending along the stalks from the crowns. The unhealthy plants produce undersized malformed fruits and eventually die. The disease causes the greatest losses in maiden plants. Although all cultivars of strawberry can apparently become infected there is a difference in the way in which they react to the disease, thus 'Cambridge Vigour' is always very severely affected whereas 'Talisman' and 'Redgauntlet' are resistant. (For information on other cultivars see East Malling Annual Reports for 1968 and 1970.)

Verticillium dahliae is a microscopic fungus but it does produce minute black resting bodies (microsclerotia) which can sometimes be detected embedded in the bark of diseased raspberry canes. The microsclerotia are released into the soil and under favourable conditions, germinate to produce fungal threads which infect the roots (and underground portions of the stems of raspberries) of hitherto healthy susceptible host plants. The fungus will also survive in the soil for long periods on the debris of infected plants. The disease is spread by the scattering of infected debris and by using planting stock vegetatively propagated on infected land.

If verticillium wilt appears on raspberries or strawberries the diseased plants should be dug up and burnt, and new certified stocks should be bought in and planted on a fresh site. If this is not possible, resistant cultivars of strawberry should be grown. No other treatment can be recommended for amateurs at the moment although soil drenching with a systemic fungicide could be considered by commercial growers.

A root disease of strawberries which is troublesome in some commercial crops is red core caused by the fungus *Phytophthora fragariae*. This should not occur in gardens because it is usually introduced into a new area by the planting of infected material and under the Red Core Disease of Strawberry Plant Order 1957 (applicable to England and Wales only) plants affected by the disease may not be sold or planted except on land already declared to be infested. Nevertheless, as this is a notifiable disease it is advisable for gardeners to be familiar with the symptoms just in case it should appear. Diseased plants are most obvious in May and June when they are seen to be dwarfed with small leaves which are often reddish, the outer ones being dead, brown and stiff. Many or all of the roots are dead and are dark brown or black, and the outer layers easily peel off, leaving the central cylinder showing as a "red core". Anyone suspecting that this disease is present in their garden is obliged by law to notify a local officer of the Ministry of Agriculture, Fisheries and Food.

So far, only diseases due to fungi have been mentioned, and there are several other fungi which have also been known to affect the roots of fruit crops, but they are not of any importance and have mostly occurred on young plants in nurseries. There is, however, a bacterial disease which occurs fairly frequently in gardens, namely crown gall, caused by *Agrobacterium tumefaciens*. This pathogen has a wide host range but, in fruit crops, is most common on raspberry, blackberry and apple. It is not considered to be a serious disease and is only likely to persist and spread in wet soils. The bacteria enter through a wound and stimulate the cells of the host to proliferate abnormally so that a spherical or convoluted gall is produced, ranging in size from about 1 cm to 20 cm in diameter. The galls may be on the roots or at the collar of the plant or even on the stems. Sometimes a chain of galls develops along a root or shoot, and such aerial galls are most frequently found on raspberry and blackberry.

There is no real evidence to show that crown gall always has an adverse effect on a diseased plant, although occasionally slight stunting occurs and there may be a reduction in crop which would not necessarily be noticed in a garden. Cane fruits having a gall at the crown, however, have been known to die. Apart from those cases where the galls have appeared on the shoots, they are very often not found until the diseased plant is lifted for some other reason. Plants found to be severely diseased should be burnt, but where only a few aerial galls have appeared on a cane fruit, it is usually sufficient to cut out affected canes. When new stocks are to be planted in soil known to be infected with *A. tumefaciens*, any cut or injured surfaces of the roots should be protected with a wound paint, and waterlogging should be prevented by adequate drainage.

It will be seen that root diseases of fruit crops, with the exception of honey fungus, should not be troublesome in gardens. In fact, more harm is done to the roots of plants by unsuitable cultural treatment than by root diseases, and most of the specimens sent to Wisley merely show signs of ill-health as a result of soil conditions that are too wet or too dry or of malnutrition. Good cultural treatment will, therefore, go a long way towards ensuring that the roots of plants remain healthy, but when a disease does occur, quick and appropriate action should prevent further trouble.

REFERENCES

MOORE, W. C. 1959. *British Parasitic Fungi*. Cambridge University Press. p. 147.
REDFERN, D. B. 1971. Chemical control of honey fungus (*Armillaria mellea*). *Proc. 6th. Brit. Insectic. Fungic. Conf. Brighton, 1971*, Vol. 2, pp. 469–474.

The Dwarf Fruit Tree Association of North America—its Origin, Growth and Development

ROBERT F. CARLSON

Professor of Horticulture, Michigan State University

TWENTY years ago, the words "dwarf fruit trees" meant smaller trees for the garden or the backyard. Today these words have specific meaning to commercial fruit growers in North America. "Dwarf" now denotes smaller compact trees planted in orchards of 500 or more trees per acre in contrast to 35 trees per acre of past years. This dramatic change in commercial fruit growing is largely due to the leadership of the Dwarf Fruit Tree Association over the past 16 years.

A humble beginning

The Dwarf Fruit Tree Association came into existence on March 4, 1958, at a small meeting of fruit growers at Hartford, Michigan. The meeting was called by the late Mr Jerry Mandigo, District Horticultural Agent, who felt growers and pomologists should get together and discuss the increasing interest in planting dwarf trees in commercial orchards. The meeting was held in an empty apple storage at the Hill Top Orchards operated by the Heuser family.

Nearly 300 persons attended the first meeting. The "pros and cons" of dwarf fruit trees and rootstock types for commercial orchards were discussed. Before the meeting broke up that day, Mr Mandigo proposed that this become an annual affair whose purpose is to keep fruit growers informed. Dr Robert Carlson was named Secretary to lead the formation and organization of this group.

Organization

On December 3, 1958, Dr Carlson called a small meeting of leading fruit growers in Grand Rapids, Michigan, to formalize some ground rules and objectives, and most important, to appoint a president and a board of directors. At this meeting several persons were named to act for a year as a governing body of the newly formed Dwarf Fruit Tree Association (DFTA). These men were: Wallace Heuser (*President*), Hartford, Michigan; Raymond Klackle (*Vice President*), Belding, Michigan; and Robert Carlson (*Secretary-Treasurer*), East Lansing, Michigan. The persons named as Board of Directors were: Jerry Mandigo, Harold Fox, Donald Spencer and Frank Green, all from Michigan; Lorne Doud, Indiana; and Gordon Yates, Minnesota.

According to the secretary's notes, it was proposed that the objectives of this newly formed association shall be ". . . to promote an understanding of the nature and use of dwarf fruit trees through research, education and dissemination of information", and that membership shall be ". . . open to anyone interested in the furtherance and development of dwarfed fruit trees".

Following this meeting the secretary proceeded to obtain papers for the incorporation of the association. The Board of Directors gave their final approval of these on September 22, 1959.

Objectives to inform and be informed

The objectives of the association to keep growers informed through annual meetings and discussion grew into a reality with great enthusiasm. The secretary edited and published the association's first newsletter, October 1958. The sub-title of this newsletter was "Information about smaller than standard trees". Among several short articles in this newsletter, the late Dr H. B. Tukey wrote:

". . . dwarf fruit trees are promising, but are they going to be subject to spring frost injury on low ground because of their low-heading? Do they need to be located on special frost-free sites? Does the fruit of different varieties ripen a day or so earlier or later? Does this markedly affect market ability? How about finish? Do fruits from dwarf trees keep in storage as well or better than from standard trees? What about mulching, irrigation, hand pollination, mechanical harvesting, thinning, insect and disease control, pruning, and harvesting?

Here is where and why the new Dwarf Fruit Tree Association is so badly needed. Let everyone make his observations and bring them to the association for dissemination and discussion. In this way, we will shake the bugs out of the dwarf fruit tree, find where they belong, and how to handle them. The formation of the DFTA could prove to be one of the important steps in the development of the fruit industry."

And Lorne Doud, a fruit grower in Wabash, Indiana, wrote:

"One of the most encouraging aspects of the modern fruit industry is the free interchange of ideas and information among fruit growers and among the research scientists who serve them. I am certain that the organization of the DFTA last spring is a big forward step in service to both fruit growers and nurserymen. It now has the opportunity to help establish clonal rootstocks in nurseries and orchards on a sound scientific and business basis.

With its meetings and published newsletter, this new organization can serve Horticulture in the Midwest by collecting and disseminating information regarding performance of scion/rootstock combinations under the widest possible variety of climatic, soil, and management conditions. In addition, it can suggest and encourage research programs and keep fruit growers and nurserymen informed of their findings.

It can further stimulate intelligent and rational interest among laymen in a subject that has sometimes been regarded with emotion. From a personal viewpoint, I am grateful to the Horticulture staff at Michigan State University for their interest in the DFTA, and I am looking forward to the chance to cooperate with them in every way possible."

Summer orchard tours were scheduled so members could see the performance of variety/rootstock combinations. The first tour was July 31, 1959, in Michigan's southwest fruit area. Each year since a similar tour has been held at other fruit areas in the United States and Canada.

International in dimension

Although several states were represented at the early meetings, membership grew steadily to include persons from most fruit growing states and Canada. Overseas countries soon joined in membership and also received the bi-monthly newsletter.

Programme speakers for the first four years were mainly from state universities having a research interest in dwarfed fruit trees. Growers and nurserymen working with smaller trees also participated in the annual programmes. Similarly, growers and pomologists from Canada were very helpful in developing programmes which would stimulate and guide the fruit industry in the use of smaller trees.

In 1962, the international aspect of the association was further aroused when Mr Tony Preston, of East Malling Research Station, was invited to be the guest speaker. His enthusiastic presentations on rootstocks and tree pruning summed up the practical approach to smaller trees. This information was especially helpful to growers then starting to use dwarf trees in their orchards. Since then several international programmes have been held including feature speakers such as Dr Donald Fisher, British Columbia; Dr A. D. Crowe, Nova Scotia; Dr Ben Roosje, Holland; Dr Donald McKenzie, New Zealand; Mr Dan Neuteboom, England; and Dr Gerhard Bünemann, Germany.

All this has helped promote interest in the association and membership has steadily increased from about 300 in 1958 to 1,200 in 1972. Of these, 119 are from Canada, 39 from other countries throughout the world; the others are from the U.S.A.

International study tours

To keep up on latest cultural and management practices of fruit growing, both at home and abroad, several international tours have

Promising New Cultivars of Hardy Fruits, pp. 29–34

Photos: Crown Copyright

Fig. 8—*above left*: apple 'Pixie'. Fig. 9—*above right*: pear EM 18. Fig. 10—*below*: plum 'Edwards'.

Promising New Cultivars of Hardy Fruits, pp. 29-34

Photos: Crown Copyright

FIG. 11—*above*: raspberry 'Malling Admiral'. FIG. 12—*below*: strawberry 'Merton Dawn'.

FIG. 13—*left*: tree of pear
'Doyenné du Comice', which
received only natural pollen
transfer.

FIG. 14—*right*: a similar tree
which received some supplementary hand pollination.

Breeding Apple Cultivars for the Future, pp. 65-74

Photos: East Malling Research Station

FIG. 15—*top*: good skin finish (*left*), conspicuous lenticels (*centre*) and severe russeting (*right*) in seedlings from 'James Grieve' × 'Starkspur Golden Delicious'. FIG. 16—*centre* reactions to *Gloeosporium perannans* following artificial inoculation; 'Cravert Rouge' resistant (*left*) and 'Ingrid Marie' susceptible (*right*). FIG. 17—*below*: collar rot, susceptible and resistant seedlings following inoculation.

been sponsored by the DFTA. In 1964, 54 persons toured leading fruit areas and visited fruit tree research stations in England, Italy, France and Holland. Then in 1968 a group of 32 fruit growers and pomologists visited Belgium, Holland, Germany, Switzerland, France, Denmark and England. The most recent study tour was in 1971 when 63 persons visited Italy, Yugoslavia, Austria, East and West Berlin, England and Scotland.

On each tour, East Malling Research Station has been on the agenda. East Malling has provided much of the rootstock information, and two series (EM and MM) were classified or bred there. These rootstocks were tested in varied soil and climatic conditions and served as the foundation for establishing sound and practical suggestions in planting commercial orchards in U.S.A. and Canada. On each visit to East Malling, everyone there has shared generously their information with members of our group. In fact, a stop at East Malling has been and will be one of the travel prerequisites.

In June 1970, 96 members of the association flew by charter plane from Chicago to Yakima, Washington. From there four buses carried the group to Wenatchee, Washington, and to Penticton and Summerland, British Columbia for detailed studies of fruit growing and fruit handling in those important fruit areas. At each stop, leading horticultural agents explained and demonstrated latest developments in dwarf fruit trees, pruning and training, care, culture and general orchard management.

Operation—action—and results

The DFTA began with action and has continued in that vein to the present. Much of this is attributed to the Board of Directors and presidents who have been willing to become involved and participate in programme developments.

The following list of presidents have served and helped keep the leadership in the association at high keel the first 16 years. They are:

Wallace Heuser, Hartford, Michigan	1958–1961
Raymond Klackle, Belding, Michigan	1961–1963
Lorne Doud, Wabash, Indiana	1963–1965
Gordon Yates, LaCrescent, Minnesota	1965–1967
George Whaley, Ruthven, Ontario, Canada	1967–1969
John Bell, Jr, Barrington, Illinois	1969–1971
Kenneth McDonald, Martinsburg, West Virginia	1971–1973

Although the presidents and the board of directors are influential in the association's functions, objectives and progress, most decision and policy makings occur when the board meets, usually twice annually. At other times during the year the secretary carries the burden of setting meeting dates, getting programme speakers, writing and publishing newsletters, organizing national and international study tours, and numerous other chores.

Accomplishments

During the past quarter of a century the fruit industry in U.S.A. and in other parts of the world has gone through revolutionary changes caused by: (1) decreased labour, (2) increased land values, and (3) changed marketing systems. To stay in business the fruit grower had to: (1) up-date his equipment; (2) increase his acreage in some cases; (3) remove unproductive standard trees; (4) change his planting schemes to increase acreage yields; and (5) decide what new varieties and variety/rootstocks combinations to plant.

The association, in addition to sponsoring expenses for many out-of-state and out-of-country speakers at annual meetings, has aided in financing publications dealing with culture and care of compact fruit trees. To date, five volumes, 554 pages, of *Compact Fruit Tree*, have been published. Several awards, with plaques, to distinguished persons including past presidents, have been awarded.

These many and varied activities to keep the fruit grower informed have been financed from the annual membership dues which began with $1.00 in 1958, raised to $2.00 in 1959, and to $3.00 in 1963. Thus, much has been accomplished during the first years of this unique association. These accomplishments have helped the grower through a rather difficult transition period from the old standard orchard to the modern orchard of several hundred trees per acre.

Direct results to the grower

The grower benefits directly as a member of the DFTA. He is informed on use of correct scion/rootstock combinations, on tree spacing, training and pruning and other cultural practices.

Before the inception of the DFTA in 1958, most apple orchards were of trees on seedling rootstocks planted 30 × 40 feet or 36 trees per acre. Today very few standard apple trees are planted. Over 70% of the trees sold by nurserymen are budded on clonal rootstocks of the East Malling (M) or Malling-Merton (MM) series. Trees of this sort are spaced on the average of 10 × 20 feet or 218 trees per acre. This spacing is adequate for currently used orchard equipment and land use. However, some orchards are of higher tree densities (500 or more trees per acre). These require smaller equipment, but nicely lend themselves to "pick-your-own" operations.

The clonal rootstocks now commonly used are M.7, M.9, M.26 and MM.106 and MM.111. The tree spacing and number of trees per acre are generally adjusted according to vigour of the scion and the rootstock, soil type and terrain, and grower preference. The experimental M.27, when available, will be tested in U.S.A. for very high densities.

Through its meetings and newsletters, the association has informed growers how to train, prune and manage these more uniform smaller and precocious trees. With increased number of trees per acre, the growers soon realized that orchard management was most important for early and high production.

As a direct result of keeping informed on latest research results with compact trees, the grower has gained not only in more efficient production, but also in yields of quality fruit. The average production 20 years ago was less than 400 bushels per acre. Now this yield has doubled, and recorded yields up to 1,500 bushels per acre are not uncommon.

Credit to national and international co-operation

A generous exchange of ideas and information has transpired since the inception of the DFTA. And this exchange between horticulture research workers and fruit growers has helped to establish sound and practical recommendations for rootstock performance as to vigour, precocity and yield, tolerance to soils and climates, resistance to diseases and insects, tree life expectancy and other varied cultural and managerial practices.

Most fruit growing countries shared their research experience with the association. This has come about rapidly through exchange of publications, guest speakers from different countries, and first hand observations during study tours within the U.S.A., Canada and Europe.

Past, present and prospective

The Dwarf Fruit Tree Association was born out of need for information. It grew because it provided practical growing and orchard management hints, and because it came up with interesting annual meetings and tours in which everyone played a part. Fruit growers participate in programmes as speakers and panel members. Only growers are qualified to serve as presidents and board members and thus have a say in the objectives.

The association at present is still concerned with annual problems dealing with production of quality fruit for a quality conscious consumer. There is no "status quo" in its membership and in its directions.

The prospective of the association at this point is to keep ahead of production problems. And judging by the past and present activities the association will grow not only in membership but in leadership for the fruit industry, in developing new ideas for the future, and setting an example in international exchange of information for the survival of a healthy and prosperous fruit industry.

Much is yet to be done in the development of compact, high density orchards for efficient management, effective use of adaptable machines and fruit quality production. Dwarfing rootstocks are also needed for all other fruit crops, such as peaches, cherries, pears, plums and apricots.

In these and other related activities, the DFTA can play an increasing role in the future.

Breeding Apple Cultivars for the Future

R. WATKINS and F. H. ALSTON

East Malling Research Station

THIS country has had apple breeding featured in the fruit research of the Long Ashton Research Station, the John Innes Institute and the East Malling Research Station for much of the last half century. The Fruit Group of the Royal Horticultural Society, since it was started just over a quarter of a century ago, has shown a keen interest in the results obtained from these breeding programmes.

In general, it is true to say that, in their early breeding programmes the three research stations tended to follow a relatively simple but practical procedure in the breeding of new apple scion varieties. This consisted of intercrossing commercially important cultivars which carried separately the characters it was desired to combine in new cultivars. This was done without understanding the inheritance pattern of the characters concerned. Although this was a reasonable way of starting a breeding programme, the limitations of working without understanding the inheritance of important commercial attributes soon become apparent.

Apple rootstocks (probably the most critical factor in determining the quality, yield, and cost of production of particular scion cultivars) were in an even worse state than apple scion cultivars as a starting point for a new breeding programme since clearly identifiable stocks were non-existent. Hence, before it was possible to start breeding new apple rootstocks it was necessary to identify from among the mixture of types available those with the best characteristics. This task of identifying and exploiting the potential of the best existing rootstocks was successfully undertaken by Hatton (later Sir Ronald Hatton) at East Malling.

M. B. Crane at John Innes was quick to realise the value to plant breeders of obtaining a better understanding of the inheritance of important pomological characteristics. In general, he interpreted the results of his research to show that resistance to pests and diseases, quality, size, shape and colour of fruit were inherited in a complex manner. His detailed assessment of a wide range of traits set the pattern for future work in even greater depth and range.

R. L. Knight, Head of the Fruit Breeding Section at East Malling until his death in 1972, continued and intensified the investigation of individual characters and together with other members of his team was able to show that the inheritance of resistance to several of the apple diseases and pests as well as other important characters was controlled by identifiable genes whose behaviour could be predicted.

As a result of this and similar work at other research establishments it is now possible to define the genetical behaviour of about three dozen characters which are significant in the production of new cultivars. Two-thirds of these have been identified since 1960.

H. M. Tydeman of East Malling, by using the highly dwarfing rootstock Malling 27 (which he bred, and which was formerly known as 3431), was able to show that seedlings grafted on it would have a much shorter juvenile period (the time from seed germination to first flowering) than seedlings grown on their own roots. This procedure shortened the generation time. Encouraged by the availability of this new technique, Knight's team started to search for and find improved expressions of useful characters in wild species, knowing that the several generations of backcrossing necessary to transfer such characters to large-fruited varieties could be achieved in a time span no longer than that needed to produce a new wheat variety.

Information on the inheritance of important apple characters (illustrated by examining Knight's *Abstract Bibliography of Fruit Breeding and Genetics to 1960*—Malus *and* Pyrus), together with new techniques designed to utilize such information, provide the breeder with the type of tools necessary to produce significantly improved new varieties. Faced with the need to extend the frontiers of knowledge even further, it is vital to try to ensure that there is no unnecessary duplication of research effort either nationally or internationally. Duplication of effort can be minimized by dividing the detailed research on the inheritance of additional economically important characters (and research on the development of new techniques) among breeders and other research workers. The results from such work when pooled will allow each breeder to be able to conduct a comprehensive national or local breeding programme within a framework of steadily expanding knowledge. Given that it continues to be possible to promote international co-ordination of research and to facilitate exchange of information and advanced genetic lines then the prospects for producing significantly improved cultivars will continue to be good.

Specialization by research stations, within the concept of a co-ordinated attack on apple breeding problems, can be illustrated by reference to the work in this country. In recent years the John Innes Institute's apple breeding programme under A. Gavin Brown has specialized in screening north American apple selections (bred for scab (*Venturia inaequalis*) resistance) for resistance to the most important apple disease in this country caused by the mildew fungus, *Podosphaera leucotricha*. The best material from this source has been incorporated into their general breeding programme and also made freely available for incorporation into the East Malling programme. In a similar way Gavin Brown's studies on the inheritance of fruit acidity (when combined with the results obtained by Hedrick and Wellington of the New York State Agricultural Experiment Station, those of Nybom at the Balsgård Fruit Breeding Institute in Sweden and reinforced by the work at East Malling) give a clear guide on how to breed for levels of acidity acceptable to the consumer. Gavin Brown has also shown how the more complex inheritance of fruit sugars relate to fruit acidity and has been able to define the combinations of sugar and acid acceptable to the consumer. Turning to the Long Ashton Research Station, it is specializing in the induction of useful mutations in varieties such as 'Cox's Orange Pippin'. Successful mutations would in turn be valuable to the East Malling breeding programme. Long Ashton is also investigating the potential of high tree density "meadow" orchards while East Malling is developing bed systems of planting with the dwarf M.27 rootstock and is breeding types specifically geared to the requirements of high density orchards. This type of co-operation both national and international sets the scene for a breakthrough to high-quality-high-yield-low-cost-apple-cultivars for the orchards and home gardens of the future.

QUALITY

The selection of new cultivars with high quality fruit is the primary target of apple breeders. There is little merit in increasing pest and disease resistance, changing tree habit, or increasing yield unless these are combined with high fruit quality. Neither is it sufficient merely to maintain currently accepted standards of quality—there is both a need and considerable scope for improvement.

Factors which affect the eating enjoyment and appearance of apples are together considered as fruit quality. The genetic basis of most of the quality components is complex. However, breeding progress has been greatly improved since some of the basic factors have been found to be simply inherited. For example, a single dominant gene Ma controls the important acidic component of flavour. The presence of this gene can be detected in the field by means of an acid indicator (bromo-cresol-green). Seedlings without the Ma factor have an unacceptable, insipid flavour, consequently it is necessary to consider the genetic constitution of potential parents with respect to this gene in order to produce the maximum number of seedlings within the acceptable range of acidity.

Variation in acidity within the range determined by the gene Ma has, as mentioned in the introduction, been studied by the John Innes Institute in relation to variation in the sugar content. The results form a basis for planning future quality testing of advanced selections.

Gas chromatography has been used to study the aromatic component of apple flavour by breeders at both John Innes and East Malling. At least 20 different components are believed to be involved. The relationship between these factors and the "aromatic" flavour, such as occurs in 'Cox', needs to be the subject of additional research. Meanwhile, selection based on taste is usually adequate for preliminary selection of seedlings. Surveys for additional sources of good flavour have shown that few varieties come up to the standard of 'Cox'. Fortunately tasting surveys in families derived from this variety support the hypothesis that at least one basic aromatic component of 'Cox' is determined by a single gene.

Flesh texture, flesh colour and core type must also be considered in association with flavour in determining eating quality. In considering these characters the fruit breeder knows that cultivars such as 'Golden Delicious' contribute fine texture and juicy flesh to a high proportion of their progeny. Similarly, the desirable yellow-cream flesh, as found in 'Cox', appears to be simply inherited while a high proportion of 'Cox' × 'Court Pendu Plat' derivatives have a desirable core type which is neat and compact.

Storage and shelf life are also important aspects of fruit quality and need to be considered with particular regard to the effect of prolonged storage on flavour.

Fruit with good eating quality needs to have an attractive appearance if it is to sell well. Therefore, preference is given to selections which combine attractive and distinctive colour features with a good skin finish free from russet (except when selection is for fully russeted types) (Fig. 15). Fortunately single genes govern major components of skin colour and also complete russet (although inheritance of the tendency to partial russet, such as occurs in 'Cox', is complex). In addition, some cultivars (like 'Northern Spy') give a high proportion of derivatives with a good skin finish in crosses with 'Cox' and are therefore valuable parents for improving fruit appearance. Russeting and cracking are not the only deleterious skin finish factors to be considered. 'Lord Lambourne' transmits very greasy skin to a very large proportion of its progeny and 'Golden Delicious' progenies have many seedlings with prominent lenticels. Knowing the inheritance patterns of these undesirable features, care must be taken to offset these characteristics when selecting parents.

Fruit shape is another important factor in considering appearance. Although preferences vary, the almost spherical shape of 'Cox' is preferred in the United Kingdom. Consequently, selections with flat fruit (like 'Court Pendu Plat'), conical ribbed fruit (like 'Delicious'), or angular fruit (like 'Irish Peach') would usually be discarded.

For those gardeners who may not wish to spray too frequently cultivars incorporating resistance to pests and disease will produce better quality fruit. The benefit of having scab resistance and resistance to certain pests under such conditions is obvious. Incorporation of mildew resistance has an indirect effect on fruit quality since it makes it possible to eliminate sprays which cause russeting. Cultivars bred to flower late in order to avoid both spring pests and late frosts have the additional advantage that the fruit develops in a warmer period and so they are less liable to russet. Resistance to storage diseases such as *Gloeosporium* is particularly important in late maturing varieties since it helps to ensure that high quality fruit, both with respect to flavour and appearance, is available as late as March and April.

Quality components which are inherited simply are of considerable value in apple breeding since they can readily be combined in their entirety with important resistance and yield components. Nevertheless, the role of minor genes in modifying or "blending" these characters must not be overlooked. Furthermore, although the identification of major genes governing such basic characters greatly facilitates breeding planning and progress, it does not obviate the need for care during selection, rather it increases the probability of achieving success.

The aim at East Malling is to produce a range of distinct cultivars, red, green, yellow and russet, together with ones which are an improvement on 'Cox', for each season of maturity. Particular attention is being paid to breeding for improved storage and shelf-life since improvements in these two characters facilitate orderly marketing. Advanced selections which combine improved colour, good skin finish, pleasing shape with good texture and flavour are now being tested. In some cases the flavour is considered to surpass that of 'Cox'.

DISEASE AND PEST RESISTANCE

The introduction of new cultivars incorporating disease and pest resistance would result in lower production costs and simplified cultural practices by reducing the number of spray applications. Such features are now being combined with high fruit quality and high yield.

Sources of resistance to the principal diseases and pests of the apple have been located through extensive surveys of cultivars and *Malus* species (Table 1). In many cases resistance has been found to be controlled by a single dominant gene—a distinct advantage in planning a breeding programme. At least half of the seedlings derived from such sources may be expected to carry resistance, leaving ample scope for selection for fruit quality and yield.

The major part of an apple spray programme is directed against fungal diseases, with 14 applications against mildew, seven against scab and three to control the storage disorder *Gloeosporium*. New cultivars have been released in the U.S.A. which carry high resistance (derived from the ornamental crab *M. floribunda*) to apple scab. Using the most advanced American selections, British breeders have combined this resistance with acceptable English quality and flavour in a number of seedlings now under test at the National Fruit Trials. These selections also carry some resistance to mildew, but not sufficient to allow for a complete relaxation of the mildew fungicide spray programme.

At East Malling a very high level of mildew resistance, found in *M. robusta* and *M. zumi* is being transferred to the cultivated apple through a series of backcrosses. It appears from other work with *Malus* species that no more than three backcrosses will be necessary to combine high resistance to mildew with commercial size and quality. In addition to mildew resistance these species have a very short juvenile phase (3 years from germination to flowering) which is transmitted to a large proportion of their progeny. Initial crosses were made in 1964, the first backcross was made in 1968 followed by the second backcross in 1972. Thus it is reasonable to expect that there will be cultivars with high mildew resistance for trial by the early 1980's. Resistance, determined by the single dominant genes Pl_1 (*M. robusta*), and Pl_2 (*M. zumi*), is being combined in the backcrossing programme with the gene V_f (*M. floribunda*) which determines scab resistance. The new cultivars of the 1980's should include some which will not require sprays for either scab or mildew.

Resistance to *Gloeosporium* (Fig. 16), collar rot (Fig. 17) and apple canker has also been introduced into the East Malling breeding programme.

Most insecticidal sprays combat two or more pests, therefore the incorporation of resistance to an individual pest may have little effect on the spray programme. In addition to specific resistance, it has been found that late flowering (normally correlated with late leafing) can provide sufficient general spring pest avoidance to make the pre-blossom insecticidal application unnecessary. A combination of late flowering and resistance to woolly aphid and sawfly would save two insecticidal applications. Work on transferring sawfly resistance to the cultivated apple is at an early stage, but late flowering has already been combined with woolly aphid resistance.

The absence of sprays, following genetic control of spring pests and mildew, would facilitate predator control of the fruit tree red spider mite. Improved orchard hygiene and the use of chemical sex attractants promise to be the most practical biological means of codling moth control. Therefore, it may not be necessary to breed for resistance to these two pests.

The number of characters that may be incorporated into one cross is limited to those present in the two parents. A series of crosses will be necessary before all the resistance factors that are available are combined. Selections combining resistance to mildew, collar rot, woolly aphid, rosy apple aphid and rosy leaf-curling aphid, have been bred at East Malling. Other selections carry late flowering, scab resistance and resistance to rosy leaf-curling aphid and further selections are available which combine mildew, *Gloeosporium* and sawfly resistance. Within a few years it should be possible to make a cross with the potential for combining the basic components of pest and disease resistance together with good yield and high fruit quality. Meanwhile, priority at East Malling is given to the production of new cultivars with high resistance to both mildew and scab since these are the most damaging factors in terms of yield and fruit quality.

YIELD

An orchard consisting of compact spur-type trees (spaced nine inches apart within rows and an average of one foot apart between rows) each carrying 16 fruits would yield 6,000 bushels per acre (at present 1,000 bushels is considered to be good). This type of orchard would allow for the good light penetration necessary for the production of top quality fruit if each tree consisted of a main stem carrying fruiting spurs but no lateral branches, since less than half of the land area would be covered by plants. If such an orchard came into production in the second growing season and had to be cut-back and allowed to re-grow after five cropping seasons then an overall yield of 5,000 bushels per acre per year would be achieved. The genetic potential necessary to breed such plants is already available to plant breeders. This provides the apple breeder with three basic options: (1) to aim for this high yielding high quality type (thus making maximum use of the genetic potential), (2) to aim for an improved conventional type, or (3) to aim for an intermediate type. At East Malling all three options are being followed in order to provide for both the short-term and possibly long-term needs of the industry. The more compact types would have the additional advantage of providing the gardener with plants which were much more manageable in small gardens than the present-day commercial varieties.

ROOTSTOCKS

At present cultivated apple trees are normally made up of two or more parts joined by grafting and, in the simplest case, consisting of two parts—a rootstock and a scion. It is rare to see scion varieties growing on their own roots since most commercial cultivars lack rooting ability. However, with the increased interest in growing trees at high densities there would be a considerable advantage to have scion cultivars which could be produced by being propagated on their own roots. Breeding has now started to produce such cultivars although it is recognized that it will be a difficult project since it will be necessary to combine features which have in the past been bred for separately, in rootstocks and scions.

To be successful in high density plantings this new type of tree will need to have many, if not all, of the following characteristics:

1. Be cheap to produce—propagate easily; require no grafting; remain only a short time in the nursery.

2. Produce high quality fruit—give the best possible consumer satisfaction; look attractive; have a good shelf life; store well.
3. Maintain a high yield per acre—fruit early in the life of the orchard; fruit regularly (avoid or resist damage by spring frosts); have a long productive life.
4. Incur low production costs—need minimal pruning and management; have few disease and pest control problems; require no supports or wires.
5. Provide size control—fill space allocated rapidly; be easily limited to area provided; be readily held to height desired.

The breeding of self-rooting fruiting cultivars will require considerable work. In the meanwhile there will be a need to continue to breed rootstocks which are cheap to produce, induce scion cultivars to produce high quality fruit, and a high yield of fruit, minimize production costs, and provide the desired control over tree size.

At the present time there is little merit in attempting to breed seed propagated rootstocks since the very wide variation between seedlings results in the production of orchards with considerable variation between plants—although in general, they tend to produce vigorous trees which on average are slower to come into production than the best vegetatively propagated rootstocks. There is, however, likely to be renewed interest in the production of seedling rootstocks when the technique of producing haploid apple plants is mastered and it becomes possible to produce homozygous diploid apple selections which when crossed with similar plants would give uniform seedling progenies. Even if such a technique is available there is no certainty that it will provide a means of producing seedling rootstocks which are cheaper than those produced vegetatively—provided we continue to improve our vegetative propagation procedures as rapidly as in the past few years. Its greatest value is likely to be as a means of combining the characters of scions and rootstocks into self-rooting types which will be vegetatively propagated.

AMATEURS, CONNOISSEURS

Fruit breeding at the official research stations has traditionally been concerned with the production of cultivars for use in the commercial fruit industry. This is likely to remain the main function, at least for the foreseeable future. The amateur however, in addition to being interested in commercial cultivars, has often shown considerable interest in selections which have had only limited use in the commercial fruit industry. For example, the deep red coloured 'Michaelmas Red', which is crisp, juicy, has a pleasant flavour and follows 'Worcester Pearmain', is an attractive cultivar which might appeal to some amateurs. Such interesting cultivars, whether they rise to major commercial prominence or not, are likely to continue to be produced as by-products of the official breeding programmes and hence to be available to amateurs. The recent increase in support for research on the needs of the home garden industry means that there is likely to be an even greater degree of deliberate selection for apple cultivars to serve such requirements.

The general availability of reliable dwarfing rootstocks provided the component necessary for producing trees suited to small gardens. The possibility of breeding compact scion cultivars which if grown in a pot on a very-dwarfing rootstock such as Malling 27 could readily be kept under two feet in height, opens the door to the possibility of growing "bonsai" apple trees but without the complexities of management traditionally associated with the special methods of culture of bonsai plants.

The connoisseur who wishes to grow a range of cultivars for each season suited to his own particular tastes and interests and who has a relatively small garden is in a position to allocate as little as one square yard per tree by using the very dwarfing rootstock Malling 27. Within a modest garden new cultivars can be tried and old ones re-tried. The maintenance of collections by connoisseurs, particularly where they include commercial cultivars as well as unusual ones are potentially valuable sources of information to plant breeders. Such information can be particularly helpful where a record of the relative performance of each tree is available for a period of several years. It is a common observation that many apple cultivars do outstandingly well occasionally, but very few do consistently well every year. 'Cox' is an example of the former, only being induced to do well in a high proportion of years by being given the very best possible care and attention. In contrast, 'Worcester' is naturally a much more reliable cultivar.

SUMMARY

The consumer will require a reasonable range of types of quality apple throughout the year. Thus there must be culinary and dessert apples with good shelf-life for the early and mid-season and types with significantly improved storage characteristics for the late and very late season. Within the dessert apple category the consumer will wish to be able to choose between red, green (yellow), russet and 'Cox' types for each season.

The grower can only provide the consumer with reasonably priced fruit of high quality if cultivars are available which give regular high yields and which consistently have a high proportion of top quality fruit. Production costs, particularly those arising from the use of hand labour, must be significantly reduced relative to the final price of the fruit. This will be achieved with orchard systems and types of cultivars geared to mechanically aided production methods. Small trees at high densities are likely to be favoured. Such small trees are likely to be chosen from the following types: standard scion cultivars on dwarfing rootstocks; compact spur-type scion cultivars on relatively invigorating rootstocks; compact types grown on their own roots.

The amateur may in the future be offered an additional choice of a micro-combination consisting of a very compact spur-type scion cultivar on a very dwarfing rootstock for use in gardens or window boxes, or even for use as potted table decorations.

The improved possibilities for small scale orchards will stimulate the interest of those home gardeners who wish to produce a range of types within each season. Choice of cultivars with resistance to pests and diseases will minimize their management problems.

The availability of miniature trees will permit the connoisseur to collect numerous unusual cultivars within even a modest sized garden. Specialized connoisseur collections would have the additional advantage of contributing to the gene pool needed by the National Fruit Trials and the plant breeders to ensure that there is adequate genetic diversity available. Such genetic diversity is essential for future progress in apple breeding.

TABLE 1. Diseases and pest resistance/avoidance in the apple and their relevance to a routine spray programme

	No. of sprays	Resistance	Avoidance
Diseases			
Scab	7	V_f	
Mildew	14	Pl_1Pl_2	
Gloeosporium	3	ex Jonathan	clean foliage
Collar rot	—	Pc	
Canker	3	ex Dunkitt	
Pests			
Apple-grass aphid			
Apple sucker			
Caterpillars	1		late flowering
Rosy apple aphid		Sm_h	
Rosy leaf-curling aphid		$Sd_1Sd_2Sd_3$	
Woolly aphid	1	Er	
Sawfly		ex *M. zumi*	
Fruit tree red spider mite	2	*Malus* spp.	predators
Codling moth		Cultivars	orchard hygiene sex attractants

Clonal Variation in 'Cox's Orange Pippin'

A. I. CAMPBELL

University of Bristol, Long Ashton Research Station

'COX'S ORANGE PIPPIN' was introduced into general commerce over 140 years ago and a century later had become the most widely grown apple cultivar in England where, during the past 20 years, more trees of 'Cox' have been planted than all other dessert apples together. Although 'Cox' has been grown in most apple producing countries of the world, it seems to succeed best in the cooler temperatures and higher humidity conditions such as prevail in this country.

The high quality associated with 'Cox' in England has outweighed the many short-comings of the variety, which include susceptibility to several common fungal diseases, irregularity of cropping and sensitivity to environmental and nutritional disorders.

FACTORS AFFECTING THE FRUIT CHARACTERS

It is well known that a great many factors can influence the size, colour, skin finish and texture of the fruit. Indeed the variation to be seen in the dishes of 'Cox' at local and national fruit exhibitions illustrates the differences that can and do occur and the numbers and interactions of the factors involved.

Experimental results have shown that the rootstocks used, the manurial programme, the ground cover, and the aspect and soil of the orchard can affect particularly the size and colour of the fruit. For example, apples from trees on M.9 rootstocks are usually larger and mature earlier than fruit from trees on more vigorous rootstocks. Many growers are also aware that summer temperatures and water supplies, biennial cropping, spray materials and system of pruning can influence the fruit quality, size and skin finish. Other less well-known causes of variation include several virus diseases, particularly star-crack virus, which causes skin blemishes, and mosaic and latent viruses which affect skin colour and fruit maturity. Low spring temperatures and cold winds can also have a greater effect on the fruit quality than is generally appreciated and recent experiments have shown that even the position of the fruit within a tree can affect the final size and flavour.

In addition to all the external factors which influence the fruit characters, growers have been aware of the many coloured mutations or bud sports that occur in 'Cox' as in other widely grown cultivars. Several of these clonal selections are very different from the original description of 'Cox's Orange Pippin' noted in *The Gardeners' Chronicle* for October 31, 1857. The fruit was then described as "a medium sized, warm-looking, brownish-red apple with yellow crisp flesh of most exquisite flavour".

COLOURED MUTANTS

In the recently published *National Apple Register of the United Kingdom* (Muriel W. G. Smith, 1971) eight coloured bud sports of 'Cox' are noted. Many of the following descriptions and data, which are based on that and other N.F.T. publications, describe the characteristics of some of these natural mutations.

'Blangsted Cox' ('Körtegard Cox'). A selection grown widely in Denmark and other northern European countries. It is less striped than normal and although similar in colour is not as bright as 'Queen Cox'.

'Bledisloe Cox'. A New Zealand selection which is said to ripen a week or two earlier than 'Cox'. It is more striped than normal but yields from this clone in trials over a six-year period have been consistently lower than those from other forms of 'Cox' (Table 1).

'Cherry Cox'. The skin of this clone is a dull red colour with a rather unattractive purplish tone in some years. It arose in Denmark and in trials over five years the clone has not yielded as well as 'Cox' (Table 1).

'Cox' (Red Sport). A mutation with a brighter coloured skin than 'Crimson Cox' or 'Cherry Cox' which was found in the 1950's near Canterbury in Kent. The yield figures from trials with this clone have been higher than those from 'Cox' (Table 1).

'Crimson Cox'. A dark red bud sport which was introduced in 1928 from Herefordshire. The skin colour is less intense than 'Cherry Cox' but the fruit has a dull appearance which has not increased the popularity of this mutation.

'King Cox' ('Scarlet Cox', 'Giles Cox'). This is reputed to be a 'Worcester Pearmain' skin on a 'Cox' which arose when some 'Cox' trees were top grafted with 'Worcester'. Studies at Long Ashton however using light and scanning electron microscopes do not support this conclusion. The fruit is attractive with a conspicuous red striping on the skin, in all other respects it looks and tastes like 'Cox'. In trials at the N.F.T. however this clone has not yielded as well as the normal 'Cox' (Table 1).

'Queen Cox'. A bright red mutation without the normal striping, which was introduced by G. A. Maclean of Abingdon in Berkshire. This and 'Cox' (Red Sport) are probably the most attractive of the natural mutations. In addition, the trial results suggest that 'Queen Cox' will give higher crops than 'Cox' (Table 1).

Striped early 'Cox' sport. An early maturing selection produced by colchicine treatment at John Innes Institute. Trials have suggested that this clone has not maintained its early ripening character but further results are necessary before final conclusions can be made.

NATIONAL FRUIT TRIALS RESULTS

An examination of the growth and cropping results of a number of the replicated N.F.T. trials (2 blocks of 4 trees) in which the mutations have been compared with a standard 'Cox's Orange Pippin' show that over a six- or seven-year period these clones have not behaved in the same way as the standard. 'Queen Cox' and 'Cox' (Red Sport) for example, have out-yielded standard 'Cox' and the trees are similar in size, but 'King Cox' and 'Bledisloe Cox' have given consistently poorer crops and the trees are considerably smaller than those of the standard 'Cox' (Table 1).

TABLE 1. Total yield and average tree size of 'Cox' mutants as a percentage of standard 'Cox' (six- or seven-year replicated trials).

	Crop yield	Tree size
Bledisloe	65	77
Cherry Cox	93	103
Cox (Red Sport)	109	107
King Cox	78	82
Queen Cox	111	99

LONG ASHTON TRIAL RESULTS

It is clear from the N.F.T. data that clones of 'Cox' can vary considerably in skin colour, yield and tree size even when grown in the same conditions.

In order to examine in more detail the extent and possible causes of these variations a replicated trial of 36 clones of 'Cox', including some of the coloured mutants, was planted at Long Ashton in 1966. The budwood was obtained from growers and other experimental stations and the trees were propagated in the Research Station nursery on two rootstocks M.26 and MM.111.

In records taken over 5 years the 36 clones have shown consistent differences not only as expected in skin colour but also, as in the N.F.T. trials, in growth and yield. Differences have also been found in time of bud break, flowering and the rate of pollen tube growth. Fruit characters, other than skin colour, such as amount of russeting, time of maturity, fruit flavour, texture, size and number of seeds have also differed. Records have been taken of the occurrence of 'Cox' spot, mildew and storage rots, and some differences in the susceptibility of the clones has been noted.

The crop weight of 16 of the selections on MM.111, including 'King Cox' (clone 4), is shown in the Text Figure. Some of the heavier cropping clones (5 and 6) have yielded almost 3 times as much fruit as the poorest croppers (8 and 15). A comparison of the trunk diameters has shown that clones 5 and 6 are among the largest trees, with a mean trunk diameter of 6·9 and 6·7 cm, whereas clone 8 has a mean diameter of 5·8 and clone 15 averages only 4·4 cm. The results from the parallel trial on M.26 follow the same pattern and the strongest clones on this rootstock are larger trees than the weakest clones on MM.111. The differences noted in tree size and cropping reflect those found at the National Fruit Trials and underline the importance of examining characters other than skin colour, when determining the full merits of mutations.

Several differences were found in the time of bud-break and other flowering characteristics: for example, there could be as much as 10 days between bud-break of the earliest and latest clones. Pink-bud and petal-fall dates could also vary by as much as 5 or 6 days and the flowers of some clones appeared to pass through certain stages in flower development more quickly than others. No differences were found in the rate of pollen germination but the pollen tube growth differed. For example, when pollinated with 'Worcester Pearmain' pollen, only 5% of the pollen tubes reached the ovary in clone 18, compared with 22% in clone 17. It is therefore not surprising that clone 18 was one of the poorest croppers whereas clone 17 was a comparatively good cropper.

Records showed that the clones differed in their sensitivity to 'Cox' spot and mildew and that the presence of the two diseases seemed to be related. However, the tree to tree variation within a clone was too great for any definite conclusions to be reached on disease sensitivity or on whether the diseases were correlated with other growth factors.

An assessment of the fruit characters after storage, showed that the skin of some clones had more russet than others, the proportion varied from 80% to 5% and the differences were consistent from year to year and not related to colour, the percentage of russet however was higher in some years than in others. The skin colour of the 36 selections varied enormously; some, like 'Queen Cox', were bright red, others, like 'King Cox', were striped clones, yet others were brownish red normal selections and a few had almost no red colour over the yellow background. The percentage of red skin varied over the fruit surface from 85% in the highly coloured clones to 10% in the poorly coloured ones. The background colour of some clones, e.g. 19, remained green for much longer than in others suggesting that the storage life of the fruit could vary, and records on storage breakdown confirmed these observations.

On two occasions, December 1969 and February 1972, a tasting panel of 30 people examined the flavour, texture and appearance of some of the clones. As was expected the panel preferred the appearance of fruit from the bright red clones more than the standard 'Cox', although they disliked the very dark skinned ones. Flavour differences were small and varied within the fruits from single trees, so that no clear differences were apparent in the scoring. The texture scores, however, probably reflecting the ripeness of the fruit, varied considerably. Clones 5 and 17 scored consistently well whereas 3, 18 and 19 always scored badly. Clone 18 may have been over-ripe and 19 was probably under-ripe.

An examination of the known viruses present in the clones was made in 1966 and again in 1972, using a standard range of indicator plants. Viruses were suggested as a possible reason for the differences in growth and cropping of clones of 'Cox' trees noted by Goodchild and Moore (*J. hort. Sci.*, 1971, Vol. 46, pp. 13–16). Although all the clones in this trial were infected with at least three latent viruses, the differences in their performance could not be associated with any known virus infections.

Some of the heavier cropping clones in the trial have recently been heat-treated and a comparison of the growth and cropping of these with the EMLA clones has now been planned. Transmission experiments have also been carried out to examine the possibility that the differences found were due to an unknown transmissible factor.

FUTURE PROSPECTS

Further research work has been started at Long Ashton to induce a greater range of mutations, particularly with a view to increasing the cropping potential of 'Cox's Orange Pippin'. Gamma irradiation from a cobalt 60 source is being used and preliminary results suggest that differences in fertility can be induced. In addition, nearly 200 dwarf mutants of 'Cox' have also been produced after irradiation and the fruit from these is at present being assessed for colour, shape and season of maturity. The compact mutants appear to be very stable and by selecting clones with different growth patterns a range of vigour can be obtained; two of these are shown in Figs. 18 and 19. Great differences are obvious in the irradiated material in a wide range of other characters, particularly leaf shape and pose and fruit shape, colour and date of maturity. Preliminary results also suggest that some 'Cox' mutants will have greater tolerance to fungal diseases and nutritional disorders than the clones in use at present.

It seems likely that induced mutations of 'Cox's Orange Pippin' will be available within a few years with improved colour and skin finish and perhaps with a higher crop potential than the clones now in use. It also seems probable that the number of different types of rootstocks being used could be reduced by selecting compact or dwarf forms of

'Cox' and some of these could be very suitable for garden use. The selection of clones which could be harvested earlier or later than normal seem a distinct possibility and the results suggest that the storage period can also be extended by selecting clones which mature more rapidly or more slowly than normal.

If these promising preliminary results are maintained and extended then 'Cox's Orange Pippin' could continue to be the most popular apple in this country and be the mainstay of fruit industry for a further 100 years.

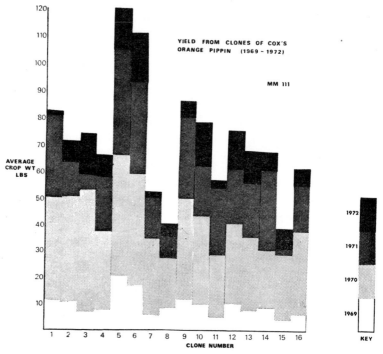

TEXT FIGURE. Average yield from sixteen clones of 'Cox' over four years.

Growing Apple Cultivars on Their Own Roots

E. H. WILKINSON

Wye College, University of London

TRADITIONALLY, apples are propagated by uniting the scion with a rootstock by budding or grafting. Both are lengthy techniques involving the production of rootstocks and their establishment for one year in the nursery, followed by budding or grafting, and then an additional year to allow for the growth of the maiden shoot. All this makes a maiden tree a comparatively costly article. Since apple cultivars can only be perpetuated in a stable form by vegetative propagation, methods permitting rapid and plentiful multiplication at low cost must be favoured for commercial use.

As the swing from extensive to intensive systems of culture has gained momentum, growers have become aware of the increasingly large amount of capital required for establishing such orchards. Thus, within this economic context, a distinct need has arisen to take a fresh look at propagation techniques to see whether a simpler, cheaper method could be devised in order to make establishment costs more realistic.

Before discussing this possibility, it would be of interest to ask why it is necessary to bud and graft apples. The answer usually given is to obtain the uniformity of growth and cropping imposed on the scion by the rootstock. This, of course, is true but the main reason is much more fundamental and is that it provides the only commercially reliable and efficient method available since, over the centuries, attempts to propagate by simpler or more direct means have proved to be either inadequate or impossible.

The prime purpose of the rootstock, therefore, is to nurse the scion throughout its life, a function which has tended to be ignored or taken for granted, because of the obvious commercial benefits bestowed by the range of rootstocks now available.

At this point one may speculate what the present position might have been if apple cultivars had always had the inherent ability to root from cuttings as readily as, for example, the black currant. The need for rootstocks would not then have arisen and it is safe to speculate that in these circumstances the majority of apple orchards would have consisted of cultivars growing and cropping on their own roots at least up to the end of last century. In these conditions, it is difficult to guess whether the incentive to investigate and discover the controlling influences of rootstocks would have arisen, but if it had, the benefits to be derived would have had to be weighed against an obvious increase in time and cost to produce such trees.

Still assuming that apples could be grown on their own roots present-day thinking immediately associates this with scion-rooting and, therefore, a state to be avoided. Can it be said, however, that all instances of scion-rooting have been detrimental to tree performance in orchards so affected? We suspect there are, scattered throughout the British Isles, numerous examples of scion-rooted apple trees which have been retained because either the grower was unaware it had taken place or that they performed adequately in this state.

Growing tree fruits on their own roots, however, is not uncommon in England and, in certain districts, it is an accepted commercial practice with plum cultivars such as 'Yellow Egg' or 'Pershore', 'Warwickshire Drooper', 'Kentish Bush' and also prune-damsons. It may be assumed that this arose from the capacity of the original seedlings and their progeny to produce suckers so that their collection offered the simplest and cheapest means of multiplication.

With apples, however, we have no knowledge of a modern planting of any commercial significance which was established with trees originally propagated on their own roots although there are records extending back to the seventeenth century where, in this and other countries, lesser known cultivars were successfully fruited after being raised from cuttings and layers. This was based on their capacity to produce "burr-roots" or "burr-knots" which are tuberous swellings on shoots and branches, with papilla-like outgrowths regarded as incipient roots with arrested development, capable of resuming growth to produce functional roots when placed in moist soil.

This phenomenon is associated with, and indicative of, free rooting characteristics and cultivars such as 'Burr Knot' ('Bide's Walking Stick'), 'Nurse Garden', 'Gennet Moil', 'Sweeting', 'Oslin', 'Kentish Codling' and 'Warner's King' have, in the past, been successfully propagated from cuttings. In 1926, Hatton stated he had records from many country districts where local apple cultivars were handed round from garden to garden by means of root-knotted branches. He also pointed out that the Codling group of apples, in particular, have always been traditionally associated with burr-knots and have been widely used as rootstocks on that account. In fact, the presence of burr-knots formed one of the principal bases of rootstock selection in Europe for what became known as the Paradise varieties.

In contrast, modern cultivars lack the capacity to produce burr-knots and are extremely difficult to root from cuttings. Thus, it can be said that the lack of apple cultivars growing on their own roots today, and the total dependence on budding and grafting for their multiplication, can be explained by the difficulty of inducing cuttings to initiate roots with any degree of certainty even when traditional techniques including stooling and layering are used.

One may ask, however, whether the technical advances made in recent years now make the propagation of apples from cuttings more of a possibility and, if so, would any advantages accrue and would it be wise or foolhardy to establish commercial acreages with trees of this type?

A possible solution to the first of these questions lies in the work carried out at East Malling Research Station where it was shown that careful integration of the correct physiological status of the mother tree, with precise control of the rooting environment in storage bins, induced ready rooting in hardwood cuttings of certain clonal apple *rootstocks*.

Since clonal apple rootstocks and cultivars originated from selected individual seedlings of the same species it could be argued that cuttings of certain cultivars might also respond to this particular technique, but apparently this is not the case, as stated in the annual report of East Malling Research Station for 1964: "Some 30 scion varieties of apple have been propagated on their own roots: none was found to root as readily as even the shyest rooting commercial rootstock."

A few years ago we became interested at Wye in the possibility of propagating apples from cutttings and, despite the difficulties encountered by previous workers, we proceeded with our investigations in order to gain experience of the problems involved.

All trials were carried out using basal hardwood cuttings 12 to 30 inches long according to the material available, collected either from virus-free mother trees or young trees in the nursery or from fruiting trees up to 33 years old. Most cuttings were taken in autumn (October–November) and given a basal dip of indolyl butyric acid (IBA) in 50% ethanol; 2,500 ppm IBA was used most commonly but 5,000 ppm and 10,000 ppm were tried more recently. The treated cuttings were then placed in a coarse sand/peat compost (8 inches deep) and remained there for 12 to 16 weeks at a basal temperature of 20°C.

Irrespective of the source of cuttings or the variation in treatments given, results were as follows: number of cultivars tested, 72; number of cuttings used, 4,330; mean rooting response for all cultivars, 9·4%. (For comparison, hardwood cuttings of 14 clonal apple rootstocks were included and gave a mean rooting response of 56%, i.e. approximately six times greater than cultivars, thus confirming the findings of East Malling in 1964.)

Rooting ability varied considerably from 20 cultivars showing no response up to 90% for the best. Those rooting in excess of 20% were as follows:

Egremont Russet	90	Worcester Pearmain	29
Cornish Aromatic	47	Wellington	27
Grenadier	44	Lord Derby	24
Cox's Orange Pippin	41	Beauty of Bath	22
Lord Lambourne	32	Cheddar Cross	20
Miller's Seedling	32		

Unfortunately, some of the main trials were carried out under suboptimal conditions, due to problems encountered with source of cuttings and moisture content of compost, which undoubtedly caused a depression in the overall rooting response, but even if these could have been prevented, it is doubtful whether the improved response would have made this technique an attractive commercial proposition.

It is evident that a number of problems will have to be solved before growing apples on their own roots can become a commercial reality. Some of these are briefly discussed below.

Firstly, will it be possible to devise a technique guaranteeing a consistently high rooting response year by year for all important commercial cultivars? Although the storage-bin method has yielded some encouraging results it is apparent that in general they fall short of the standard required and it would appear that far greater control will have to be achieved over the various factors involved if the desired improvements are to materialize.

One approach which merits further study concerns the influence of the physiological state of the mother trees on the subsequent rooting ability of cuttings taken therefrom. At Wye investigations are proceeding whereby it is hoped to produce mother trees of this type by rooting, under mist, detached shoots induced from the roots of own-rooted cultivars and growing them on to form a nucleus of mother trees. These shoots, which arise as adventitious buds from isolated groups of meristematic cells in the bark, show juvenile characteristics and have a much greater rooting ability than softwood cuttings taken from shoots arising from normal axillary buds. It is hoped that the hardwood cuttings which will be eventually collected from these trees will retain the capacity to root more readily.

It is possible, however, that greater success may be achieved by using sophisticated techniques involving the culture of excised tissues *in vitro*, as is being tested at Long Ashton Research Station, which may lead to the development of very rapid micro-vegetative methods for multiplying desired clones.

Secondly, since rooted cuttings require a further year in the nursery for establishment, do all cultivars respond satisfactorily to this treatment? Experience to date shows a marked difference existing between cultivars in their response but further trials will be required to show if this variation is a constant varietal feature.

Percentage establishment of rooted cuttings after one year in the nursery

Miller's Seedling	93	Crispin	55
Lord Lambourne	91	Grenadier	45
Worcester Pearmain	88	George Cave	44
Lord Derby	79	Early Worcester	29
Laxton's Superb	75	Bramley's Seedling	25
Egremont Russet	60	Cox's Orange Pippin	12
Beauty of Bath	55		

Thirdly, will own-rooted trees in their permanent position grow and crop as efficiently as those on the less vigorous rootstocks in popular demand today? Information on this point should have been available from a quarter acre orchard planted in 1966–67 with a limited number of own-rooted cultivars raised from cuttings from virus-tested mother trees. Unfortunately, in its short history the depredations caused by frosts (1968 and 1972) and excessive bird damage in most seasons, make the records obtained of little value. Speaking generally, however, it can be said that vegetative response was vigorous and was accentuated to some extent in those cultivars suffering the greatest crop losses. The degree of vigour within each cultivar was however consistent thus providing uniformity, but it varied between cultivars and appeared to be related to their inherent vigour. 'George Cave', 'Laxton's Superb', 'Early Worcester', 'Lord Derby' and possibly 'Lord Lambourne' were the most vigorous with 'Grenadier' and 'Worcester Pearmain' the least. At Wye, 'Cox's Orange Pippin' made very unthrifty trees on its own roots.

'Cox's Orange Pippin', 'Laxton's Superb' and 'Early Worcester' produced little blossom throughout and rarely more than a few apples per tree each year. 'George Cave' averaged 13 lb/tree in 1970 but little else in other seasons, whereas 'Lord Lambourne' and 'Worcester Pearmain' suffered so severely from bird attack that rarely was more than 2 or 3 lb picked per tree.

The response of 'Grenadier' was the most satisfactory; 20 trees totalled 1,038 lb in the four seasons 1968–71 inclusive. In 1971, 870 lb were picked, equivalent to 43 lb/tree which, on the 12 × 6 foot plant, represents 645 bushels/acre in the fifth year from planting; more than 90% of the crop was picked without the aid of ladders. 'Lord Derby' (18 trees) totalled 602 lb, 330 lb coming from the 1971 crop at 18 lb/tree.

The size and quality of fruit was satisfactory and graded out well when sold through normal commercial channels. The few 'Cox's Orange Pippin' harvested were small, russeted and cracked.

The final question concerns pests and diseases and experience suggests that their incidence and control was no different to that in orthodox orchards. It is appreciated, however, that collar rot (*Phytophthora cactorum*) could become a problem since none of the trees has the resistance provided by the rootstock but no cases were recorded in the experimental orchard.

One final observation of interest was that no suckering occurred in any of the cultivars grown for cropping and this was confirmed in winter 1971–72 when many root systems were excavated and without exception were free of vegetative growths. Their absence on roots of undisturbed trees appears to be associated with a very efficient inhibitory effect because when detached roots were made into cuttings and placed in moist vermiculite, numerous swellings of the bark were evident after 14 days, all of which led to the emergence of single or multiple shoots within a month.

Conclusion

The concept of growing apples on their own roots is an interesting one but it has become apparent that a number of problems will have to be solved before it can become a reality. Those associated with rooting and establishment are most likely to be solved first and should provide the means of producing trees at a fraction of the cost of conventional maidens thus achieving the main objective of significantly reducing costs of orchard establishment.

Little information is available, however, on the growth and cropping potential of own-rooted trees in the orchard but it can be said that they exhibit "uncontrolled uniformity", i.e. in any given set of circumstances, all trees of the same cultivar show similar vegetative responses but the rate of growth and ultimate tree size will depend on the inherent vigour of each cultivar. In most instances examined, this is greater than if they had been planted on M.9, M.26 and MM.106.

It would appear, therefore, that in order to make own-rooted trees efficient cropping units, the lack of rootstock control will have to be replaced by the careful and intelligent use of growth and fruit-regulating chemicals and hormones. Only time will tell if this can be achieved and whether the whole concept of growing and cropping apple cultivars on their own roots is an economic possibility.

On Controlling the Size of Apple Trees

A. P. PRESTON

East Malling Research Station

IT was in 1924 that the late Sir Ronald Hatton writing in *The Garden* made some suggestions for a planned fruit garden. He later put these into practice in his own garden at East Malling. From this experience and his own research work at the Station, he drew up a set of plans for model fruit gardens of varying size while he was temporarily laid up with a bout of "rhumatiks". One of the first of these gardens was planted near the Victoria Gate in the Royal Botanic Gardens at Kew. Others followed, at Bradbourne, East Malling Research Station where they have recently been replanted within the area now known as the Hatton Fruit Gardens, and at the R.H.S. Garden at Wisley. As far as apples were concerned two principles were fundamental to the design and success of these gardens. Firstly, that a small quantity of fruit from each of a large number of cultivars should supply fresh apples from the garden over as long a period as possible. Secondly, to control tree size by the use of dwarfing rootstocks and, where necessary, by summer pruning. Thus it became possible for the private gardener to grow a wide range of cultivars not readily available from shops and which were in danger of going out of cultivation. Now, exactly thirty years after Hatton (1943) wrote "An amateur's fruit garden" for the Royal Horticultural Society's Journal, it seems appropriate to summarize recent research findings on quality of planting material, tree training, pruning and apple rootstocks, where these may be of benefit to the amateur fruit grower in controlling tree growth and cropping during the next decade or so.

PLANTING MATERIAL

The laborious task of testing and indexing apple rootstocks and scions for virus diseases has recently been undertaken jointly by the Long Ashton and East Malling research stations. This has resulted in the production of EMLA fruit trees (Campbell) comprising rootstock and scion material free from all known viruses. This plant material is being propagated rapidly by fruit tree nurserymen under strict requirements for isolation. EMLA trees should gradually become available to the amateur fruit grower and his planting material should therefore be free from the insidious effects of virus disease.

Some nurserymen are now budding their apple rootstocks one foot above ground. This not only eliminates the risk of scion rooting, which can nullify the careful choice of a dwarfing rootstock, but it also reduces the risk of a susceptible scion cultivar (e.g. 'Cox's Orange Pippin') becoming infected with collar rot (*Phytophthora cactorum*). If trees can be worked a few inches higher still, they could be planted a few inches deeper than they were in the nursery. Such trees, during their first season after planting, develop a second tier of roots just below ground level. This greatly improves the anchorage of the tree.

The primary objective of the fruit grower, whether professional or amateur, should be to cover the ground as quickly as possible with potential fruiting wood. With this in mind a recent trial compared maiden trees with feathers (the one-year lateral shoots on the first year's scion growth from budded rootstocks) as primary branches with trees without feathers. Where feathers were used as branches the trees made more shoot growth, had large trunks and at three years old, when they were lifted and weighed, they were heavier. In addition, the crotch angles of the primary branches were wider when feathered trees were used (Preston 1968). More recent experience with trees on a dwarfing rootstock has shown that the first crop from trees where feathers were used in tree training was 39% heavier than that from trees which were planted as non-feathered maidens. The shortened-back feathers provided sites for early fruit buds to form and these fruited the second summer after planting. It is therefore well worthwhile to specify feathered maiden trees when placing an order with a nursery, even if they cost a little more.

CHOICE OF ROOTSTOCK

Since there is no single "right" rootstock to cover the wide range of soil and growing conditions that can be present where fruit is to be planted a choice of rootstock has to be made. For intensively grown trees such as cordons, pyramids, spindlebushes and lightly pruned bushes, the choice at present is between the dwarfing M.9 and the semi-dwarfing M.26. The relative sizes of 'Cox' trees on these rootstocks at seventeen years of age are shown in Fig. 1 together with a tree on M.7 for comparison. Where conditions suit M.9 this rootstock is highly satisfactory giving good tree size control and yields of high quality fruit. But on some stiff boulder clays, or thin sandy soils, tree size and fruit size can be disappointing and in these conditions the more vigorous M.26 might be more suitable. Our experience with trees on M.26 has been that, initially, they grow vigorously and then settle down and yield crops with good fruit size and colour. This rootstock makes a tree intermediate in size between those on M.9 and M.7, but as Fig. 20 shows, tree size on M.26 is nearer to one on M.7 than on M.9.

The title of this volume implies a glimpse into the future so that it may not be out of place to mention a new dwarfing apple rootstock that may not be readily available to amateurs for some years. M.27 was raised at East Malling by Mr H. M. Tydeman from a cross between

M.13 and M.9. This rootstock is very dwarf and it has been extensively tested at East Malling in three field trials. Fifteen-year-old trees were half the size of those on M.9 growing under comparable conditions. For the professional fruit grower this new rootstock has two possibilities; firstly, for use in very intensive bed systems of planting similar to those at present under test at East Malling, and secondly, for use on those farms in England and abroad where even trees on M.9 grow too strongly. Six-year-old trees of 'Cox' on M.27, M.9a and M.26 are shown in Fig. 21. What are the chief characteristics of this new rootstock, and has it possibilities for the amateur fruit grower? Firstly, it can hold a wide range of the more common apple cultivars at no more than 3 or 4 feet in height, making a flat-headed "table-top" tree when mature. Secondly, it can drastically reduce the size of vigorous triploid apple cultivars such as 'Holstein Cox'. Thirdly, it is almost completely free from the troublesome habit of suckering from underground. Lastly, and perhaps this is the rootstock's most unusual feature, at about the fifth or sixth year shoot growth virtually ceases and detailed winter or summer pruning of leaders and laterals is unnecessary. In fact we have found that an occasional thinning out of spurs or shortening back the longer spur systems is the only pruning that is necessary once the tree is established and the main branch framework secured. A comparison of the amount of shoot growth on six-year-old 'Cox' trees on M.27, M.9a and M.26 (Fig. 21) shows that, whereas pruning back of the numerous laterals on the trees on M.9a and M.26 was necessary the following winter, no such treatment was needed by the trees on M.27 which had reached maturity early. The yields from trees on M.27 are naturally lower *per tree* than those from larger trees on M.9 and M.26. The average annual yield of 'Cox' on M.27 over fifteen years was 10 lb per tree, and during the last five years of the trial (years 11 to 15) the crop averaged 16 lb per tree (Preston 1971). On account of their final size trees on M.27 can be spaced closer together and the yield from a row of trees should not be less, and can be much more, than that from trees on more vigorous rootstocks which need wider spacing. At East Malling we have some demonstration plots of 'Cox', 'James Grieve' and 'Golden Delicious' on M.27 covering a wide range of tree spacings; these include a very close spacing of 20 inches apart (Fig. 22) in an attempt to exploit fully the vigour of this new rootstock. These trees have been successfully held for the past three years by short stakes at every tenth tree, the trees being tied to a double length of polypropylene binder twine secured to the stakes. Our experience with trees on M.27 has shown that they are not best suited to methods of pruning involving many unpruned leaders and laterals. On account of their precocity and high yield in relation to tree size such laterals often break away from their parent branch under weight of crop. However, a simple method of pruning where all leaders and laterals are shortened back by half their length, cutting always to either an underneath or sideways-placed bud, ensures a good supply of short cropping branches. Because trees on this rootstock normally stop shoot production quite early, it is essential to secure framework branches and their attendant short fruiting laterals, where they are required within five years of planting. Corrective pruning, such as the removal of very upright shoots, is sometimes required.

LATE SUMMER PRUNING

The summer pruning of bush apple trees in the garden, to induce fruitfulness and restrict tree size, is normally carried out in late July when new shoots are shortened back to five leaves above the basal cluster (Beakbane). Once the trees have reached their allotted room, however, it is possible to contain them by cutting back all one-year shoots to their point of origin about one month before harvest. With late-ripening cultivars this is normally done during the third week in August. My colleague, Mr M. A. Perring, and I have been experimenting with this method on bush trees of 'Cox'. We have found that, not only is fruit colour improved, but that bitter pit, a storage disorder, is markedly reduced in a year when this is prevalent. Furthermore, this late summer pruning has not resulted in a second flush of growth, even in a year when August and September were abnormally wet months. We are now using this late summer pruning technique on 'Egremont Russet' bushes. With this cultivar our aim is not only to reduce bitter pit and restrict tree size, but also to improve fruit size. In a heavy cropping year 'Egremont Russet', like 'Laxton's Superb', normally carries very small apples on one-year laterals. Removal of these laterals the previous August by late summer pruning should lessen the proportion of small fruit in the total crop. This simple method of removing all one-year shoots in mid-August is well worth the consideration of growers anxious to hold their trees at their present size.

During the past six years my colleague, Mr H. W. B. Barlow, and I have been investigating the possibility of holding tree size by using the late summer pruning technique but, in this case, pruning the trees with an electric garden hedge cutter. Such a method sounds more suited to the ranch-farming methods of apple growing practised by some of our American cousins, and it must be anathema to the private gardener used to lavishing tender loving care on his fruit trees. However, it often occurs that, at a critical time for orthodox summer pruning, a spell of ill health or a call to overseas for the grower upsets the pruning routine. In these cases the use of an electric hedge cutter in late August may prove helpful. The first seven trees of 'Cox' in Fig. 23 have been pruned in this manner for the past six years. These are followed in the photograph by seven trees pruned at the same time but by using hand secateurs, followed again by another batch of trees pruned by hedge cutter. The spread of the trees has been contained each year at about one metre (Fig. 24). Fruit size and colour have been good and little damage occurred to the fruits when the hedge cutter was used. After five consecutive years' pruning solely with a hedge cutter, it was necessary the following winter to thin out, by secateur, some of the weaker laterals that had accumulated in the centres of the trees.

SHOOT AND FRUIT COMPETITION

There is much truth in the old dictum that "growth and fruitfulness are opposed to one another" and it is usually the aim of the professional fruit grower to strike a balance between cropping and shoot growth by pruning and fruit thinning. Trees making too much shoot growth often fail to retain an initially promising fruit set to harvest time. In a series of experiments at East Malling recently (Quinlan and Preston) involving the removal of one-year shoots or shoot tips at different times during the growing season, the seat of competition between shoots and fruitlets has been located at the shoot tip. In a comparison between the removal of complete shoots and the removal of shoot tips fifteen days after blossoming both treatments improved fruit set. But whereas shoot removal caused a heavier "June drop" compared with untreated trees, shoot tip removal increased both the number of fruits retained to harvest and crop weight. Shoot tipping and the removal of any regrowth is laborious and has to be done by hand (finger and thumb), but the method might be useful for the amateur fruit grower to try on a cultivar that sets well but fails to retain much of its crop beyond the "June drop" period. Furthermore, the annual practice of shoot tipping considerably restricts tree size (Figs 25, 26).

REFERENCES

BEAKBANE, A. B. 1947. Intensive methods of apple and pear growing. *J. Roy. hort. Soc.*, Vol. 72, pp. 145–154.
CAMPBELL, A. I. 1972. 'EMLA' fruit trees. *Agriculture, Lond.*, Vol. 79, pp. 334–340.
HATTON, R. G. 1943. An amateur's fruit garden. *J. Roy. hort. Soc.*, Vol. 68, pp. 361–374.
PRESTON, A. P. 1968. Pruning and rootstock as factors in the production of primary branches on apple trees. *J. Roy. hort. Sci.*, Vol. 43, pp. 17–22.
PRESTON, A. P. 1971. Apple rootstock 3431 (M.27). *Rep. E. Malling Res. Stn 1970*, pp. 143–147.
QUINLAN, J. D. and PRESTON, A. P. 1971. The influence of shoot competition on fruit retention and cropping of apple trees. *J. Roy. hort. Sci.*, Vol. 46, pp. 525–534.

Pear-Apple Hybrids

A. G. BROWN

John Innes Institute, Norwich

FROM time to time fruits are produced which are claimed to be crosses between apples and pears. Invariably these turn out to be either apples or pears and not hybrids. Some are apples like the old 'Lemon Pippin' which has oval fruit with a bulbous protuberance round the stalk giving a somewhat pear-like appearance. Others are apples that taper markedly to the calyx end of the fruit rather like a pear in reverse since the stalk is at the broad end. Among the pears are cultivars like 'Bergamotte d'Esperen' which are quite apple-shaped. Frequently the claim is even made for apples that are said to taste like pears and *vice versa*.

Many serious attempts have been made to hybridize apples and pears. In Russia Cernenko in 1936 pollinated the 'Tonkovetka' pear with mixed apple pollen. Many of the 25 fruits which resulted were seedless but some 65 seeds were obtained of which 16 germinated. The cotyledons were like those of the pear but the true leaves were intermediate between pear and apple. Most of the seedlings did not get beyond the second or third leaf stage owing to the root system being defective. Later Goroskova reported that 5,000 apple flowers pollinated with 'Tonkovetka' pear produced very few seeds and, most of the seedlings produced died because the root system was defective.

In 1952 Mr M. B. Crane and E. Marks first reported the production at the John Innes Institute of intergeneric hybrids between cultivated pears and apples. This happened more or less by accident for, in an attempt to produce apomictic seeds in pears by pollinating pear flowers with apple pollen and treating the styles and ovaries with hormone, they produced true hybrids. Further crosses were made. Pollen tube growth and embryo sac development were studied and it was found that only pears which could produce parthenocarpic fruits were suitable parents for pear-apple hybrids. Later the author reported the production of seeds from crosses between tetraploid pears and apples. It is many years since the first hybrids were made and in all nearly 1,000 seedlings have been produced.

Many will have forgotten and others will be quite unaware of the excitement these first hybrids aroused and of the great amount of publicity, often quite frivolous, that they received. Enquiries are still made about the fate of the "papples" and this short account will complete the story for the time being.

The cultivars used as female parents have been very limited. The diploid cultivar 'Fertility' was used in the first crosses and proved so

Clonal Variation in 'Cox's Orange Pippin', pp. 75–80

Photos: Long Ashton Research Station

FIG. 18—*above*: one-year-old trees of 'Cox', (*left*), three trees of an irradiated compact form (*right*) three trees of a standard form. FIG. 19—*below*: one-year-old trees of 'Cox', (*left*) a standard form, (*right*) an irradiated form showing extreme dwarfing (scale: each band is 10 cm.).

Controlling the Size of Apple Trees, pp. 87–91

Photos: East Malling Research Station

Fig. 20—*top*: seventeen-year-old bush trees of 'Cox' on M.9 (dwarfing), M.26 (semi-dwarfing) and M.7 (semi-vigorous). Fig. 21—*centre*: six-year-old bush trees of 'Cox' on M.27 (very dwarfing), M.9 (dwarfing) and M.26 (semi-dwarfing). Fig. 22—*below*: part of a two-year-old bed of 'Cox' with 'James Grieve' pollinator, both on M.27, rows 4½ feet apart with trees at 20 inches apart.

Controlling the Size of Apple Trees, pp. 87–91

Photos: East Malling Research Station

Fig. 23—*top*: mature hedge of 'Cox', the first seven trees pruned by electric hedge cutter for six years, the next seven trees secateur pruned, followed by more hedge cutter pruned trees.

Fig. 24—*right*: the hedge in Fig. 23 held to about one metre wide.

Controlling the Size of Apple Trees, pp. 87–91

Photos: East Malling Research Station

The effect of shoot tip removal on seven-year-old trees of 'Cox' on M.26.
FIG. 25—*above*: shoot tips removed at the fourth leaf above the basal cluster.
FIG. 26—*below*: normal winter pruning.

Intensive Culture of
Plums, pp. 96–99
*Photos: East Malling Research
Station*

Fig. 27—*above*: half
standard 'Victoria' trees
at six years old on root-
stocks of the E.340 series
compared with St.
Julian A control.

Fig. 28—*left*: summer-
pruned trees of 'Victoria'
on St. Julian A to show
the central-leader tree
form, (*left*) at four years
(*right*) at five years.

Breeding Sweet Cherries, pp. 100–113

Photos: John Innes Institute

FIG. 29—*Above*: A. dwarf seedling (*left*), normal (*right*); both five months old and from the same family, B. flowers dwarf. *Left*: rugose leaves of dwarf seedlings. *Below*: dwarf seedlings showing variation in vigour; the seedlings are ten years old and on their own roots.

Breeding Sweet Cherries, pp. 100–113
Photos: John Innes Institute

FIG. 30—*right*: leaf trace inoculations of maiden seedlings, (*centre*) resistant seedlings, (*right and left*) susceptible seedlings (see p. 106).

Soft Fruit Breeding, pp. 121–135
Photo: Scottish Horti-cultural Research Institute

FIG. 31—*below*: segregation for resi-tance to leaf spot disease in a progeny elated to *Ribes dikuscha*. Two sus-ceptible segregates have lost their leaves prematurely.

**Soft Fruit Breeding,
pp. 121–135**

*Photos: Scottish Horticultural
Research Institute*

FIG. 32—*left*: development of
more than one lateral from a
node of 'Glen Clova' raspberry.

FIG. 33—*below*: 'Marmion'
strawberries (*left*) showing field
resistance to red core disease
in conditions which cause
'Montrose' (*right*) to succumb.
'Templar' and 'Talisman' in
the background both show
good field resistance.

successful that it has been very widely used in the experiments, together with its giant sport the 2-4-4-4-diploid-tetraploid chimaera 'Improved Fertility'. 'Doyenné du Comice' and 'Conference' have been used but with very limited success and 'Dr Jules Guyot' and 'Louise Bonne of Jersey' failed completely. The apple cultivars used as male parents were 'Crawley Beauty', 'Cox's Orange Pippin' and 'Merton Worcester', all diploids, and two tetraploids of Swedish origin 'Alpha 68' and 'B.T.37/60'.

The hybridizations were all made on pot-grown trees in a cool greenhouse. The technique used throughout was to pollinate emasculated pear flowers with apple pollen and, immediately after pollination, to treat the base of the styles and the ovary with an aqueous solution of β-naphthoxyacetic acid at 40 ppm. This treatment was repeated after 24 hours. Where the two forms of 'Fertility' were used the crosses were always successful and the fruit set was similar to what would be expected following pear × pear pollinations. The average number of seeds per fruit was 6·2 compared with 7·4 from pear × pear and the percentage germination of the pear-apple hybrids was 85·7 compared with 83·3 for pear. At all stages the hybrids were equal to normal pears. The seedlings grew quite normally for a time then, as mentioned in the earlier reports, the root system became defective and most of the seedlings died when they were about a month old.

To try to overcome this, seedlings were grafted on seedling apples and pears. Pear and apple seeds were sown and brought into the greenhouse about a fortnight before the hybrids so that they were a little in advance and suitable to use as stocks on which to graft. The grafting method was one evolved by Mr R. J. Garner at East Malling. The tip of the hybrid seedling was cut off with two or three leaves and the base of the stem cut to a wedge shape. The apple or pear seedlings to be used as stocks were cut off just above the cotyledons and a vertical cut made in the stem. The scion was inserted in the cleft, held in position with a cotton thread tie and the union securely held by binding with a small piece of self-adhesive crepe rubber. The grafted seedlings were put into a shaded propagating frame. This method was remarkably successful and very few grafts failed.

These grafted plants made quite satisfactory growth during their first season. They went dormant in the autumn and received the normal winter chilling requirements to break dormancy in the spring. Most failed to respond and only a few grew in the second year. The most successful cross from the point of view of survival was 'Improved Fertility' × 'Alpha 68' where, out of a family of 90 seedlings, 14 survived for four years. There is no doubt that, apart from a defective root system which can be overcome by grafting, the above ground part of the plant is all wrong too. Plants which did survive for four years never looked as if they would make a tree. The growth was stunted, the leaves small and the plants seemed to have lost the ability to produce lignin with the result that the growth was rubbery and no longer rigid.

Comparing seedlings grafted on apple with those on pear it was found that those on apple were more successful than those on pear. Each year approximately half of the seedlings were grafted on each stock and of the 22 seedlings which survived four years or more 19 were on apple and three on pear stocks. The one seedling that remained alive for six years was, however, on pear.

Of the 128 plants of the family from 'Fertility' × 'Cox's Orange Pippin', 38 were planted out in the nursery and all died during the following winter. Of the remainder in pots 16 survived and four of these were growing sufficiently well to permit the removal of propagating material. A total of 35 M.2 rootstocks were budded. These made a few inches of growth during the following season after which they died. Similarly 32 M.2 rootstocks were budded with material from 'Improved Fertility' × 'Alpha 68' and like the previous family all died after making a few inches of growth.

Since our initial successes others have repeated our crosses with equally disappointing results and none of the seedlings have ever lived long enough to flower. The plants, however, while they were alive proved very interesting in many ways.

Half of the family of 'Fertility' × 'Merton Worcester' seedlings were inoculated by spraying with a spore suspension of apple scab (*Venturia inaequalis*) and the other half with pear scab (*Venturia pirina*). The seedlings had just reached the first true leaf stage which is the normal time to test apples and pears for susceptibility to scab. Although minute necrotic pits were observed it was not found possible to produce sporulating lesions with either fungus. It appears, therefore, that the hybrids are resistant to both forms of scab.

Biochemical studies of the phenolic substances found in the leaves of apples and pears have been made by several investigators. Apple leaves contain as their principal phenolic the glucoside phloridzin. The pear leaf contains three phenolics in quantity, chlorogenic and isochlorogenic acids and the glucoside arbutin. The two glucosides are quite specific. Phloridzin is always found in apple leaves and never in pear, and arbutin is always found in pear and never in apple. In pears grafted on apple rootstocks the arbutin remains in the pear scions and phloridzin in the apple and neither pass across the graft union. Dr A. H. Williams at Long Ashton Research Station examined leaves of some of our pear-apple hybrids and found that all the phenolics of both apple and pear were present. It would appear that certain phenolics when brought in contact with each other are toxic. This provides a possible explanation for the poor growth and eventual death of the pear–apple seedlings since in these plants the phenolics of pear and apple are brought together in one plant.

A number of intergeneric hybrids do exist within the Pomoideae and most of these have occurred naturally. *Sorbaronia dipelii* (*Sorbus aria* × *Aronia melanocarpa*) is quite fertile and produces seeds freely, *Amelosorbus* (*Amelanchier* × *Sorbus*), *Sorbopyrus auricularis* (*Pyrus communis* × *Sorbus aria*) produces a few fruits but few seeds and *Pyronia veitchii* (*Cydonia oblonga* × *Pyrus communis*) is also fertile.

There was much speculation in the press at the time when the pear-apple hybrids were first made about the probable taste of the fruit and what they should be called. Papple was the most usual suggestion. To end in a lighter vein I would like to include a little fantasy (50 years hence) from the pen of Gordon Rowley which appeared in the *John Innes Society Journal*:

"Have a plummigranate," she said.

I gazed at the bowl of choice fruits, each as large as a football and reluctantly declined. "Too rich for me, I'm afraid. What are the smaller fruits?"

"Damages."

"Damages?"

She smiled, sensing my perplexity, "Damsons crossed greengages, you know. The new John Innes Hybrid No. 6,927,146. Wonderful things they turn out nowadays."

"True," I replied, helping myself to another damage. "Take the prunectangerine, for instance."

"Pleasant enough," she mused, "But give me the old peacherriplumcot every time. A whole meal in every fruit."

"They claim that for gilberts, too."

This time it was her turn to look puzzled.

"Haplo-grapes crossed with tetra-filberts, you know," I replied, with an air of feigned authority. "2n = 47, and an obligate apomict. When you finish the grape there's the nut waiting in the middle."

"Sounds delightful," she said, "but for sheer deliciousness there's one dish you can't beat."

"Curranges?"

"No. We had it at the Crane Memorial Banquet last Friday. Took two weeks to prepare, and they say it cost twice its weight in dollars."

"Glacé grapricot with figgage sauce and octoquince au gratin?"

"Nothing so common as that."

"You don't mean . . . ?"

"Of course! What else?—mock apple!"

Intensive Culture of Plums

A. BERYL BEAKBANE AND MORWENNA M. FULLER

East Malling Research Station

IN growing a crop intensively one is attempting to increase the productivity of a given area of land. Since the amount of land that can be devoted to fruit in gardens is usually restricted, it is obviously important to aim at high productivity. With this end in view, a close plant of small, easily managed trees is most desirable. In fact, the potential value of high density planting for all fruit crops—not only those grown in gardens—is now recognized by the International Society for Horticultural Science and a special working group has been set up by the Society to study it. One of the first essentials for success in such a project is to acquire trees which have an inherent capacity to remain small while, at the same time, bearing heavy and regular crops. For apples, this is already a practical possibility. Well grown trees on Malling 9 will remain small while still producing sufficient annual shoot growth to support high quality fruit. No plum rootstocks giving a comparable degree of control over scion growth are yet available in commerce. The clone St Julien A has proved to be of value where trees of intermediate vigour are required, but it is in the semi-dwarfing, rather than the dwarfing, class and trees worked on it do not, as a rule, begin to bear a significant crop until about the seventh year. In 1966, Gilbert drew attention to this lack of a dwarfing rootstock for plums and he suggested that the best that could be done was to work trees on St Julien A and grow them in the compact form obtainable by pyramid culture (Beakbane and Preston, 1962).

NEW PLUM ROOTSTOCKS

An account of an expedition to France to seek suitable parent plants for new races of plum rootstocks was published in 1948 (Beakbane and Thompson). From seed parents selected at this time, a new range of plum rootstocks known as the E340 Series (Beakbane, 1969) has been raised and has reached the stage at which the effect of individual clones on the growth and fruiting of plum scions is being assessed in field trials at East Malling Research Station, and at the Experimental Horticulture Station at Luddington. One of the new clones E340/4.6 appears to be a promising dwarfing rootstock (Fig. 27) with the capacity to induce precocity in the scion (Beakbane and Fuller, 1972). This clone may provide a degree of control over growth and fruiting that will place it in a vigour class for plums somewhere between Malling 9 and the even more dwarfing Malling 27 for apples. It is capable of bearing fruits on the main stems of two-year-old trees and at seven years old, the amount of fruit borne in relation to head capacity was more than twice that for comparable trees on St Julien A (Text Figure). Meanwhile, until the clone E340/4.6 is released to the industry as we hope it may be in a few years, the intensive culture of plums must still be based on the use of the rootstock St Julien A. The choice of tree form is therefore especially important.

TREE FORMS FOR PLUMS

Most of the plums grown in England are on invigorating rootstocks and trained as half-standards, a form of tree that is not only slow to crop and difficult to manage but is also particularly susceptible to branch breakage under the weight of the crop (Beakbane and Preston, 1962). The introduction of new dwarfing rootstocks for plums may influence the form of tree selected for intensive planting. The use of the semi-dwarfing rootstock St Julien A has already begun to popularize the pyramid form (Fig. 28). When dwarfing rootstocks are available, it may be possible to consider other forms including those based on the free spindlebush (Walker, 1966).

The summer-pruned pyramid
One-year-old trees should be planted at 9 to 12 feet apart, preferably in autumn. Pruning in the first spring consists of heading the trees back to about 5 feet from ground level in late March, and cutting back laterals arising from the main stem to 8 to 10 inches. Summer pruning is carried out about the third week in July. The length to which the shoots should be cut will depend on the nature of the scion and rootstock varieties, but for 'Victoria' on St Julien A branch leaders should be shortened to 8 and laterals to 6 inches. The cut is made just beyond a downward- or outward-pointing bud in order to encourage horizontal growth. These short branches forming a wide angle with the trunk are stronger than long pendulous branches, possibly partly because a reduction in shoot length by pruning is not followed by an equivalent reduction in thickening. After the first season, the central leader is not pruned until April when it is shortened to one-third of its length. This operation is repeated annually until the tree reaches the desired height, after which time the central leader should be shortened to one inch, or less, in May. Any vertical shoots competing with the leader should be removed.

Trees to be grown in the pyramid form should not be staked unless grown in a very windy situation. Staking of any form of plum tree introduces the risk of infection by fungal and bacterial diseases through wounds caused either by the ties or by the stake itself. Staking is usually adopted to prevent trees leaning or falling over. It has, however, been shown that if young trees are never supported they build up a

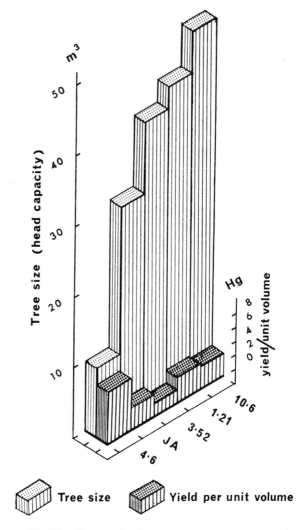

TEXT FIGURE. Yield in relation to head size of tree. The effect of four plum root-stocks from the new E.340 Series on the growth and yield of 'Victoria'. Control rootstock 'St Julien A'. Age of trees 7 years.

root system and branch framework that is capable of standing alone. The tops of the trees should be free to move and so set up stresses that will result in the build-up of a good taper to the trunk (Leiser *et al.*, 1972).

REFERENCES

BEAKBANE, A. B. 1969. A new series of potential plum rootstocks. *Rep. E. Malling Res. Stn 1968*, pp. 81–83.

BEAKBANE, A. B. and FULLER, M. M. 1972. A dwarfing plum rootstock. *Rep. E. Malling Res. Stn 1971*, pp. 151–153.

BEAKBANE, A. B. and PRESTON, A. P. 1962. Three tree forms for plums. *Rep. E. Malling Res. Stn 1961*, pp. 57–60.

BEAKBANE, A. B. and THOMPSON, E. C. 1948. Exploration for fruit tree rootstocks. *R.H.S. Fruit Yearb. 1948.* pp. 14–19.

GILBERT, E. G. 1966. Tree fruits for the garden (excluding cherries). *Fruit Present and Future.* R.H.S. London, pp. 39–62.

LEISER, A. T., and others. 1972. Staking and pruning influence trunk development of young trees. *J. Amer. Soc. hort. Sci.*, Vol. 97, pp. 498–503.

WALKER, J. H. 1966. New developments in fruit tree shaping. *Fruit Present and Future.* R.H.S., London, pp. 63–71.

Recent Advances in Breeding Sweet Cherries at the John Innes Institute

P. MATTHEWS

John Innes Institute, Norwich

T HE main problems facing the sweet cherry industry today are the susceptibility to bacterial canker of the most widely grown varieties and the lack of dwarfing rootstocks. Another problem the cherry grower has to contend with is cross pollination since all cherry cultivars are self-incompatible. This requires careful orchard planning and the selection of cross-compatible cultivars which may be uneconomic. In this context the development of self-fertile cultivars could be significant.

SELECTION OF MERTON CULTIVARS

For a number of years work on the sweet cherry has been carried out at the John Innes Institute. Between 1920 and 1937, 28 selections were made from 1,028 seedlings on the basis of size, flavour, appearance and productivity, and from these, eight Merton cultivars were selected and named (Table 1). Significant acreages are now being grown of 'Merton Bigarreau', 'Merton Favourite' and 'Merton Glory'. More than 50 parents were used in these crosses and the most successful, judged by the number of times they occur as one of the parents of a useful selection, were 'Napoleon', 'Noble' and 'Schrecken'. Between them these appear as one or both parents of 19 selections, so producing on average a much higher proportion of useful seedlings than did the other parents.

Between 1948 and 1962, many seedlings were obtained from crosses where one or both parents were Merton cultivars. Similar selection criteria were used, 1,298 seedlings were evaluated and ten were thought to be worthy of further assessment in the National Fruit Trials. Undoubtedly the most successful parents in this series of crosses were 'Merton Glory' (which appears as one parent in five selections sent for trial) and 'Merton Heart'. One combination deserves special mention, the seedlings of 'Merton Heart' × 'Wellington B' were all of extremely high quality; in a family of 32, six were regarded as being of value, including one which has been sent for trial. Another family of 22 seedlings derived from 'Emperor Francis' × 'Bedford Prolific', also deserves a special mention. Five were selected and two named and released, viz., 'Merton Premier' and 'Merton Reward'. In addition to these families very high percentages of seedlings with above average

TABLE I. Merton cultivars raised at the John Innes Institute

Cultivar	Seedling no.	Parents	Season	Juice colour	Incompatibility group	Bacterial canker
Merton Bigarreau	193	Knight's Early Black × Napoleon	M	B	II	S
Merton Bounty	490	Elton Heart × Schrecken	M	B	II	R
Merton Crane	519	Napoleon × Schrecken	M	B	II	S
Merton Favourite	185	Knight's Early Black × Schrecken	EM	B	II	S
Merton Glory	1278	Ursula Rivers × Noble	EM	W	O	R
Merton Heart	404	Schrecken × Elton Heart	EM	B	VI	R
Merton Late	659	Belle Agathe × Napoleon	L	W	IX	S
Merton Marvel	868	Noble × White Bigarreau	LM	W	III	R
Merton Premier	418	Emperor Francis 'A' × Bedford Prolific	EM	B	IV	R
Merton Reward	414	Emperor Francis 'A' × Bedford Prolific	LM	B	IX	R

commercial qualities have been recovered from 'Ursula Rivers' × 'Van', 'Ursula Rivers' × JI Sdg. 1464 ('Noble' × 'Napoleon'), and 'Van' × 'Late Black Bigarreau'.

SELF-FERTILITY AND ITS EXPLOITATION

Spontaneous self-fertile mutations of the S-gene (controlling sterility) are known to occur, and compatible mutations can be induced by X-rays. Three self-fertile mutations, seedlings 2420, 2434 and 2538 were isolated by Lewis and Crowe (1954). Progenies derived from these have now been analysed (Matthews, 1971b), and these studies have led to a precise understanding of the nature of self-fertility in the cherry and to greater precision in the exploitation of such mutations in breeding programmes (Table 2; Text Fig. 1).

All three self-fertile seedlings carry an unmutated S_3-allele as well as the mutant self-fertile allele (SF). Therefore to obtain families in which all the seedlings are self-fertile, the mutants should only be crossed with cultivars belonging to groups II, III, IV, V and VI all of which also carry S3 (Text Fig. 1).

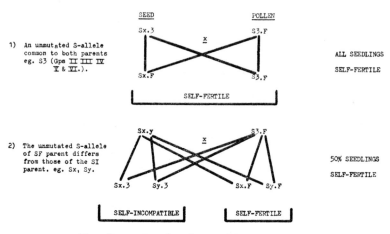

TEXT FIG. 1. Breeding from self-fertile seedlings.

The advantages of self-fertile cherries have still to be proven. However it seems likely that orchards of self-fertile cherries will be more efficiently pollinated especially in unfavourable weather conditions. This should result in increased yields coupled with regular cropping. In addition, uneconomic pollinators could be removed allowing the development of the single cultivar orchards.

The three self-fertile seedlings raised by Lewis and Crane have been used by Lapins (1971) in Canada to obtain 1,500 self-fertile seedlings from which one selection has been raised and released, 'Stella' (JI 2420 × 'Lambert').

TABLE 2. Parentages and genotypes of John Innes self-fertile
seedlings (Matthews, 1971b)

Seedling	Parentage	Genotype (S-allele)
2420	Emperor Francis × Napoleon X-Ray Pollen	3·4*
2434	Emperor Francis × Napoleon X-Ray Pollen	3·4†, 3·3†
2538	Self, from Merton 42 (Schrecken × Gov. Wood)	3·6, 3·3*, 3·3†

* Self fertility is due to loss of pollen activity.
† Self fertility is due to loss of pollen and style activity.

Self fertility has been introduced in the cherry breeding programme at the John Innes Institute where the three original seedlings, 2420, 2434 and 2538 have been systematically crossed, as pollen parents, with cultivars having high resistance to bacterial canker. From this series of crosses more than three thousand self-fertile seedlings have been raised from which two selections have so far been made and sent for trial. In these selections self-fertility is combined with resistance to bacterial canker, high productivity and large fruit size.

BREEDING BACTERIAL CANKER RESISTANT CHERRIES

Bacterial canker is caused by *Pseudomonas morsprunorum* and the related pathogen *P. syringae*. Field observations of mature orchards have consistently indicated considerable differences in resistance between cultivars (Grubb 1949). A breeding programme aimed at producing a range of resistant cultivars was initiated in 1958. The first step was to determine the relative resistance of a representative collection of the principal cherry cultivars.

A mixture of *P. morsprunorum* isolates varying in virulence, were inoculated into the bark of ten 2 year-old shoots of each variety. From the resulting cankers a mean canker length was derived for each variety. In this way 113 cultivars were screened for resistance (Table 3). Resistance varied continuously from those in which cankers were small (10·0 to 15·0 mm) and poorly developed, to highly susceptible ones in which the cankers were very large (40·0 to 150·00 mm), and well developed, producing symptoms of wilt, and frequently killing whole branches. On the basis of these results cultivars have been placed into five resistant classes; 1, very high resistance to 5, very low resistance. The principal sources of resistance are to be found amongst the 38 cultivars in classes 1, 2 and 3, which field observations indicate are seldom seriously damaged in English orchards.

As well as surveying sweet cherry cultivars some 42 *Prunus* species were also screened for resistance to *P. morsprunorum*. Most are grown either for their fruits or as ornamentals. A few, such as *P. pseudocerasus*, *P. mahaleb* and *P. cerasus* have been used by East Malling in interspecific crosses with *P. avium*, to produce dwarfing rootstock selections for the sweet cherry (Tydeman and Garner, 1966). The range of resistance found amongst these species, as might be expected, greatly transcends that found in cherry cultivars. An arbitrary classification has been adopted and species have been placed into five resistance groups (Table 4). Species in group 1 are extremely resistant to *P. morsprunorum*; it was found impossible to induce cankers of any significance in these species.

The genetics of resistance to the pathogen was studied in a group of 1,231 fruiting seedlings growing on their own roots. Inoculation methods were identical to those used in establishing varietal and species

TABLE 3. The relative resistance to bacterial canker (*Ps. morsprunorum*) of sweet cherry varieties based on the mean canker length from 10 inoculations of 2-year-old shoots (Matthews, 1969)

Resistance to bacterial canker

Class 1 *Very high*	Class 4 *Low*	Class 4—*contd.*
Black Elton	Baumann's May	Waterloo
Black Oliver	Bedford Prolific	Wellington 'A'
Caroon 'B'	Big. de Schrecken	Werder's Early Black
Chapman 'B'	Bing	Windsor 'A'
Cleveland Big.	Black Circassian	
Guigne de Winkler	Black Cluster	Class 5
Hedelfingen falso	Black Tartarian 'A'	*Very low*
Ludwig's Big.	Black Tartarian 'B'	Allman Gulrod
Maiden's Blush	Bowyer Heart	Big. Gaucher
Merton Premier	Bradbourne Black	Black Downton
Nutberry Black	Bullock's Heart	Black Eagle 'A'
Purple Griotte	Caroon 'A'	Burcombe
Reidern 2nd Early Black	Cryall's Seedling	Carnation 'C'
Sam	Dun Mazzard	Florence
Smoky Dun	Early Amber	Governor Wood
Strawberry Heart	Elton Heart	Kentish Big.
Turkish Black	Emperor Francis	Knight's Elton 'B' and
Yellow Spanish	F 12/1	'C'
	Guigne d'Annonay	Lambert
Class 2 *High*	Hedelfingen	Late Amber
Big. Jaboulay	Hooker's Black	Lester
Big. Reverchon	Judy's Fancy	Merton Big.
Frogmore Early	Knight's Big.	Merton Favourite
Heinrich's Riesen	Knight's Early Black	Merton Late
Kassins Fruhe Hertz	Malling Black Eagle	Mezel B No. 1
Merton 42	Merton Bounty	Mezel B No. 2
Merton Heart	Merton Crane	Napoleon
Merton Marvel	Merton Premier	Roundel
Noir de Guben	Monstreuse de Mezel	Semis de Burr
Rockport Big.	Mumford's Black	Sparkle
Velvet	Noble	Tillington Black
Victoria Black	Noir de Schmidt 'A'	Vernon
Wellington 'B'	Norbury's Early Black	Weston's Amber
	Ohio Beauty	White Big.
Class 3 *Moderate*	Peggy Rivers	
Bohemian Black Big.	Ramon Oliva	
Bolium	Rodmersham Seedling	
Late Black Big.	Ronalds Heart	
Merton Glory	Smoky Heart	
Merton Reward	Stark's Gold	
Newington Late Black	Sue	
Old Black Heart 'B'	Turkey Black Heart	
	Turkey Heart	
	Van	

TABLE 4. Relative resistance of *Prunus* species to bacterial canker (*Pseudomonas morsprunorum*), based on ten bark inoculations of each species. Species in groups 3, 4 and 5 span the range of resistance found in sweet cherry varieties, Table 3

Group 1. No cankers produced.
  P. curdica, P. insititia, P. pleuroptera, P. conradinae, P. lusitanica, P. laurocerasus.
Group 2. Inoculations rarely produce cankers, those produced were always very small.
  P. spinosa, P. cerasifera, P. cocomilia, P. mexicana, P. mandschurica, P. fruticosa.
Group 3. Inoculations produced cankers which were small and poorly developed, frequently gumming.
  P. × blireana, P. enzliana, P. incisa, P. nipponica, P. × juddii, P. serrulata, P. mahaleb, P. emarginata, P. virginiana.
Group 4. Inoculations produced large, well developed, clearly defined, gumming cankers up to 35·0 mm long.
  P. bokhariensis, P. mume, P. × amygdalo-persica, P. davidiana, P. serrula, P. latidentata, P. × yedoensis, P. cerasus, P. pilosiuscula, P. serotina.
Group 5. Inoculations produced large gumming cankers which frequently killed the inoculated branch.
  P. domestica, P. hortulana, P. persica, P. tenella, P. triloba, P. besseyi, P. sargentii × subhirtella, P. cantabrigiensis, P. avium actiana, P. × fontanesiana, P. padus.

---

resistance. In all, 22 families were analysed derived from parental varieties representative of all resistance classes, and in all possible combinations. Considerable variation between seedlings for resistance was found. The distribution of seedlings in the different resistance classes is illustrated for families derived from intercrossing cultivars with different levels of resistance (Text Fig. 2). In these, as in all other families so far analysed, variation in resistance is continuous, showing partial dominance of low susceptibility.

The results obtained from these crosses showed that reasonable numbers of resistant seedlings could be obtained either from open pollinated cultivars or from crosses between those of resistant classes 1, 2 or 3 which could yield up to a maximum of 17% of resistant seedlings (Table 5).

Results from earlier selection work at the John Innes Institute show that only 1% of seedlings from crosses between superior cultivars are likely to be commercially useful. This fact coupled with the relatively low percentage of resistant seedlings produced from any one cross meant that to be successful in combining resistance with quality and productivity large numbers of seedlings would have to be raised.

A leaf trace or node inoculation method simulating natural infection was developed in order to screen large numbers of maiden seedlings. Five-month-old, pot-grown seedlings are inoculated at five nodes with a mixture of *P. morsprunorum* isolates representing different

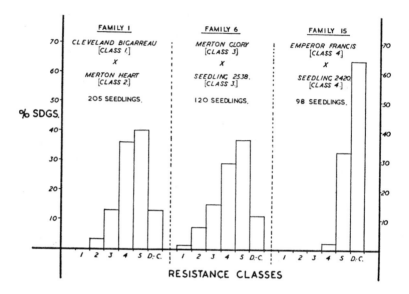

TEXT FIG. 2. Resistance to bacterial canker in sweet cherry progenies derived from parents differing in resistance, based on bark inoculations of 2-year-old wood. D-C: inoculated branches dead or cankers continuous.

pathotypes and screened for resistance 5 months later (Fig. 30). Seedlings unaffected by these inoculations are planted and left for 2 to 4 years after which they are reinoculated via the bark in a manner similar to that used in the assessment of varietal resistance. Seedlings found to be resistant to both modes of inoculation are grown to fruiting and selections made on the basis of fruit quality, size and productivity.

Inoculations of fruiting seedlings have shown that the methods used measure two uncorrelated facets of resistance; resistance to infection (node infections) and resistance to growth or spread of the pathogen

TABLE 5. The frequency of seedlings resistant to bacterial canker in families derived from crosses between varieties of different resistance classes. Data summarized from 22 families (Matthews, 1969)

Type of cross (resistance classes)	Total inoculated	% Seedlings in resistance classes			Total % Classes 1, 2 and 3
		1	2	3	
1, 2 or 3 × 1, 2 or 3	581	0·2	3·8	12·9	17·0
1, 2 or 3 × 4 or 5	92	0·0	0·0	2·2	2·2
4 or 5 × 4 or 5	470	0·0	0·0	0·5	0·5

(bark inoculations). It is thus possible to find seedlings and cultivars which are highly susceptible to infection but which are highly resistant to spread of the pathogen, e.g. 'Early Rivers', and others highly resistant to infection but highly susceptible to canker development. This second situation occurs in 'Roundel' and F 12/1 which are both commonly found to be free of infection but on which large cankers develop when bark tissues are artificially inoculated.

In breeding for resistance, the parent cultivars were either selected primarily for high resistance, fruit quality taking second place, to give progenies containing large numbers of resistant seedlings, or selected with greater emphasis being placed on fruit quality to give progenies with relative few seedlings of high resistance and with the expectation that a high proportion would be of good quality.

Where possible, specific crosses were made between cultivars known to give good quality seedlings. Otherwise large numbers of seedlings were obtained from open-pollinated resistant cultivars. In all nearly 27,000 seedlings have been raised and screened for resistance. In particular, large, open-pollinated families were screened derived from 'Caroon B', 'Emperor Francis', John Innes Seedling 1045 ('Hedelfingen' × 'Jaboulay'), 'Merton Bigarreau', 'Merton Favourite', 'Merton Glory', 'Merton Late' and 'Yellow Spanish' whilst families of 300 or more seedlings were raised from the following crosses: 'Hedelfingen' × 'Frogmore Bigarreau', 'Merton Glory' × 'Merton Reward', 'Merton Late' × 'Merton Glory', and 'Van' × 'Frogmore'. In the attempt to combine self-fertility with resistance, large families of self-fertile seedlings were obtained from 'Caroon B' × JI 2434, 'Merton Premier' × JI 2538 and 'Turkish Black' × JI 2538.

Up to and including the 1972 fruiting season 55 selections had been made and sent to the National Fruit Trials for assessment. These span the season from early to late and for each season there are both black and white cherries. In addition to the selections sent for trial 62 secondary selections have been made and are being kept under observation for a further period. Predominant amongst the parents of selections are the varieties JI 1045, 'Merton Glory', 'Merton 42' ('Schrecken' × 'Govenor Wood'), 'Merton Premier', 'Ursula Rivers' and 'Van'. Many of the white cherry selections show very obviously their 'Merton Glory' parentage which they closely resemble in both fruit size and appearance.

With the availability of such a wealth of material, increasing emphasis is now being placed on other characters such as resistance to cracking, precocious bearing, ease of fruit detachment for mechanical harvesting, tree shape and structure and tree size. Amongst the many thousands of seedlings which have been raised considerable variation in vigour has been seen between seedlings. Upright and vigorous seedlings, currently of little value, are particularly common in progenies derived from 'Merton Heart' which itself possesses this character. On the other hand small and relatively slow growing seedlings, not to be confused with genetic dwarfs (see below) occur in the progenies of many cultivars, especially those of 'Merton Glory'. Small tree selections of this type with large fruits and resistance to bacterial canker have been made and are included in those at present under trial at Brogdale. If they maintain their small stature they could be exploited either as small tree scion varieties on F 12/1, or grown on their own roots, or used as semi-dwarfing rootstocks. They are of course resistant to bacterial canker.

It is well known that certain cherry cultivars, for instance 'Napoleon', are precocious in bearing. This character appears to be strongly inherited, and is a particularly important one to the commercial cherry grower. Certain of the bacterial canker resistant selections on trial are now known to possess this attribute and all resistant seedlings are being assessed for this character.

As well as the small tree selections now on trial, resistant seedlings with marked dwarf or slow growing habits but lacking desirable fruit characters, have been picked out and sent to East Malling for testing and evaluation as dwarfing rootstocks.

DWARFING ROOTSTOCKS

Distinctive dwarf seedlings were frequently recorded in seedling progenies raised in the incompatibility studies. These dwarfs were severely limited in shoot growth with rugose leaves which sometimes showed evidence of chlorosis (Fig. 29, A, centre). Dwarfs are distinct from small tree segregants which have already been noted. They were first observed in the cross 'Black Tartarian' × 'Napoleon' and they have now been recorded in a large number of intervarietal crosses in which they segregate in frequencies varying between 50% to 1·0%. On the evidence obtained from intervarietal crosses, back-crosses and intercrossing dwarfs it is now clear that the dwarf phenotype is determined by two genes, one of which is a recessive suppressor of the other (Matthews, 1971a).

Considerable variation occurs in vigour of dwarfs which is dependant on the parental cultivars (Fig. 29). After 10 years growth on their own roots, dwarfs are between 20% and 50% smaller than their normal sibs, they possess an extended juvenile period and it may be up to 8 years before they flower. Flowers differ from normal in that the petals are reduced in size, remain cupped as in the bouquet stage with the style and stigma protruding through incurved petals (Fig. 29, B).

Clearly recognizable segregations of 1 normal to 1 dwarf and 3:1, 13:3 and 7:1 occur in families derived from cultivars heterozygous for the dwarf determining genes. Typical examples of such segregations involving widely grown cultivars are illustrated in Table 6.

More than 100 cultivars have been surveyed for the presence of

TABLE 6. Examples of dwarf segregating families where the ratios of normal to dwarf seedlings are 1:1, 3:1, 13:3 and 7:1; from Matthews (1971a)

Cross	Normal	Dwarf	Ratio
Knight's Early Black G × Kassins Fruhe Hertz	33	33	1:1
Bradbourne Black × Merton Favourite	19	18	
Napoleon × Merton Heart	41	16	3:1
Late Black Bigarreau × Knight's Bigarreau	83	27	
Hedelfingen × Guigne d'Annonay	71	15	13:3
Late Black Bigarreau × Cryall's Seedling	84	22	
Noir de Guben × Early Rivers	194	27	7:1
Merton Late × Merton Heart	267	36	

dwarf determining alleles; these are now known to occur in 48 varieties (Table 7). Similar dwarf segregants were found in progenies derived from a Duke cherry 'Empress Eugenie' considered to be a hybrid between *Prunus avium* and *P. cerasus*.

As potential dwarfing rootstocks, genetic dwarfs show great promise (Table 8). A small trial conducted at the John Innes Institute with 'Merton Glory' as scion variety has shown that trees worked on "dwarfs" are significantly reduced in height and spread, are less vigorous, have a flat tree shape and are reasonably well anchored. Fruits from dwarf trees were of equivalent size, rather bolder in colour, and ripened 2 or 3 days earlier than fruits from the control 'Merton Glory' on F 12/1 trees.

The promise of a commercially useful dwarfing rootstock shown by this trial and the development of a series of clonal dwarfing rootstock selections by East Malling Research Station (Tydeman and Garner, 1966) led to the planting in 1968, of a much larger trial at the National Fruit Trials (Table 9). Seedling dwarfs of four vigour classes were selected, which were by-products of breeding for resistance to bacterial canker and consequently possessed some measure of resistance. Each vigour class is represented by sixteen trees, half of which are worked with 'Merton Glory' and the other half with 'Merton Bigarreau'. Already after only 4 years considerable differences in tree size have developed between the different series of rootstocks.

Particularly impressive are the reductions in tree stature resulting from growing 'Merton Glory' on genetic dwarf seedlings derived from open pollinated 'Merton Favourite' (D) (Table 9) and on the East Malling hybrid clonal rootstock selection from *P. avium* × *P. pseudocerasus* (E). Trees on the *P. avium* × *P. pseudocerasus* (E) selection are distinctly precocious in bearing as are those on the genetic dwarf

TABLE 7. Cultivars heterozygous for dwarf determining alleles
(Matthews, 1971a)

Baumanns's May	Late Black Bigarreau
Baker's Self-fertile	Lester
Bigarreau Gaucher	Ludwig's Bigarreau
Bigarreau Napoleon	
Bigarreau Reverchon 'A'	Maiden's Blush
Black Circassion	Merton Bounty
Black Tartarian 'A'	Merton Favourite
Bowyer Heart	Merton Glory
Bradbourne Black	Merton Heart
	Merton Late
Carnation 'C'	Mezel B No. 1
Cleveland Bigarreau	Mezel B No. 2
Cryall's Seedling	Mumford's Black
Early Rivers	Noir de Guben
Emperor Francis	Nutberry Black
Empress Eugenie	
	Ramon Oliva
Frogmore Bigarreau	
Florence	Sam
	Sparkle
Guigne d'Annonay	
Guigne de Winkler	Turkey Heart
	Turkey Heart 'B'
Hedelfingen	
	Ursula Rivers
Judy's Fancy	
	Van
Kassins Fruhe Hertz	Victoria Black
Knight's Bigarreau	
Knight's Early Black 'G'	White Bigarreau
	Windsor

rootstock seedlings derived from 'Merton Favourite' (D). Considerable variation exists in tree sizes of 'Merton Glory' and 'Merton Bigarreau' within each of the four vigour classes of genetic dwarfs. This is to be expected since each tree on a genetic dwarf rootstock is a unique rootstock/scion combination and not identical as are trees worked on the East Malling clonal rootstocks.

The *P. avium* × *P. pseudocerasus* (E) rootstock has one great advantage over that of any genetic dwarf in that it can be easily propagated by traditional methods. Conventional layering techniques are inadequate and unsuitable for the propagation of genetic dwarfs, only at an occasional node are roots produced. Selection of genetic dwarfs

TABLE 8. Comparative effects of genetic dwarfs and F 12/1 as rootstocks of the sweet cherry (Trees 8 years old. Scion variety 'Merton Glory'. Three trees each rootstock)

Characters	Rootstocks	
	F 12/1	Dwarfs
Trunk circumference (cm)		
(a) Ground level	49·30	29·20
(b) at 1 metre	40·50	23·00
Spread (metres)	5·16	3·60
Height (metres)	4·90	3·18
Spurs	4,135·00	1,201·00

for layering ability has been attempted from a pool of 750 dwarfs obtained from a variety of different parent combinations, but has proved unsuccessful. However it was observed that dwarfs from different parental combinations differed in the ease with which they rooted and in the nature of the rooting systems which were produced. It has also proved impossible to propagate dwarfs either from hardwood or softwood cuttings.

Should genetic dwarfs prove to be the only really efficient dwarfing rootstock system then a return to seedling rootstocks as opposed to clonal rootstocks might be an acceptable method of obtaining orchards of dwarf trees. The simplest and cheapest way to obtain dwarfs would be to stratify stones from open pollinated heterozygous cultivars (Table 7).

Stones should be taken from ripe fruits, kept moist and stratified in sharp sand, 200 stones to a standard seed box. They should be kept outside throughout the winter until the first week of March when the

TABLE 9. Origins of genetic dwarfs and clonal rootstocks in the dwarf-rootstock trial set up in 1968 at the National Fruit Trials

Seedling Genetic Dwarfs: John Innes Institute.
A: Napoleon × JI 4865 (Ursula Rivers × Merton Late)
B: Judy's Fancy × JI 4865 (Ursula Rivers × Merton Late)
C: Hedelfingen × Merton Heart
D: Merton Favourite (open pollinated)

Clonal Selections: East Malling Research Station
E: *P. avium* × *P. pseudocerasus* selection, from F 299/2. Fb 2/58 No. 21
F: *P. avium*, mazzard selection from selfing F 1/3. Fd 1/57
G: *P. mahaleb*, selected clone from Pont de la Maye, Bordeaux. S.L. 69

embryos start to germinate. At this stage the small seedlings may be pricked off into soil blocks. After 6 weeks dwarfs can easily be distinguished by the puckering of the first true leaf.

Seedling families of this type have been raised from a number of cultivars found in commercial orchards (Table 10). In these families, depending on variety, between 1% and 21% of seedlings are dwarf.

TABLE 10. The segregation of dwarf seedlings in progenies from open pollinated cultivars of sweet cherries (Matthews, 1971a)

Fam.	Variety	Normal	Dwarf	% Dwarfs
46/69	Bradbourne Black	1,554	27	2
71/62	Late Black Bigarreau	272	9	3
22/64	Merton Favourite	890	102	10
41/62	Merton Glory (Replicate I)	224	7	3
42/62	Merton Glory (Replicate II)	893	56	6
23/63	Merton Glory (Replicate III)	2,257	56	2
21/64	Merton Glory (Replicate IV)	168	8	5
80/62	Merton Late	929	18	2
45/59	Napoleon	176	6	3
32/64	Nutberry Black (Replicate I)	97	2	2
38/63	Nutberry Black (Replicate II)	309	2	0·6
56/60	Turkey Heart	1,172	318	21

As alternatives, large numbers of dwarfs could be obtained from specially selected crosses in which either 50% or 25% of seedlings are dwarfs, or from specially set up isolation plots of 100 or more dwarf trees. Trees for these plots should be obtained from late or mid-season cultivars so as to ensure high levels of germination, since the germination of stones from early ones is virtually nil because the embryo is immature when the fruit is ripe.

It takes up to 4 years to produce a dwarf rootstock of workable size, therefore any stocks produced would be expensive. However, if trees were really dwarfed to a size where they could be netted to avoid bird damage the increased return from greater productivity would be attractive and make exploitation along these lines worthwhile.

Some of the likely advantages of dwarf trees would be:

(i) ease of picking; hence lower costs
(ii) ease of spray application and more efficient coverage
(iii) trees could be netted, this is now economically feasible; as a consequence losses due to birds would be eliminated, leading to significant increases in productivity, possibly as high as 40%
(iv) closer planting would lead to higher yields in the early establishment of orchards

(v) induction of precocious bearing, again leading to an increase in yields during the early establishment of an orchard.

REFERENCES

GRUBB, N. H. 1949. *Cherries*. Crosby Lockwood, London.
LAPINS, K. O. 1971. Basic improvements in sweet cherry through breeding. *Canada Agric.*, Vol. 16, part 2, pp. 2–7.
LEWIS, D. and CROWE, L. K. 1954. Structure of the incompatibility gene. IV Types of mutations in *Prunus avium* L. *Heredity*, Vol. 8, pp. 357–363.
MATTHEWS, P. 1969. Breeding for resistance to bacterial canker in the sweet cherry. *International Society for Horticultural Science Symposium on Cherries and Cherry Growing, Inst. Obstb. Gemuseb. Bonn, June 1968*, pp. 152–165.
MATTHEWS, P. 1971a. The genetics and exploitation of dwarf seedlings in the sweet cherry. *Proc. Angers Fruit Breeding Symposium (Eucarpia), 1970*, pp. 319–335.
MATTHEWS, P. 1971b. The genetics and exploitation of self fertility in the sweet cherry. *Proc. Angers Fruit Breeding Symposium (Eucarpia), 1970*, pp. 307–316.
TYDEMAN, H. M. and GARNER, R. J. 1966. Breeding for testing rootstocks for cherries. *Rep. E. Malling Res. Stn 1965*, pp. 130–134.

Fruit Cultivars and their Suitability for Home Freezing

MARGARET LEACH

Head of Home Food Preservation Section, University of Bristol, Long Ashton Research Station

THE work of the Home Food Preservation Section at Long Ashton Research Station has for over 20 years included quality assessment of preserves made on the domestic scale from various cultivars of different fruits. Apart from jam making, fruit bottling was formerly the main method of preservation available in the home although home canning machines were obtainable where the quantity of fruit justified the cash outlay. In both bottling and canning processes it was necessary to apply heat to ensure keeping quality and the rise in temperature inevitably caused some softening of texture and change in flavour. Tougher fruits benefited from the slight softening but with some berry fruits it was a disadvantage.

With the introduction of freezing as a preservation method, the fresh flavour of material so treated was soon realized. Horticulturists with their appreciation of quality were quick to purchase home food freezing equipment so that they could spread the enjoyment of short season produce over a longer period. Commercially much more attention has been given to vegetables than to fruit so the home grower will often be able to freeze from his own garden fruits rarely available from frozen food cabinets.

Large-scale supplies of some frozen fruits are lacking because of their "luxury" cost and fragility and here again the small scale grower is at an advantage.

It would be unfair to suggest that the freezing process has no effect on the produce. During the inevitable formation of ice crystals there is disruption of the cellular structure of the fruit and, on thawing, there will be leakage or drip. The faster the freezing takes place, the less this damage will occur and very fast methods such as liquid nitrogen sprays are used now for large scale work. At home it must be ensured that the freezer is at a low temperature with the Fast Freeze switch, if fitted, in the "On" position when the fruit is put in. The quickest way to freeze fruit at home, is to spread it out on clean trays which are placed in the coldest part of the freezer. Metal baking trays are suitable and if there is doubt about their cleanliness they can be lined with kitchen foil. As soon as the fruit is really firm, it should be transferred quickly to boxes or bags, and as much air as possible excluded before sealing. Not only is this a quick method but it gives a free running pack. Two points must be remembered: (1) this method is not suitable for light fruits because they would discolour, and (2) the fruit must be packed and sealed as soon as it is firm to prevent dehydration. For this tray method of freezing, the fruit may be slightly damped with clean cold water and rolled in caster sugar before spreading out to freeze. This sugar coating helps to speed freezing and to retard enzymic changes. A steady temperature should be maintained in the freezer as fluctuations, particularly above 0°F (− 18°C), will cause an increase in the size of ice crystals with consequent loss of quality due to excessive drip on thawing.

The alternative method of preparation for freezing fruit is to pack it into polythene bags or rigid containers and seal before freezing. Light fruits should be submerged in sugar syrup and this is best achieved by using a rigid container. As liquids expand on freezing, a ½ to 1 inch headspace must be left; it will be found that a piece of clean crumpled greaseproof paper placed under the lid will prevent the fruit from rising. A sugar syrup (½ to 1 lb of sugar per pint of water) makes a good protective cover for frozen fruit but the sweetness of the syrup does not penetrate into the fruit as is the case in bottling. With plums, gooseberries and loganberries it has been found that more than half the members of a tasting panel preferred these fruits bottled in syrup rather than frozen in a similar syrup. For those who find the frozen fruit tart, there is no reason why it should not be gently stewed with sugar, packed, cooled and then frozen. One advantage of this method is space-saving in the freezer.

At the present time, there is much interest in the use of unrefined sugar and honey. Part or all of the white sugar used for freezing can be replaced by these but it is recommended that a small sample be tried out first. Flavour will be affected and it is a personal decision whether it is acceptable.

Although fruit is usually put into the freezer in mealtime quantities, it can be frozen in larger units if required for jam making later on. There are several advantages in doing this. In the first place it cuts out the necessity of making jam in the height of the warm weather when there is already a great deal of outside work to do. A boiling of jam can be made as required during the cooler times of the year. With central heating jam made in the summer and stored under traditional cellulose covers tends to shrink and solidify after a few months' storage so that jam freshly made from frozen fruit will have a flavour and texture advantage over jam made when picked. It is advisable to allow a little extra fruit when making jam from the frozen state as the pectin which is necessary for a good set tends to weaken during freezer storage. Black currant skins tend to toughen and it is recommended in the case of tough varieties to give a quick ½ minute dip in boiling water with immediate rapid cooling before freezing. If convenient a 1 minute steam blanch gives a rather better result. If time is short, currants for subsequent jam or jelly making can be frozen on their stalks. It is comparatively easy to rub the frozen fruit off the stalks before heating them but it will be found a cold occupation unless gloves are worn!

For jam making, the frozen fruit is put directly in the preserving pan with water as required and heated gently until it thaws; for dessert purposes the best result is obtained if the unopened pack is placed overnight in a domestic refrigerator. If fruit has to be thawed quickly, it will tend to soften badly if it is not used as soon as it is ready. In a refrigerator it keeps its quality for a longer period. In an emergency fruit can be thawed by placing the unsealed pack in cold running water.

Before giving recommendations for actual cultivars, it should be stressed that two other factors are probably of equal importance. Firstly, the fruit must be in prime condition and secondly it must be prepared for freezing as soon as possible after picking with particular care to keep it cool during handling.

Apples

Slices—for subsequent use in pies, charlottes, etc., slices are required and in order to retain whiteness, these must be blanched for $\frac{1}{2}$ to $1\frac{1}{2}$ minutes depending on cultivar and thickness of slice. In a three-year trial of 14 cultivars the following scored well: 'Bramley's Seedling', 'Corry's Wonder' (very good for colour), 'Oxford Friend' and 'Martin No. 1' (both good for colour) and 'Sowman's Seedling' (good flavour, weak colour).

Pulp—this is produced by stewing the fruit with the minimum quantity of water, with or without the addition of sugar according to taste, until an even texture is obtained. It is much more quickly prepared than slices and is useful for apple sauce and in many desserts. 'Bramley's Seedling', 'Woolbrook Russet', 'Oxford Friend' and 'Martin No. 1' all scored well for colour and flavour and had good "body", an important point in pulp.

Raw—there is much interest in freezing raw dessert apples. A whole frozen apple quickly discolours and softens on thawing and cannot be recommended. Sliced raw apple in a mixed fruit salad in syrup is acceptable if eaten as soon as thawed. There are divided opinions about freezing grated apple. The fine shreds may enable the fruit to be eaten while still frozen and therefore still white and firm. A peeled raw cooking apple completely encased in pastry can be frozen uncooked and will make an acceptable apple dumpling or apple jack after cooking for approximately 45 minutes at 400°F from frozen.

Blackberries

Given a good season, wild fruit has a fuller, less acid, flavour than the cultivated cultivars but the latter tend to give a more even product. 'Himalaya Giant' is particularly acid but freezes satisfactorily as do 'Ashton Cross' and 'Merton Early', but with this fruit the result is poor unless from a really good sample.

Black currants

Although this fruit freezes well raw, it is never used for dessert and it can therefore be cooked before freezing. It also freezes well as a puree, in which form it is useful for fruit fool, mousse, ice cream. The vitamin C value of black currant is valuable and 'Baldwin', 'Boskoop' and 'Westwick Choice' are particularly good, with 'Cotswold Cross', 'Malvern Cross', 'Mendip Cross', 'Seabrook's Black' and 'Wellington XXX' all good. 'Edina' is weak in vitamin C compared with other cultivars but may be chosen by those who prefer a less robust flavour.

Blueberries

This fruit is fairly rare in England. Although at first it may not be enthusiastically received, tests have shown that preference for it grows with familiarity. It freezes well and keeps its attractive bloom when thawed. There are many satisfactory cultivars. 'Bluecrop' and 'Jersey' give good results; the former has a considerably larger berry than the latter. Blueberry pie is a favourite transatlantic dessert and an excellent pie filling can be made by mixing together 1 oz sugar with 1½ teaspoonsful cornflour or arrowroot and stirring this into 6 oz blueberries and 2 teaspoonsful of lemon juice. This mixture can be put into a small pie, frozen raw and subsequently baked from frozen or packed and frozen on its own or made from partially thawed fruit.

Cherries

Any cherries can be used in a fruit salad but for packing alone cherries of the 'Montmorency' type in syrup are recommended. The stones should be removed if the fruit is to be stored for more than 2 or 3 months.

Damsons

See under plums. Choose a true damson such as 'Shropshire Damson'.

Gage plums

See under Plums.

Gooseberries

Dessert fruit are not recommended for freezing but cooking cultivars freeze well. There is a tendency for the skins to toughen and a quick ½ minute dip in boiling water with subsequent thorough cooling before freezing will prevent this. As gooseberries are light in colour they should be cooked from frozen as quickly as possible to off-set darkening. Where the crop is heavy, spare fruit can be frozen for jam or chutney making later. Most cultivars freeze well and 'Careless', 'Keepsake', 'Lancer' and immature 'Leveller' are recommended.

Loganberries

This fruit retains its colour, texture and flavour well in freezing and is very palatable providing really ripe fruit is used.

Mulberries

As with loganberries the result is good if the fruit is really ripe. It may be advisable to spread a clean sheet of polythene under the tree and to use fallen fruit for freezing. The large core detracts from the pleasure of eating and frozen puree of raw sieved fruit can be recommended.

Peaches

'Hale's Early' is a good cultivar for freezing. It is customary to peel the fruit. The skin can be loosened by a $\frac{1}{2}$ to 1 minute dip in boiling water and immediate cooling in running cold water. Care must be taken to use really ripe fruit, to avoid overblanching and to keep the fruit under liquid to prevent discoloration as explained above for light fruits. The addition of ascorbic acid (vitamin C) to the covering syrup helps to retain the light colour without detracting from the flavour. Recommended quantities are 300 mg ascorbic acid to approx. 6 fl. oz of syrup which will be sufficient for 10 oz of fruit. 100 mg tablets of ascorbic acid are available from chemists. Unless peaches are small, it is usual to halve them and remove the stones.

Pears

There is little advantage in freezing cooking pears which store well. Dessert pears can be peeled and halved or sliced and treated as for light fruit but it is generally considered that the thawed fruit is too soft to be attractive. A few slices of dessert pear in a mixed pack of frozen fruit salad are acceptable. 'Williams' Bon Chrétien' and 'Doyenné du Comice' retain texture better than some other cultivars.

Plums

So far as freezing is concerned, the main consideration is the colour of the fruit. Deep red and black cultivars can be frozen plain whereas light plums and gages have to be submerged in syrup. As plums are fairly bulky it may be advantageous to freeze a selected few in syrup and stew or pulp the main quantity before freezing it in required size packs. Raw plums thawed for dessert use will quickly discolour if allowed to come in contact with air. Although this darkening is not so evident on deeper coloured fruit it will be noticeable in the interior. 'Victoria' and the gages retain a good proportion of their fresh flavour if frozen for dessert but the softness of their texture may be unacceptable.

Quinces

Only a few ornamental quinces have sufficient characteristic flavour to justify their use in apple pie. Where true quinces are available, two or three slices may be put with 1 lb apple slices, blanched and frozen together. If preferred small packs of cubed and cooked quince may be packed and frozen separately.

Raspberries

This is probably the most rewarding frozen fruit. After removal of stalk, avoid washing the fruit unless essential. Damp lightly, coat with caster sugar and freeze on trays recommended above. If preferred the fruit can be frozen plain. Most cultivars give a very palatable product. Tests in hand indicate that 'Malling Enterprise' is particularly good for freezing as it is for preserving generally.

Red currants

These can be frozen in quantity for subsequent jelly making. For dessert purposes they are rather soft once fully thawed but a small pack of good sized fruit coated in caster sugar will make an attractive decoration for a dessert or fruit cup.

Rhubarb

Early pink stems cut into 1 to $1\frac{1}{2}$ inch lengths can be frozen either plain, coated with sugar or in sugar syrup. It is difficult to exclude the air and dehydration is a common fault with rhubarb frozen plain. This tends to give an appearance which is often confused with mould, therefore the addition of sugar or syrup is suggested. 'Timperley Early', 'Champagne' and 'Linnaeus' are recommended.

Strawberries

It is fair to assume from the scarcity of this fruit in commercial packs that it does, alas, present difficulties. Many American recipes use sliced strawberries or strawberry puree but traditionally in England, the berry is required whole. Herein lies the difficulty with frozen fruit, as it tends to collapse once fully thawed. Small to medium sized berries should be chosen in ripe but firm condition. Experimental work has shown a preference for fruit frozen in a 60% syrup, i.e. in the *proportion* of 60 oz ($3\frac{3}{4}$ lb) sugar to 40 fl. oz (2 pints) water. However, fruit coated with caster sugar was also acceptable and this may be easier at home. Fruit should preferably be thawed overnight in its sealed pack in the refrigerator and only removed immediately before serving. Tasting panel tests, using eleven cultivars for three years, gave preference to 'Templar', 'Cambridge Rival' and 'Cambridge Favourite'. 'Cambridge Vigour' did well in previous tests. 'Senga Sengana' scored above average for texture but its flavour was not always well liked. For those who grow 'Royal Sovereign', this excellent berry should be sliced before freezing. Raw strawberry puree tends to develop a "banana" off flavour after about 6 months' frozen storage and this can be minimized by using ascorbic acid in the proportions given under peaches.

White currants
Can be frozen as recommended above for dessert red currants. This is usually a scarce fruit but if in plentiful supply makes an attractive jelly with equal part of red currants.

Whortleberries
Known by various names up and down the country, this fruit can be treated as blueberries.

It is realized that this list does not cover all English fruits but it is anticipated that adventurous fruit growers will be adventurous fruit freezers too, and take the opportunity to experiment. No good quality produce can become harmful through the freezing process so there is no risk—only the probability of a successful novelty.

Recent Developments in Soft Fruit Breeding

D. L. JENNINGS, H. J. GOODING* AND M. M. ANDERSON
Scottish Horticultural Research Institute, Dundee

I N *Fruit, Present and Future*, published in 1966, Knight and Keep wrote on breeding new soft fruits. Sufficient progress has been made in the intervening years to justify another review, and this is also an opportunity to discuss some of the new breeding objectives that have arisen. Knight and Keep dealt mainly with breeding in progress at East Malling Research Station but we are mostly concerned with work at the Scottish Horticultural Research Institute. Raspberries, black currants and blackberries are bred at our main station near Dundee, and strawberries at the Institute's West of Scotland Unit near Ayr.

Two recent developments have influenced breeding objectives. Firstly, the trend towards machine harvesting requires that breeders give greater priority to the selection of plant characters which facilitate this operation, for example, easy abscission in raspberries and black currants and suitability for once-over harvest in strawberries. Secondly, entry into the European Economic Community influences our outlook in several ways; increasing competition from European strawberry growers is expected, particularly from those in southern Europe where the climate provides considerable early-season advantages. Our growers can expect an advantage late in the season, and so breeders are giving special attention to late cultivars. Strawberries with a deep red internal colour are also needed to compete in European markets, whilst the possibility of greater restriction in the use of colour additives for processed fruit leads to selection of raspberries and strawberries with deeper natural colour.

RASPBERRIES

Since Knight and Keep's review, several new raspberry cultivars have been introduced. 'Glen Clova' bred at the Scottish Horticultural Research Institute, became available to growers in 1971, 'Malling Orion' and 'Malling Admiral' will be available in 1973 and 1974 respectively, and 'Phyllis King', bred by a private breeder, is expected to be commercially available in 1974. 'Glen Clova' was released to give Scottish growers an early cultivar capable of being used for canning, freezing or the fresh market; the new 'Malling Admiral' caters particularly for English growers, because it ripens late and does not clash seriously with the strawberry harvest. Early results (Potter) suggest that

* West of Scotland Unit, Auchincruive.

'Glen Clova' and 'Malling Orion' have high yield potential and growers can look forward to yield increases of about 30% after changing to these. Raspberry production thus becomes an economic alternative to strawberry production in England. 'Malling Admiral', though possibly not so productive as these cultivars, represents a big improvement in fruit quality, especially in fruit texture. 'Glen Clova' and 'Malling Admiral' have both given especially good results in tests of their suitability for jam manufacture and canning: in particular, they gave jams in which the seed showed less tendency to become transparent and whose flavour and colour were preferred to those of the older cultivars.

No cultivars have yet been released for their particular merits for machine harvesting. Fruits of most cultivars can be shaken from the plant easily enough when they are sufficiently ripe, but by this stage their quality has usually deteriorated. They tend to break up or "bleed" and are prone to fruit rot and mildew. Cultivars are therefore required whose fruits will either shake off easily at an earlier stage in their development, or else show less deterioration as they reach a more advanced stage of ripeness. Cultivars possessing both of these attributes are preferable, and, in addition, their ripe fruits should retain a good red colour and not develop an unattractive bluish tinge. Fruit rots and mildew become important when harvesting is delayed, and though these diseases can be controlled by suitable chemical sprays, there is reason to believe that sprays achieve a better control if the cultivar is resistant. *Botrytis* is the main cause of fruit rot, and sources of resistance have been found in the Canadian cultivars 'Carnival' and 'Matsqui' and in the American 'Cuthbert' (Daubeny *et al.*, 1969; Barritt); 'Glen Clova' possesses some resistance (Topham), but probably less than 'Matsqui'. Resistance in the fruits is not closely related to resistance in the stem and probably acts in part by delaying the change from the quiescent to the aggressive phase of the fungus. Resistance may break down when the fruit becomes overripe or when rainfall is heavy, but this delay is nevertheless a valuable contribution to the control of the disease. Further progress is possible if this form of resistance is combined with factors which enable the fruit to escape infection, such as inflorescence types in which flowers and fruits are well spaced to minimize contact between healthy fruits and infected fruits or "plugs". This is favoured by the long stiff stalks associated with the large-fruited mutant described below. Resistance to mildew has also been studied (Keep, 1968a; Daubeny *et al.*, 1968), but here again resistance in the leaf and stem is not closely related to resistance in the fruit, which seems to be associated with properties of its skin (Jennings *et al.*, 1969).

The problem of controlling the raspberry beetle has also received increased attention. Chemical control is effective, but the public are becoming increasingly opposed to the possible contamination of fruits with sprays, and the prospect of cultivars with built-in resistance has become attractive both because it avoids all possibility of contamination and for economic reasons. There are several sources of resistance, notably *Rubus phoenicolasius* (Rietsema; Jennings and Taylor, 1969), *R. coreanus* and *R. crataegifolius* (Keep and Briggs). The inheritance of resistance is probably complex in each case, and since none of these species is closely related to the raspberry it will need several backcrosses to transfer resistance and restore the horticultural qualities.

The components of yield in raspberry include the number of laterals per cane, the number of fruits per lateral and the size of individual fruits. Knight and Keep (1966) described the attempt of the East Malling breeders to increase the number of fruits per lateral. At the Scottish Horticultural Research Institute we are giving special attention to the other two components. The higher yields recorded for 'Glen Clova' owe much to the cultivar's capacity to produce more than one fruiting lateral per node (Fig. 32). For good expression of this characteristic a cultivar must first produce several strong buds at each node, and then induce more than one of them to develop into a fruiting lateral. Keep (1968b) has shown that in certain cultivars strong development of secondary buds is controlled by two genes. The cultivar 'Lloyd George' has these genes, but only a small proportion of its nodes develop more than one lateral because the capacity to develop frequent "multi-lateral" nodes as in 'Glen Clova' appears to be inherited independently. It appears to be a recessive character and to be controlled by a number of genes. The fact that both buds frequently develop may of course be a disadvantage in years when spring frosts are prevalent, because the presence of a dormant second bud has hitherto been considered an insurance against injury to the primary one.

The discovery of a gene giving a large increase in fruit size offers the possibility of a big advance with this yield component. This gene, which was discovered as a mutant in a commercial plantation of 'Malling Jewel', influences many aspects of development because it probably controls the production of a plant hormone (Jennings, 1966). In particular, it prolongs the growth of the receptacle to give an elongated cone bearing 50% more drupelets than the normal form, each individual drupelet being so enlarged that the fruit tends to be doubled in size. The length and diameter of fruiting laterals relative to that of the canes is also increased and this results in the fruit being well displayed to pickers, while an increase in fruit-stalk length reduces the chances of the fruit coming into contact with fruit rots. The prospect of making such a large improvement in fruit size by selecting for a single gene is exciting, but, unfortunately, it often affects fertility, and progress is slow because the breeder has in addition to select for improved fruit set and regular drupelet size.

For good expression of these yield components it is essential for the plant to remain healthy. Knight and Keep (1966) described how resistance to viruses, virus vectors and fungal diseases of the canes is being bred into new cultivars both at East Malling and in Scotland. We are also taking special account of hardiness. A problem here is that much selection is done in years when the incidence of winter injury to the canes is not high, and it is not possible to recognize variation in hardiness. Frequently it is not until later years that promising material is subjected to testing conditions and variation in hardiness is revealed. It seems that damage is frequently done in early winter in material where the processes of acclimation do not start early enough (Jennings *et al.*, 1973). European breeders have made considerable use of germ plasm obtained from southern latitudes of America, where climatic conditions in August and September are very different from ours. Such material frequently continues to grow throughout September and is ill-prepared for early November frosts, unlike adapted cultivars which cease extension growth during August. It is notable that cultivars which have shown exceptional hardiness in Scotland stop growing and become dormant particularly early. It is hoped that such material will not only make improvements in cane hardiness possible, but that recognition of the importance of this early acclimation will enable us to recognize hardy forms even in years when winter injury does not occur.

STRAWBERRIES

There are three state-sponsored strawberry breeding programmes in Britain, located at widely separated centres but all with objectives related both to the present needs of the industry and to those imposed by our entry into the EEC. The programme at Auchincruive, the site of the West of Scotland Unit of the Scottish Horticultural Research Institute, has always concentrated on producing cultivars resistant to red core, our major strawbery disease. Since the Unit started in 1930 it has produced the cultivars 'Auchincruive Climax' (1947), 'Talisman' (1955), 'Redgauntlet' (1957), 'Templar' (1964), 'Crusader' (1966), 'Marmion' (1969) and 'Montrose' (1969). The programme at the John Innes Institute, Norwich is a continuation of the one initiated by Boyes at Cambridge in 1930 (Williams), which resulted in the Cambridge series of cultivars, the best known of which is 'Cambridge Favourite'. Since its transfer to the John Innes Institute, the programme has provided 'Merton Princess' (1961), 'Merton Herald' (1964) and 'Merton Dawn' (1969). Strawberry breeding was started at Long Ashton Research Station, Bristol in 1963 (Wilson, 1964) and the first selections produced are now at the stage of advanced trials.

Some 18,500 acres of strawberries were grown in Britain in 1970 giving an output of 44,000 tons valued at £10 million. More than half of this acreage is in eastern and south-eastern England and about 40% of the total crop is used for processing. The industry relies, perhaps inadvisedly, on two main cultivars—'Cambridge Favourite' and

Fungal Diseases of Raspberry, pp. 136–139

Photos: East Malling Research Station

FIG. 34—*above*: canes of raspberry 'Malling Jewel' affected by spur blight. FIG. 35—*below left*: young green canes showing nodal lesions of *Didymella applanata*. FIG. 36—*below right*: green canes showing nodal infections by spur blight.

Ever Changing Strawberry, pp. 140–144

Photo: John Innes Institute

FIG. 37—*above*: strawberry seedling showing uniformly medium sized fruits, simultaneous ripening and a suitable strig type for mechanical harvesting.

Late-Season Strawberries, pp. 145–147

Photos: Crown Copyright

FIG. 38—*below*: general view of experimental area showing the black polythene covering in position providing short-day treatment.

Late-Season Strawberries, pp. 145-147

Photo: Crown Copyright

FIG. 39—*above*: general view of flowering response to short-day treatments on spring-planted, deblossomed runners; plants of 'Redgauntlet' given (*left*) fifteen, (*centre*) twenty, (*right*) twenty-five short days. FIG. 40—*below*: flowering response to short-day treatments in autumn planted runners of 'Redgauntlet', (*left*) deblossomed in spring, (*right*) cropped. Both plots given twenty short days.

Producing Early Strawberries, pp. 148-152

Photos: Crown Copyright

FIG. 41—*above left*: putting out the polythene tunnels. FIG. 42—*above right*: wire hoop and polypropylene twine tie to hold polythene to hoop. This allows the tunnel to be ventilated by pushing up the plastic. FIG. 43—*below*: it is important to use a tunnel just big enough to cover final size. Plants in smaller tunnel on right are constricted.

'Redgauntlet'. Before these cultivars became available in 1954, average crop yields were only about 36 cwt per acre, but nowadays with virus-free modern cultivars, yields of 6–10 tons per acre are common (Reid). This great improvement can be attributed to the use of improved cultivars, the benefits of certification schemes (Ministry of Agriculture, 1970) and, more recently, better disease control, particularly of *Botrytis*. Although the cropping area fell from about 30,000 acres in 1925 to only 18,500 acres in 1970, production has increased from an average yield of 30 cwt per acre in 1948 to over 60 cwt in 1970.

Now that increasing quantities of early strawberries are being imported from France and Italy, the current gap in our supply lies in August and early September. Emphasis is therefore placed on selection for late main-crop cultivars and for double-cropping forms like 'Redgauntlet', though preferably with an earlier second crop. Another new requirement is for red fleshed cultivars, which are preferred in the EEC both for processing and for the fresh market. New cultivars like 'Marmion', 'Merton Dawn' and 'Montrose', though high yielding and fairly late, do not have this character. Even in Britain, where pale-fleshed cultivars are acceptable on the fresh market, there is likely to be a change of preference, especially for canning, because colour additives are not required with dark-fleshed cultivars. The likely preference is for cultivars which when canned give a natural bright product without artificial colour, instead of appearing an unattractive reddish brown. With these changes in mind, many of the selections being tested at the National Fruit Trials were chosen because of their red flesh, bright appearance and improved tolerance in transport.

Harvesting is one of the biggest problems of the modern strawberry grower and accounts for 60% of the total cost of growing the crop. Breeders are therefore working towards large-fruited selections which can be picked more efficiently, and also towards those which might be suited to mechanical harvesting. For the latter purpose the requirement is for very firm-fruited, easily decapped cultivars capable of being harvested in one operation. Whilst concentrated ripening is desirable for this, the ability of ripe fruit to hold its quality on the plant seems to be of primary importance. Fruit of different cultivars differ considerably in "shelf-life" and tests have been devised which reveal those selections in which this characteristic is best. Good shelf-life also means resistance to the inevitable bruising that mechanical harvesting will entail. Resistance to *Botrytis*, which seems to be a component of long shelf-life, is also important and sources of resistance to this pathogen are available. The problem lies in incorporating all of these qualities into a single genotype and combining them with disease resistance and high yield.

Breeding for resistance to diseases has always been a primary objective of the Auchincruive breeding programme and a high threshold of fitness has been aimed at in new cultivars. Resistance to red core disease has been emphasized, but progress has also been made in breeding for resistance to *Botrytis*. In earlier work, resistance to red core disease was sought by attempting to breed for immunity from specific strains of the causal organism *Phytophthora fragariae*, but this proved an unpractical goal in view of the large number of races present in Britain. More recent selection has therefore been for plants with field resistance, which may be defined as an ability of the plants to crop acceptably even when infected by the disease. Several cultivars, notably 'Cambridge Favourite', have a measure of this kind of resistance, and it is also possessed by the new cultivar 'Marmion' which thrives on the severely infected soil of our testing ground at Auchincruive, in contrast to the susceptible 'Montrose' (Fig. 33). Field resistance occurs to a higher degree in certain clones of *Fragaria virginiana* and *F. chiloensis* and these are now being used extensively in breeding.

The nature of this field resistance has also been studied (Gooding, 1971, 1973), and it is hoped that the knowledge gained will result in more effective screening of seedling progenies. It was found that field resistance operates by several different mechanisms. In the case of one *F. virginiana* derivative it appeared that the fungus was inhibited from producing the symptom of red stele in more than a small proportion of roots. Seedlings with resistance derived from this potent source are now becoming available for test after breeding for 20 years to eliminate the small, soft fruit characteristic of the wild species; several of them have inherited the fine flavour of *F. virginiana* as well. With cultivars such as 'Crusader' and 'Templar', field resistance was apparently due to a greater capacity to produce roots; with 'Cambridge Favourite' the mechanism of resistance is still not fully understood but it may be related to drought resistant properties inherited from *F. chiloensis*, which thrives under strand conditions in the wild.

Verticillium wilt is the second most important strawberry disease and occurs particularly in eastern England. 'Redgauntlet', 'Talisman' and the new cultivar 'Montrose' each possess some resistance to it and the breeders at Long Ashton are selecting for this resistance. Aphid-borne virus diseases are no longer of major importance in Britain but nematode-transmitted viruses are being given more attention. Of these, raspberry ringspot and tomato black ring viruses are sources of trouble in Scotland and advanced selections are field-tested for their reactions to them, as well as to arabis mosaic virus which is common in southern England (Gooding, 1969). Certain other diseases are of minor importance here, though major problems elsewhere. For example, crown rot caused by *Phytophthora cactorum* is always a potential menace, particularly in Europe, and resistance to it is highly desirable if British propagators are to export homebred cultivars. A search for sources of resistance is therefore being made (Gooding, 1972).

Breeders often try to re-design a crop to meet likely future requirements. This is being attempted at Auchincruive by assessing the feasibility of breeding plants whose fruits are held off the ground and hence more amenable to mechanical harvesting. *Fragaria vesca* (diploid) and *F. elatior* (hexaploid) are being used for this because of their strong peduncles, while some segregates from the conventional breeding programme are also promising for this purpose. The usual method is to produce synthetic hexaploids by crossing tetraploid forms of *F. vesca* produced by colchicine treatment with normal octoploid cultivars. These plants can produce unreduced hexaploid gametes which, when pollinated by tetraploid gametes from octoploid cultivars, produce decaploids (Scott).

Another possible novel approach being examined is to develop breeding lines which may be crossed to give F_1 hybrids that are acceptably uniform when grown from seed. Success with this project would help to solve the problems of mechanical harvesting, as high seed rates could be used to achieve close spacing. New cultivars with fruits tending to be borne well above the ground would be grown, and this tendency would be aided by the close spacing, because the crowded petioles would help to support the fruit stalks. The crop would probably be treated as an annual or biennial. Since our climate tends to induce more concentrated cropping than that of more southerly countries we might well be able to exploit such features to our economic advantage.

BLACK CURRANTS

Although several new black currant cultivars have been introduced in the last 50 years they have not displaced 'Baldwin' and 'Wellington XXX' as Britain's leading cultivars. Yields generally have remained both too low and too variable. Some 11,000 acres are grown and the average annual production is about 22,000 tons, but yields drop markedly in years of spring frost as in 1967, for example, when spring frosts reduced the crop to 6,800 tons. Yield losses occur when unfavourable weather at flowering time adversely affects pollination and fruit set, or through the effects of reversion virus, American gooseberry mildew (*Sphaerotheca mors-uvae*) or leaf spot (*Pseudopeziza ribis*). Improved cultivars would be particularly welcome now that we have produced mobile machines capable of harvesting the crop by shaking conventionally-grown bushes. The use of these machines on improved cultivars selected for their suitability for machine harvest might well result in Britain becoming the main supplier of black currants to the EEC, as production on the continent is declining because of labour shortages and because plantations there are usually too small for the machines to operate economically.

It is generally agreed that major improvements in black currants are unlikely to be attained from a mere reshuffling of the genes present in British cultivars, because our cultivars show such limited variation

(Spinks; Tydeman). The breeding programme of the Scottish Horticultural Institute is therefore making considerable use of cultivars of foreign origin, especially those from Scandinavia, Finland and the U.S.S.R., hitherto unused as parents for crossing with British cultivars. It is also attempting to transfer entirely new characteristics of major importance from other *Ribes* species. Sterility barriers are a problem when crosses are attempted between species belonging to different sections of the genus (Keep, 1962), so attention was at first confined to crosses between species within the *R. nigrum* section, where the hybrids produced are more or less fertile. Workers at East Malling Research Station have given greater emphasis to crosses between distantly related diploid species, sometimes using modern colchicine techniques to obtain fertile tetraploids, and have had notable success in transferring gall mite immunity from the gooseberry (Knight and Keep, 1957), and also in transferring characters from the red currant. Much of this work is essentially of a long term nature, but it promises dramatic improvements in productivity, crop management techniques and resistance to pests and diseases.

Spring frosts cause the biggest losses in yields, and cultivars differ in their response to spring frost damage, 'Wellington XXX' being notoriously susceptible while 'Greens Black' ('Hatton Black'), 'Roodknop' and 'Consort' are reputed to be somewhat resistant. The reasons for these differences are probably complex, as no known cultivar has flowers which are inherently resistant to spring frost. It is not surprising therefore that breeders have achieved most success by breeding for a frost-escaping mechanism such as late flowering, which occurs in progenies of *R. nigrum* crossed with the North American black currant species *R. bracteosum* (Knight, 1972). Unfortunately, late-flowering plants are invariably late ripening, which is a feature of the selections now under trial. Hybridization with the red currant may eventually provide opportunity for a more direct form of frost resistance.

Black currant cultivars vary in self-fertility from highly self-compatible types like 'Baldwin', 'Brödtorp' and 'Kajaanin Musta' to partially self-compatible types like 'Boskoop Giant' and self-sterile types like 'Coronet' (Tamás, 1965). Fruit set nearly always benefits from cross-pollination (Baldini and Pisani; Hofman), but since plantations of clonally propagated plants usually provide opportunity only for self-pollination, the first requirement of a cultivar is an ability to set fruit consistently after self-pollination. If possible, it should do this even when adverse weather during flowering and fruit-setting tends to increase "running-off" (Teotia and Luckwill; Wright). In such conditions in Scotland a selection derived from crossing among three black currant species—*R. nigrum* ('Brödtorp'), *R. dikuscha* and *R. hudsonianum*—has shown a remarkable ability to set fruit. The Finnish cultivar 'Brödtorp' also has good self-compatibility, apparently because it synthesizes large amounts of auxin even after self-pollination (Tamás, 1967). Its strigs are remarkably uniform in berry size, a characteristic of highly self-compatible cultivars, and the fruit is outstanding for its uniform ripening. It also hangs well when ripe. 'Brödtorp' has therefore been used widely in breeding, both in Britain and abroad, and many of its progenies have inherited this self-fertility and other desirable characteristics. Unfortunately, they have also inherited its very undesirable spreading habit of growth. It produced particularly productive progenies when crossed with the Swedish cultivar 'Janslunda', 'Baldwin' or *R. bracteosum*, but in progenies of all crosses with erect-growing British cultivars this productivity was closely associated with a spreading growth habit. This type of habit is a serious disadvantage in a field crop, particularly for machine harvesting by shaking as the available machines can only engage erect-growing branches, but productive erect growing types have now been obtained by crossing 'Brödtorp' derivatives with derivatives of the extremely erect growing Canadian cultivar 'Consort' which belongs to the species *R. ussuriense* (Anderson, 1972). Selections from these crosses and several other 'Brödtorp' derivatives from other research stations are currently on trial in Britain.

Considerable improvement in fruit size has been obtained in crosses with 'Janslunda'. In several progenies, notably the one from crossing 'Janslunda' with 'Brödtorp', fruit size was nearly twice that of 'Baldwin'. Even larger berries of up to 25 mm in diameter have been reported in wild populations of *R. nigrum* in the U.S.S.R. (Zhukovsky), and the recently introduced Dutch cultivar 'Black Reward' also has very large berries. Other improvements in strig characteristics are being achieved in crosses with *R. bracteosum*. Long strigged plants with up to 26 flowers per strig have been reported (E.M.R.S., 1969) and some have the additional merit that their berries absciss easily and leave a dry scar similar to that of a blueberry. This is a desirable feature for mechanical harvesting by shaking. Some of these hybrids also have strigs with the so-called "handle" of *R. bracteosum*, that is to say, a basal area free from berries which facilitates hand picking. This feature is likely to appeal to growers who provide "pick-your-own" facilities. One or more of these characteristics also occurs in *R. sanguineum*, *R. sanguineum albidum*, *R. longeracemosum*, *R. multiflorum* and other red currant species.

Finally, to maximize productivity, a high number of fruit buds must develop both on one-year-old shoots and on the fruit spurs of two and three-year-old branches. This usually means a high ratio of fruit to vegetative buds. 'Greens Black' and 'Baldwin' are useful donor parents for these characteristics (Wilson and Adam, 1966, 1967), which complement improvements in fruit size and strig length obtained either the from 'Brödtorp' × 'Janslunda' cross or from *R. bracteosum*.

In addition to providing new cultivars adapted to machine harvesting, plant breeders are also attempting to reduce the costs of production by breeding for resistance to pests and diseases, thus eliminating or reducing the necessity for sprays. The main diseases are reversion, American gooseberry mildew and leaf spot, which are all difficult and expensive to control by sprays. Fortunately, sources of resistance to all the major diseases and pests are available to the breeder, in both closely related and more distantly related species.

The hybrid obtained from crossing the black currant with the gooseberry is immune from infestation by black currant gall mite (*Phytoptus ribis*) and second backcross derivatives of it have remained free from infestation after exposure for up to nine years (Knight, 1971). Two eastern Siberian black currant species, *R. ussuriense* and *R. nigrum sibiricum*, are also resistant to galling by the mite; in these species infested buds show a hypersensitive type of reaction in autumn, presumably in response to the feeding of the mites, which are unable to reproduce and survive overwinter (Anderson, 1971). *Phytoptus ribis* is the only known vector of reversion virus, and this work is a classical example of controlling a disease by breeding for resistance to its virus-transmitting vector. However, it is likely that the disease can also be controlled by breeding directly for resistance or tolerance to it, as graft-inoculation tests indicate that both *R. nigrum sibiricum* and the gooseberry are either resistant or highly tolerant (Posnette; Tiits). Resistance is thought to be a recessive character in the gooseberry cultivar 'Green Ocean' (Knight, 1966), and a dominant one in *R. nigrum sibiricum* (Anderson, unpubl.).

Cultivars susceptible to infection by the leaf spot fungus (*Pseudopeziza ribis*) produce sporulating lesions on their leaves which are consequently shed prematurely with adverse effects on yield (Corke). However, segregates from crosses between the black currant and the resistant *R. dikuscha* show only restricted non-sporulating lesions, and their leaves rarely show premature defoliation (Fig. 31). These hybrids are sub-fertile but fertility has been restored by two backcrosses. This form of resistance from *R. dikuscha* is controlled by two complementary genes (Anderson, 1972), and contrasts with the form found in certain *R. nigrum* cultivars which merely reduces the intensity of defoliation. The latter form is apparently conferred by minor genes (Wilson et al., 1964). Other sources of resistance include *R. sanguineum*, *R. glutinosum* and *R. cereum*. These three species are particularly useful because they also contribute resistance to mildew, black currant gall mite and the currant-lettuce aphid *Hyperomyzus lactucae* (Keep, 1962).

Much of the breeding material so far described has resistance to mildew derived from 'Brödtorp', the Swedish cultivar 'Öjebyn', *R. dikuscha* or *R. nigrum sibiricum*. The mildew fungi notoriously occur in races or biotypes, however, and the species infecting black currant seems no exception, because some of the plants hitherto considered to be highly resistant to existing forms have recently borne sporulating lesions, suggesting that a new form of mildew may be present. However, higher levels of resistance or immunity occur among other resistance sources available.

BLACKBERRIES

Blackberries are of relatively minor importance in Britain, as only about 1,000 acres are grown compared to some 8,000 acres of raspberries. In the U.S.A., blackberries are a crop of major importance, but neglect of the crop is typical of European countries. The British climate is very suitable for blackberry growing, however, and offers several advantages over that of potential continental competitors. The canes do not suffer excessive winter injury as in eastern Europe, and we do not have the hot dry summers which adversely affect fruit development and yield in some parts. Probably the main reasons why blackberries are not grown more extensively are the difficulties of managing their sprawling, highly spined growth, and their late ripening, particularly in northern areas. Many growers may be attracted to the crop if an erect, spinefree, early ripening cultivar became available so that management techniques could approximate more closely to those used for growing raspberries. There would be advantages in diversifying the crops grown. For example, blackberries will probably be harvested in the future by machines developed for harvesting raspberries, so a grower with both crops will be able to extend his season of operation and spread the capital costs of his new machine over the two crops.

Previous attempts to improve blackberries in Britain have relied almost entirely on indigenous species. These sources have yielded cultivars with good fruits and a very valuable gene for spinelessness, but there has been little improvement in earliness. The gene for spinelessness was found in a wild form of the diploid *Rubus rusticanus* known as *R. rusticanus* var. *inermis*, and is the most widely used source of this character. Other sources include the triploid *R. canadensis*, the diploid 'Whitford's Thornless' and the octoploid 'Austin Thornless' (Hull, 1967). None of these sources is ideal because our blackberries are predominantly tetraploid, but the 'Austin Thornless' source is useful because its spinelessness is determined by a dominant epistatic gene (Hull, 1961) and a tetraploid spine-free derivative of it has been produced and kindly supplied to us by Dr J. W. Hull of Illinois. However, this material is not sufficiently hardy in Scottish conditions and its value is sometimes reduced by sterility. Most emphasis is therefore being placed on breeding with the recessive form of spinelessness originally found in *R. rusticanus* var. *inermis*. This form first became important when an unreduced germ cell of this diploid species functioned in a cross with the tetraploid *R. thrysiger*, and gave a fertile tetraploid hybrid which was released to growers as the cultivar 'John Innes'

(Crane and Darlington). The cultivar was spined, because the gene for spinelessness is recessive, but spine-free forms were obtained by further breeding, and one of them was released as the cultivar 'Merton Thornless' (John Innes Institute, 1938). 'Merton Thornless' itself did not make a big impact because it is late in ripening and prone to winter injury, but it led to big advances in Maryland, where Scott and Ink (1966) crossed it with several American cultivars and after several generations of breeding produced the cultivars 'Thornfree' and 'Smoothstem'. These are both spineless, with hardiness adequate for most but not all parts of the U.S.A. Their growth habit is semi-erect and much superior to that of 'Merton Thornless', though further improvement is possible. When tested in Britain they proved very hardy but still too late for most purposes.

The American cultivars 'Early Harvest' and 'Darrow' are our best sources of erect habit. Their growth is rigorously erect and they are sources of other improvements as well. They have the capacity to spread by suckers, which means that planting material can be produced in spawn beds using methods which are traditional for raspberries. Only one progeny has so far segregated for this character, giving non-suckering to suckering segregates in a ratio which suggests that the difference may be determined by a recessive gene. However, though it ripens early in areas of America where it is adapted, 'Early Harvest' is so ill-adapted to Scottish conditions that it either flowers very late or else fails to initiate any flower buds and produces blind laterals. Most of the hybrids derived from it have also tended to be late flowering. The cultivar 'Darrow' has been introduced more recently to the breeding programme and there is reason to believe that it will be better adapted to our climate than 'Early Harvest'.

The problem of earliness is complex, because not only do blackberries flower later than raspberries but many require some 55 to 75 days after pollination to produce ripe fruits, compared to only 30 to 35 days for raspberries. It seems likely that additional sources of germ plasm will be required. Several cultivars from the north-west coast of America, such as 'Marion', 'Chehalem' and 'Aurora' ripen as early as raspberries, but they are either hexaploids or octoploids and are not good parents for improving tetraploid material. The earliest British cultivar is 'Bedford Giant', which requires only about 45 days to ripen, but this too is hexaploid and is probably derived from a raspberry-blackberry hybrid (Crane, 1935). An attempt is being made to transfer earliness from tetraploid raspberries to blackberries and the hybrids obtained so far have been early and erect but with fruits totally unacceptable for flavour and colour. Several backcrosses to the blackberry will be required to correct these shortcomings.

Selection for good flavour and other fruit qualities is particularly important for blackberries, because an increase in their production will only be justified if consumers are persuaded to increase their demands.

The preference is for the wild bramble flavour which is commonly thought to be superior to that of named cultivars. Early ripening in itself may lead to improved flavours, because the higher temperatures prevailing in August would probably favour the production and accumulation of more sugars in the fruit, but deliberate breeding to improve fruit quality is also essential. It may also be possible to breed for smaller pyrenes (seeds) which may make blackberries acceptable as fruits for jam. The cultivar 'Chehalem' for example has very small pyrenes and is a possible parent for this purpose.

Breeding for disease resistance in blackberries may assume importance as breeding proceeds. Blackberries frequently become infected with virus diseases but little is known of the viruses involved or of their vectors. Some of the viruses can be transmitted from brambles to black raspberry seedlings by *Amphorophora rubi* (Cadman) so resistance to this vector is desirable, and an attempt is being made to transfer the gene A1 for resistance to *A. rubi* from tetraploid raspberries.

REFERENCES

ANDERSON, M. M. 1971. Resistance to gall mite (*Phytoptus ribis*) in the Eucoreosma section of *Ribes*. *Euphytica*, Vol. 20, pp. 422–426.

ANDERSON, M. M. 1972. Resistance to black currant leaf spot (*Pseudopeziza ribis*) in crosses between *R. dikuscha* and *R. nigrum*. *Euphytica*, Vol. 21, pp. 510–517.

ANDERSON, M. M. 1972. Black currant. *Rep. Scot. hort. Res. Inst. 1971*, p. 37.

BALDINI, E. and PISANI, P. L. 1961. (Research on the biology of flowering and fruiting in black currants.) *Riv. ortoflorofruttic. ital.*, Vol. 45, pp. 619–639.

BARRITT, B. H. 1971. Fruit rot susceptibility of red raspberry cultivars. *Plant Dis. Reptr*, Vol. 55, pp. 135–139.

CADMAN, C. H. 1957. Plant Pathology. *Rep. Scot. hort. Res. Inst. 1956*, pp. 26–27.

CORKE, A. T. K. 1963. Black currant leaf spot. The influence of biological factors on control. *Proc. 2nd Brit. Insectic. & Fungic. Conf., Brighton, 1963*, pp. 203–212.

CRANE, M. B. 1935. Blackberries, hybrid berries and autumn-fruiting raspberries. *Cherries and Soft Fruits*, R.H.S., London. pp. 121–128.

CRANE, M. B. and DARLINGTON, C. D. 1927. The origin of new forms in Rubus. *Genetica*, Vol. 9, pp. 241–278.

DAUBENY, H. A. and PEPIN, H. S. 1969. Variations in susceptibility to fruit rot among red raspberry cultivars. *Plant Dis. Reptr*, Vol. 53, pp. 975–977.

DAUBENY, H. A., TOPHAM, P. B. and JENNINGS, D. L. 1968. A comparison of methods for analyzing inheritance data for resistance to red raspberry powdery mildew. *Can. J. Genet. Cytol.*, Vol. 10, pp. 341–350.

EAST MALLING RESEARCH STATION. 1969. Fruit Breeding. *Rep. E. Malling Res. Stn 1968*, pp. 22–25.

GOODING, H. J. 1969. The problems faced by strawberry breeders. *Grower*, Vol. 71, pp. 591 and 594.

GOODING, H. J. 1971. Studies on field resistance of strawberry varieties to *Phytophthora fragariae*. *Euphytica*, Vol. 21, pp. 63–70.

GOODING, H. J. 1972. Strawberry. *Rep. Scot. hort. Res. Inst. 1971*, pp. 41–42.

GOODING, H. J. 1973. Methods of evaluating strawberry plants as parents for transmission of field resistance to *Phytophthora fragariae* Hickman. *Euphytica*, Vol. 22, pp. 141–149.

HOFMAN, K. 1963. (Fruit set in a number of black currants.) *Fruitteelt*, Vol. 53, pp. 334–335.

HULL, J. W. 1961. Austin Thornless as a parent in breeding blackberries. *Proc. Amer. Soc. hort. Sci.*, Vol. 78, pp. 245–250.

HULL, J. W. 1967. Sources of thornlessness for breeding in bramble fruits. *Proc. Amer. Soc. hort. Sci.*, Vol. 93, pp. 280–288.

JENNINGS, D. L. 1966. The manifold effects of genes affecting fruit size and vegetative growth in the raspberry. 1. Gene L_1. *New Phytol.*, Vol. 65, pp. 186–187.

JENNINGS, D. L., CARMICHAEL, E. and COSTIN, J. J. 1972. Variation in the time of early acclimation of raspberry canes in Scotland and Ireland and its significance for hardiness. *Hort. Res.* (in press).

JENNINGS, D. L. and TAYLOR, C. E. 1969. Raspberry resistance to diseases and pests. *Rep. Scot. hort. Res. Inst. 1968*, p. 41.

JENNINGS, D. L., TULLOCH, B. M. M. and TOPHAM, P. B. 1969. Raspberry, resistance to diseases and pests. *Rep. Scot. hort. Res. Inst. 1968*, p. 41.

JOHN INNES HORTICULTURAL INSTITUTE. 1938. Pomology Department. *Rep. John Innes hort. Inst. 1937*, pp. 12–15.

KEEP, E. 1962. Interspecific hybridization in *Ribes*. *Genetica*, Vol. 33, pp. 1–23.

KEEP, E. 1968a. Inheritance of resistance to powdery mildew, *Sphaerotheca macularis* (FR.) Jaczewski in the red raspberry, *Rubus idaeus* L., *Euphytica*, Vol. 17, pp. 417–438.

KEEP, E. 1968b. The inheritance of accessory buds in *Rubus idaeus* L. *Genetica*, Vol. 39, pp. 209–219.

KEEP, E. and BRIGGS, J. B. 1972. Disease and pest resistance: Raspberry beetle (*Byturus tomentosus*). *Rep. E. Malling Res. Stn 1971*, p. 107.

KNIGHT, R. L. 1966. Fruit breeding. *Rep. E. Malling Res. Stn 1965*, pp. 27–32.

KNIGHT, R. L. 1971. Fruit breeding. *Rep. E. Malling Res. Stn 1970*, pp. 93–102.

KNIGHT, R. L. 1972. Fruit breeding. *Rep. E. Malling Res. Stn 1971*, pp. 101–109.

KNIGHT, R. L. and KEEP, E. 1957. Fertile black currant–gooseberry hybrids. *Rep. E. Malling Res. Stn 1956*, pp. 73–74.

KNIGHT, R. L. and KEEP, E. 1966. Breeding new soft fruits. *Fruit Present and Future*. R.H.S., London. pp. 98–111.

MINISTRY OF AGRICULTURE, LONDON. 1970. Strawberries. *Bull. Min. Agric. Lond.* No. 95.

POTTER, J. M. S. 1972. Four new raspberries, Report on cultivar trial II. 1968–71. *Brogdale*, pp. 1–16.

REID, R. D. 1967. West of Scotland Unit. *Rep. Scot. hort. Res. Inst. 1966*, pp. 72–76.

RIETSEMA, I. 1936. (Mosaic disease of raspberries.) *Fruitteelt*, Vol. 26, pp. 206–212.

SCOTT, D. H. 1951. Cytological studies on polyploids derived from tetraploid *Fragaria vesca* and cultivated strawberries. *Genetics*, Vol. 36, pp. 311–331.

SCOTT, D. H. and INK, D. P. 1966. Origination of Smoothstem and Thornfree blackberry varieties. *Fruit Var. hort. Dig.*, Vol. 20, pp. 31–33.

SPINKS, G. T. 1947. Black currant breeding at Long Ashton. *Rep. Long Ashton Res. Stn*, pp. 35–43.

TAMÁS, P. 1965. (Soft fruits.) *Rep. Balsgård Fruit Breeding Inst. 1964*, 24–26.

TAMÁS, P. 1967. (Soft fruits.) *Rep. Balsgård Fruit Breeding Inst. 1967*, 21–23.

TEOTIA, S. S. and LUCKWILL, L. C. 1956. Fruit drop in black currants. 1. Factors affecting "running off". *Rep. Long Ashton Res. Stn 1955*, pp. 64–74.

TIITS, A. 1970. Studies on the etiology and pathology of the black currant reversion. III. Further information on the reactions of currant species to the pathogen of reversion. *EMSV Ta Toimet Biol.*, Vol. 19, pt. 2, pp. 183–186.

TOPHAM, P. B. 1970. Grey mould resistance. *Rep. Scot. hort. Res. Inst. 1969*, p. 42.

TYDEMAN, H. M. 1938. Some results of experiments in breeding black currants. II. First crosses between the main varieties. *J. Pomol.*, Vol. 16, pp. 224–250.

WILLIAMS, H. 1952. *Rep. John Innes Inst. 1951* and subsequent reports.

WILSON, D. 1964. *Rep. Long Ashton Res. Stn 1963*, p. 15, and subsequent reports.
WILSON, D. and ADAM, J. 1966. The inheritance of some yield components in black currant seedlings. *J. hort. Sci.*, Vol. 41, pp. 65–72.
WILSON, D. and ADAM, J. 1967. A comparative study of vegetative growth and flower bud differentiation in black currant varieties. *Rep. Long Ashton Res. Stn 1966*, pp. 104–111.
WILSON, D., CORKE, A. T. K. and JORDAN, V. W. L. 1964. The incidence of leaf spot and mildew on black currant seedlings. *Rep. Long Ashton Res. Stn 1963*, pp. 74–78.
WRIGHT, S. T. C. 1954. Studies of fruit development in relation to plant hormones. III. Auxins in relation to fruit morphogenesis and fruit drop in the black currant, *Ribes nigrum*. *J. hort. Sci.*, Vol. 31, pp. 196–211.
ZHUKOVSKY, P. M. 1965. Main gene centres of cultivated plants and their wild relatives within the territory of the U.S.S.R. *Euphytica*, Vol. 14, pp. 177–188.

Fungal Diseases of Raspberry

R. T. BURCHILL
East Malling Research Station

THE raspberry is grown successfully in most counties of the United Kingdom, with the largest acreage in Perthshire and Angus, followed by Kent, Norfolk and Worcestershire.

Raspberries grow and crop best in conditions of moderate summer temperatures and an adequate supply of water, particularly at the time of fruit swelling. Canes may be killed by severe frosts during the dormant season, particularly when these occur before the canes are sufficiently hardened, or when a period of mild weather during the winter is followed by very cold conditions.

The acreage grown in England and Wales is restricted by high labour costs which make the crop less attractive to growers than other soft fruits, particularly strawberries. In general, yields have been low, the average production during the period 1962–68 being under two tons per acre.

In the earlier part of the century many of the cultivars which at first cropped freely, rapidly became infected with virus diseases, resulting in loss of vigour and cropping capacity. Lately, however, with the improvement in the health of the planting material and, in particular, the availability of virus-tested stocks and new heavy cropping cultivars, yields per acre have improved. The planting of stock as free as possible from virus is one of the most important factors in the successful culture of this crop.

The chief commercial cultivars are now included in the Ministry of Agriculture's Certification Scheme, which ensures the maintenance of health standards. Stocks carrying the Special Stock Certificate are raised from virus-tested plants.

FUNGAL DISEASES

In the United States of America, over eighty different fungi have been recorded as diseases of cultivated brambles, approximately thirty of these causing losses of measurable economic importance. In addition there are several disorders that are not linked with any pathogen and others that are attributed to faults in the physical environment of the plant.

In Great Britain, W. C. Moore lists twenty-three diseases in his book *British Parasitic Fungi*. Many of these are rare, but a few often cause considerable losses.

Root diseases

Many fungi that are associated with the rotting of roots and the crown of raspberry plants are not active parasites but follow damage caused by unfavourable soil conditions such as waterlogging. Attacks by *Armillariella mellea* (the honey fungus) can usually be traced to dead tree stumps which serve as a long-term food base for the fungus.

Blue stripe wilt (*Verticillium dahliae*) is present in some plantations. Signs of this disease first appear on the foliage of young canes about the end of June. Some leaves develop yellow strips between the main veins; later the strips turn brown while the parts of the leaf adjoining the veins remain green, resulting in a striped appearance. Usually these symptoms are confined to one side of the plant and are followed by a wilting of the leaves; a bluish stripe sometimes starts at the base of the cane and extends upwards. When the discoloration encircles the cane all the leaves wither and it dies.

Infection comes from the soil, the fungus attacking the roots and underground portions of the stems and later extending into the young canes.

As the disease is soil-borne, it is not amenable to control by the ordinary spraying methods. It is important therefore to ensure that canes are not taken from an infected plantation for planting in another area, and that healthy material should not be planted in soil where there is evidence of infection.

Recently a wilt caused by *Fusarium avenaceum* has been reported in Scotland by W. R. Jarvis. The first symptoms of the disease appeared in the spring when many of the lateral buds failed to grow; later, lateral branches that were in full fruit suddenly wilted and died. Usually all the laterals on a cane were affected but rarely did all the canes on a stool wilt. The fungus was occasionally isolated from the roots of affected plants and from their associated soil.

Other fungi reported as being responsible for root infections of raspberry include violet root rot (*Helicobasidium purpureum*), white root rot (*Rosellinia necatrix*), and black root rot (*Thielaviopsis basicola*). *Phytophthora* spp. have also been reported.

Cane diseases

Cane blight (*Leptosphaeria coniothyrium*) affects the fruiting canes during summer. The leaves wilt and the canes become brittle and are easily broken, usually at ground-level. In Great Britain the fungus may infect canes damaged by the raspberry cane midge (*Thomasiniana theobaldi*). Control of this pest with gamma-BHC (Lindane) sprays often prevents fungal infection.

Spur-blight (*Didymella applanata*) infects buds, nodes and sometimes the internodal regions of raspberry canes during the summer. It may also infect canes damaged by cane midge. At first the infected areas on young canes are purple, contrasting with the green background of the cane (Figs. 34–36). Later, when the canes turn brown, the infections become pale grey or white and studded with black dots, the fruiting bodies of the fungus. Although the canes are not usually killed, the crop is diminished because the buds at the affected nodes either die or produce weakened fruiting laterals in the following season.

Recent experiments at the East Malling Research Station have shown that applications of fungicides, such as dichlofluanid (Elvaron) or benomyl (Benlate), at fortnightly intervals from the time when the young canes appear until two weeks before harvest, effectively controlled spur-blight. Few buds died on sprayed plants and in the following season fruiting laterals were produced along almost the entire length of the cane. This resulted in crop yields of over seven tons per acre on the treated plots compared with four tons per acre on the unsprayed plots.

Grey mould (*Botrytis cinerea*) is a common parasite of many cultivated plants. On raspberry, it frequently attacks the berries, but in wet seasons it often infects the cane, producing lesions similar to those described for spur-blight. The canes may be killed when infection is severe. Satisfactory control of both cane and berry infections has been obtained with the spray programme developed for the control of spur-blight.

Cane spot or anthracnose (*Elsinoe veneta*) may infect stems, leaves, leaf-stalks and fruits of raspberry. Small circular spots with a white centre and dark edge develop on leaves, while fruit infection causes mis-shapen berries. Most infections occur in the stem, however, where the fungus produces numerous small lesions throughout the summer from May to October. Initially the infections appear as small circular purple spots which gradually increase in size during the summer. Later the spots become sunken and the bark splits to form shallow pits or small cankers. Severe attacks greatly impair the growth and cropping of the plants and may kill the upper parts of the cane. The spray programme developed for the control of spur-blight seems to provide effective control of this disease.

Leaf diseases

Besides spur-blight and cane spot, two other fungi attacking leaves are rust (*Phragmidium rubi-ideai*) and powdery mildew (*Sphaerotheca macularis*). Rust, although fairly common, is rarely severe but occasionally may cause defoliation.

Similarly, powdery mildew is seldom serious, but when it spreads to the berries they are small and malformed. Furthermore, the white mould makes the berries unattractive. Regular applications of powdery mildew fungicides during the growing season have effectively controlled the fungus.

Flower diseases

Stamen blight (*Hapalosphaeria deformans*) flattens the stamens against the petals and gives the flower a saucer-shaped appearance. The anthers become swollen, brown and fail to dehisce. The presence of the fungus gives infected flowers a white powdery appearance. Fruits produced by diseased flowers vary considerably in the amount of malformation; they ripen unevenly and are frequently hard and difficult to remove from the receptacle. Only the flowers and fruits are affected by the fungus. Experiments by I. G. Montgomerie at the Scottish Horticultural Research Institute have shown that sprays of captan or dichlofluanid (Elvaron) applied during the summer reduce the incidence of this disease.

Fruit diseases

Raspberry fruits are among the most perishable of fruit crops. Warm, wet weather at harvest favours the development of fruit rots. Grey mould (*Botrytis cinerea*), the most frequent rot occurring in the field and in the store, may be satisfactorily controlled by the application of the appropriate fungicides during the pre-harvest period.

The other damaging fungi recorded on stored fruit include species of *Alternaria*, *Penicillium*, *Cladosporium*, *Rhizopus* and *Mucor*.

Many of these diseases may be avoided by picking only sound, firm fruit. Care should also be taken in picking and handling to avoid bruising, as damaged fruit is readily infected. Unnecessary delay in processing and marketing should also be avoided.

CONCLUSION

Most of the raspberry diseases mentioned may be controlled with a suitable programme of fungicide sprays applied at the appropriate time during the season; however, the most effective control measures are those taken before the diseases become serious. Careful selection of the planting sites and of cultivars that are resistant to the major diseases is important in determining subsequent growth and high yield.

The plant breeding programmes at the East Malling Research Station and the Scottish Horticultural Research Institute are ensuring the production and release of many new cultivars resistant to most diseases.

Finally, having obtained healthy plant material it is important to observe the management practices that promote vigorous growth, such as a satisfactory soil, adequate supply of water, drainage and cultivation, as these all contribute to the production of healthy raspberry crops.

The Ever-changing Strawberry

HEDLEY WILLIAMS
John Innes Institute, Norwich

BEFORE speculating on the likely future development of the garden strawberry in Great Britain a brief look at the past will not come amiss, for examining the ways the crop has responded to past events will help us in our predictions. The early history in this country up to 1913 has been well related by Bunyard. The strawberry as we know it is of very recent origin, resulting from chance crosses of two wild American octoploid species when they were brought together for the first time in Europe at the end of the eighteenth century. *Fragaria virginiana*, from eastern north America, contributed hardiness, good constitution, good colour and acidity, and *F. chiloensis*, from the west coast of south America, complemented it by contributing large fruit and sweetness. The hybrids often excelled both parents in vigour, yield and quality and the extreme variability released has been the basis of further breeding work ever since. The new varieties were taken back to the U.S.A., and with further infusions of wild germplasm a fairly similar development took place there (Darrow).

Up to the early years of this century the strawberry was considered to be an easy crop to grow because it had fewer pests and diseases than most other fruits. It seems that in crossing the Atlantic the parental species had managed to leave most of their troubles behind. Unfortunately the constant interchange of plants brought its penalty in that the pathogens caught up, and the nineteen-twenties and thirties were years of great trouble and frustration for growers in Britain. Old cultivars disappeared because they would not grow any more. New cultivars lasted but a few years, and there was a constant stream of introduction in the hope of finding one that would last. Looking back we now realize that virus diseases were one of the main causes of failure. At that time little was known about plant virus diseases and they were recognized only after the work of Harris at East Malling (Harris and King), which paralleled American work (Plakidas). These diseases were shown to be spread by the strawberry aphid, which, being confined to the cultivated strawberry in this country, must have followed it from America. It was not recorded until 1912 (Theobold). Other troubles were also rampant, but they were gradually sorted out and the causal agents identified by research workers. Nematodes, mites, beetles, leaf diseases and fruit rots all took their toll. In Scotland, and later England, red core disease appeared, causing partial losses in some places but catastrophic losses in others (Hickman). Eventually most of these troubles were brought under control by the system of certified stocks whereby a grower could at least start off his plantation with reasonably healthy material.

But by this time most of the older cultivars had disappeared from cultivation. Instead of the innumerable cultivars of earlier times the choice was virtually limited to two, 'Royal Sovereign' and 'Huxley'. 'Royal Sovereign' was grown for dessert because of its size, light colour and good flavour. 'Huxley', although darker and smaller, gave a much greater yield and was much used for processing. Unlike 'Royal Sovereign', it was virus tolerant and stood up well when many other varieties failed. It had an interesting origin for it was raised in California by a nurseryman-breeder called Albert Etter who had used wild *F. chiloensis* amongst others. His selections never had much success in America and he never knew of the success of 'Huxley' in Britain. However, his cultivars have since had extensive influence in both U.S. and British breeding.

One of the longer term effects of the increased incidence of disease was the cessation of private breeding. A promising seedling would become diseased by the time it was propagated. Since the early nineteen-thirties breeding has been almost entirely in the hands of research stations where there is a reasonable prospect of maintaining virus-free stocks of potential new cultivars.

After the war a new era dawned with the introduction of the first cultivars bred at research stations. 'Auchincruive Climax' was the first, introduced in 1947. It combined very good quality and size with an even greater yield than 'Huxley', and gained popularity so rapidly that it was hailed as the wonder strawberry and soon conquered more than half the acreage. Unfortunately, it then suffered a catastrophic genetic breakdown known as June yellows. Stocks lost vigour, and within a few years it had disappeared (Williams). It was replaced by 'Red-gauntlet' which is still with us. The Scottish breeding work still continues under the aegis of the Scottish Horticultural Research Institute. Breeding work at Cambridge started about 1930. An early seedling was released in 1937 as 'Early Cambridge' and grown in Hampshire for some years, but the bulk of cultivars came out about 1948. There were about thirty of them in the first instance and some of them are still important, including, of course, 'Cambridge Favourite', our leading cultivar. The author took over the Cambridge breeding work from Dr Boyes in 1951, and since then it has been carried on at the John Innes Institute. More recently strawberry breeding has been started in Eire and restarted at Long Ashton, so there should be no future shortage of home-bred varieties. In the last twenty years many European countries have started breeding projects, and the impact of cultivars, such as 'Gorella', is beginning to be felt. In the United States strawberry breeding has been carried out on a large scale for many years. Among the more important aspects of the work is the use of wild selections to bring in new desirable characters. Unfortunately, none of the United States cultivars is of direct use to us in our climate, but their use as parents in breeding has given some of the best results. 'Redgauntlet', 'Gorella', 'Cambridge Favourite' and 'Cambridge Vigour' are some of those with an American parent.

Apart from new cultivars, great cultural changes have come over the commercial plantations since the war. Yields have doubled, and yet production costs have gone down. This is why strawberries are one of the few foods that have held their price nearly steady, and they are now relatively much cheaper than they once were. The improved health of planting stock and the development of systemic insecticides enable virus diseases to be fairly well controlled so that plantation life is now longer. A great deal of hand labour was once required to control weeds, but now herbicides are universally used, and even the de-runnering can be largely achieved with the use of paraquat. It is now possible to grow strawberries with no cultivation at all after the original planting (which can also be done by machine). The effective weed control together with the spread of the use of irrigation has made matted beds a good proposition, and the resulting higher plant population is largely responsible for yields that at one time would have been considered impossible. New knowledge of the way *Botrytis* infects the fruit, showing the necessity of starting to spray at flowering time (Jarvis), and also the use of new fungicides, have drastically reduced the tithe that fruit rots used to claim each year. The present state of the crop should be a source of considerable satisfaction to those who want to defend investment in research. This is not to say that further changes are unnecessary, and the rest of this article will be devoted to prediction and speculation about strawberries and how they will be grown.

We have seen how the labour requirements in growing the crop have been cut. This is unfortunately a disadvantage when it comes to harvest time when all available hands are needed. Casual labour for picking is becoming more expensive and more difficult to obtain every year and in many places the labour supply is the limiting factor to expanding production. Because of this many growers are finding it more profitable to open at least part of their plantations to the public for them to pick their own fruit. This trend will certainly continue. Some are planting special areas, centred on a car park and picnic site, with a succession of fruits throughout the season. At the same time the National Institute of Agricultural Engineering is progressing with the development of a strawberry picking machine. The feasibility of this depends upon basic research on the plant. It has been known for some years that cutting all the foliage off strawberry plants immediately after harvest is rarely very detrimental to the following year's crop, and in fact often increases it. A harvesting machine can thus operate by cutting off all the fruit and foliage and separating the fruit. Fruit for processing seems likely to be picked by such a machine within a few years. From the breeders' point of view special cultivars will be needed to suit the machine, and active work is in progress at the John Innes Institute to produce some (Fig. 37). Firstly, since all the fruit will be picked at one time, selections ripening most of their fruit simultaneously must be sought. Secondly, the machine has to lift the fruit off the ground, and for this the fruit is required to be bunched at the end of the strigs with a clear length of stem for the elevator and cutter to operate on. Thirdly, a range of selections ripening at different times will be needed. All these needs seem capable of fulfilment, given time. The prizes involved are large since the cost of hand picking can be more than half the total cost of production.

With the production of special cultivars for machine harvesting, and the fruit from them destined for processing, strawberries will have achieved the schism that occurred in some other fruits generations ago, the division into dessert and processing cultivars. The strawberry has always been a dual-purpose fruit, or rather a dessert fruit that has been processed. From many points of view the characters desired in fresh fruit are opposed to those best for processing. Large size, for example, commands a premium in the punnet, but a can with only two or three large, sagging berries would cause complaint. The present cultivars are not particularly suitable for processing, and various devices are used to make them acceptable. One of these, which seems unnecessary, is the addition of artificial colouring to cans. When canned without added colour 'Cambridge Favourite', almost the only variety used in this country, yields pale gray fruit floating in what looks like weak prune juice! We now have many selections at the John Innes Institute with dark flesh, and these yield a syrup that matches the dyed product. In such cases the fruit tends to be darker, but at least it looks natural, and is no darker than the fruit in jam. The reason strawberries like this are not already cultivated commercially is that the dark colour of the fresh fruit makes them less attractive for dessert. The prospect of special processing cultivars for mechanical harvesting opens the way for this darker colour to be combined with the other characteristics needed.

The strawberry seems then about to go three ways. There will still be supplies of dessert fruit in the shops in season, but the rising picking costs will mean that they will become more and more expensive. The quality will probably improve because it will not pay to use expensive pickers on inferior fruit. For cheaper supplies of fresh fruit members of the public will increasingly pick their own. This will be made easier by special plantations, sited near to centres of population, that will grow a range of fruits. The bulk of processing fruit will be from specialized varieties grown on a large scale, probably on a contract basis, and harvested mechanically.

Our entry to the EEC should not make a great deal of difference to the supplies of fruit in the shops, although it will call for adjustments in the industry. Freed from any restrictions on entry, early fruit from southern Europe may compete much more with our own tunnel-grown fruit. The crucial point of competition could well be whether British fruit arrives at the market in better condition than the imported. On the other hand we should be able to export (dark fleshed) processing fruit, and perhaps also late dessert fruit to follow the European season. For some years a project has been under way at John Innes to breed very late strawberries. The autumn fruit seen for sale comes mainly from plants that were fruited under tunnels early in the year, and if the early fruit decreases this supply will tend to dry up. Autumn fruiting cultivars have been in existence for over half a century both in Europe and the U.S.A., but have never been very successful commercially as the average fruit size is small and the extended season adds to the picking costs. Perhaps further improvements could be effected to make them economically viable. Another, but as yet experimental, method of obtaining late summer fruit is to black out the plants in spring to induce them to form flower initials (Clements). A more remote but still real possibility is that we may learn to control the season of flowering with a spray, delaying the July crops by whatever amount we wish.

Looking back at the changes in the past it is clear that the only certain thing about the future is that it will be different from today. But although over-population presses, and the cow is threatened with extinction in favour of beef flavoured vegetable protein, I feel that we will still somehow find room for a few plants to provide the "Queen of Fruits" to eat with the synthetic cream.

REFERENCES

BUNYARD, E. A. 1913. The history and development of the strawberry. *J. Roy. hort. Soc.*, Vol. 39, pp. 541–552.

CLEMENTS, R. F. 1972. Short day treatment may be the answer to producing second crop Redgauntlet. *The Grower*, Vol. 77, pp. 765–768.

DARROW, GEORGE, M. 1937. Strawberry improvement. *U.S.D.A. Yearbook of Agriculture 1937*, pp. 445–495.

HARRIS, R. V. and KING, M. E. 1940. Review of research on strawberry virus diseases, 1932–1939. *Rep. E. Malling Res. Stn 1939*, pp. 66–69.

HICKMAN, C. J. 1940. The red core root disease of the strawberry caused by *Phytophthora fragariae* n. sp. *J. Pomol.*, Vol. 18, pp, 89–118.

JARVIS, W. R. 1962. The infection of strawberry and raspberry fruits caused by *Botrytis cinerea* Fr. *Ann. appl. Biol.*, Vol. 50, pp. 569–575.

PLAKIDAS, A. G. 1927. Strawberry xanthosis (yellows), a new insect-borne disease. *J. agric. Res.*, Vol. 35, pp. 1057–1090.

THEOBOLD, F. V. 1912. A new strawberry aphis. *Entomologist*, Vol. 45, p. 223.

WILLIAMS, H. 1955. June yellows: a genetic disease of the strawberry. *J. Genet.*, Vol. 53, pp. 232–243.

Production of Late-season Strawberries

R. F. CLEMENTS

A.D.A.S. Regional Fruit Specialist, Cambridge

EVER since strawberries were first cultivated in English gardens they have been a distinctly seasonal crop. In prose and verse the strawberry season has heralded the coming of summer, the harbinger of other fruitful pleasures, a season with the promise of richness and pleasure and a fullness yet to come. A season marking both the memory and the year. Thus "when as the rye reach to the chin, and chopcherry, chopcherry ripe within, strawberries swimming in the cream, and schoolboys playing in the stream . . .". *The Old Wives Tale* (1595) captures the spirit and pleasure of the summer season that ripening strawberries announce.

In the sixteenth century there were no strawberries as we know them today. Our native species, the wood strawberry *Fragaria vesca* and the "hautbois" *F. elatior* had been cultivated in gardens for years but the horticultural skills of Elizabethan gardeners could do little to improve species so lacking in intrinsic merit. Some success must, however, have attended their efforts, for in *Richard III* Gloster says to John Morton— "My Lord of Ely, when I was last in Holborn, I saw good strawberries in your garden there." But the large-fruited strawberry is of comparatively modern origin, and derives from hybridization between the North American meadow strawberry and the Chilean beach strawberry. From these have arisen all the modern types which in their individual characters show such extraordinary diversification.

In spite of efforts by plant breeders to develop early and late varieties to extend the period of production, the entire season, in commercial terms is generally only a month long. Continuity is mainly achieved by covering, situation and latitude, so that the earliest crops are from cloches in favoured areas in south and west England and the latest from the extensive fields of East Anglia and Scotland. In gardens advantage can be taken of various methods of production: forcing with heat, frames, cloches, polythene tunnels and growing in the open which, combined with selection of suitable cultivars, will produce fruit over a very long season.

The breeding of new strawberry cultivars has been intensively pursued for many years throughout the world, to achieve cultivars adapted to local conditions. American efforts have resulted in many well-known cultivars, such as 'Tioga' and 'Fresno' which now occupy a significant part of the world acreage and feature strongly in winter imports to the United Kingdom.

In the United Kingdom the most significant maincrop cultivar is

'Cambridge Favourite' and for this there seems no immediate replacement. In south Hampshire protected cropping is based on 'Redgauntlet', a cultivar which with 'Cambridge Vigour' finds favour in the Tamar Valley and Cheddar, two other areas of intensive early production. During the past twenty years the majority of commercially available cultivars have been tested at the A.D.A.S. Experimental Horticulture Stations and though some have merit for garden culture the commercial dictates of yield potential, fruit size, appearance, ease of picking and ability to travel may have excluded many otherwise promising kinds.

Strawberry breeding in this country at present seeks early and late cultivars which combine all the market qualities and hopefully, the elusive flavours of the past. Concurrent with this work is an effort to select everbearing kinds capable of producing commercial yields throughout the English summer—an extended season achieved at little cost.

Everbearing or perpetual cultivars have the capacity to initiate flowers irrespective of day length at any time during the spring, summer or autumn. Most strawberry cultivars grown in England initiate flowers in shortening days during August until November for flowering the following spring and initiate runners mainly in long days in summer. Recently there has been much interest in the everbearing types which in the past have generally produced only small picks over a long season. The cultivars available have been more suitable for the amateur gardener than the commercial grower, for example the American 'Red Rich'. In recent trials the German cultivar 'Gento' and the new Dutch ones 'Ostara', 'Revada' and 'Rabunda' appear promising. From the Grand Manil Station in Belgium a range of interesting 'Manil' cultivars have appeared, including several late-season ones. It is clear that in the short term the economic success of out-of-season production—in the sense of extending the season both early and late—depends on incurring the minimum of extra costs in the techniques adopted. Thus the use of heat and artificial light for promoting growth and flower truss development is probably uneconomic.

Some cultivars, and particularly 'Redgauntlet' have the ability to produce a commercial second crop *late* in the year in September–October. Second crop production occurs in this cultivar because flower initiation in spring is not inhibited by long days (over 12 hours) as it is in other cultivars. In natural day lengths second crop flower initiation depends on stresses created within the plant by the presence of swelling fruit of the first crop. If the first flowers are removed, the second crop flowers are poor and the plant becomes vegetative. In English conditions this second crop is only produced in satisfactory quantities if the spring crop has been advanced by protection, thus enabling flowers to be initiated in time to produce ripe fruit before the autumn frosts. 'Redgauntlet' grown unprotected will often flower in the autumn but the ability to harvest the second crop, which may develop from early September onwards, depends on the autumn weather.

Experiments in Belgium, Holland and at Efford E.H.S. have recently been directed towards understanding the factors that influence second cropping with the object of improving yields and affecting harvest dates of this cultivar. It has been found that when plants are subjected to a period of artificial short days, flower initiation occurs independently of the condition of the plant (Figs. 38–40). When plants were covered with black polythene sheeting (5 pm to 9 am) from the time of early first flowering, so as to give 20 short days of only 8 hours duration, second crop flowers were induced. Approximately 100 days elapsed between time of starting short days and second harvest. At Efford, in 1971, short days from April 22 resulted in ripe second crop fruit on August 5. This was three weeks earlier than from untreated plants and the total yield was 20% greater.

This technique introduces a measure of control over second crop production and, although tested in the first place on autumn-planted, spring-cropping runners grown under low plastic tunnels, it offers interesting possibilities for other planting times and high tunnel work. The most recent development is in connection with spring planted runners. These must of necessity be de-blossomed to aid establishment and in doing this the stimulus to second flower production is removed, but if these plants are given artificial short days then initiation will occur in spite of the removal of flowers.

This technique has already been tried on a commercial scale with plants set out in the field and covered as individual rows under low tunnels, but perhaps of greater importance is a method where plants have been covered in a nursery bed and planted in the field in an induced state in early June for cropping that autumn.

Looking to the future one can see scope for combining short day treatments with high tunnel growing. Plants could be set out in the autumn, covered by tunnels in late winter, cropped and given short day treatments in the spring and an early second crop secured in late summer. Alternatively plants in nursery beds in spring might be given short day treatments and set out in the field at a spacing suitable to permit high tunnel coverage. Covering could be in late summer if required by weather conditions, or in late winter as is normally done. Such plants would crop in the autumn for the first time and again in the spring. They could then be given short day treatment for a further autumn crop. Either method would make full use of the comparatively expensive high tunnel and exploit its inherent virtues in extending the strawberry season both early and late.

Producing Early Strawberries

HILARY M. HUGHES
A.D.A.S. Regional Fruit Specialist, Bristol

THE greatest change in strawberry growing over the last decade, in common with that of most soft fruits, has been the elimination of cultivations. But the use of herbicides for the control of weeds in strawberries, perhaps the biggest problem in the production of this delectable fruit, has enabled maincrop strawberries to be grown by good arable farmers as well as specialist producers. This new type of growing, combined with the availability of healthy clonal planting material through the Ministry of Agriculture certification schemes, and more efficient pesticides has increased yields from some 17,000 acres in England and Wales and ensured adequate supplies during the main season. At times indeed there may be glut conditions; it may be said that given adequate soil and moisture the production of strawberries is straightforward, provided knowledge is carefully applied, and the real problem with this crop now is that of marketing.

With this competition from farmer growers the smaller strawberry grower and the amateur gardener now have much more interest in out-of-season strawberries. These may be fruits produced early in the year before the maincrop, by protecting the plants with glass cloches, polythene tunnels or plastic houses, or after the maincrop period during August, September and October by the use of everbearing cultivars, or the production of an autumn crop from certain cultivars such as 'Redgauntlet'. Entry into EEC may mean that more early strawberries will be available from the more favoured areas on the continent and only time will show whether the efficiency of the English grower, his nearness to markets, and the freshness of the English produce will enable producers of early strawberries to compete successfully with the imported product. There is, understandably, some apprehension about the possibility of increased imports amongst producers of early strawberries in the favoured areas of the south west and south England.

The plastic explosion

Travellers in the south of the country cannot fail to be impressed by the seas of plastic tunnels over strawberry crops glimpsed across the fields. There are considerable acreages of protected strawberries in south Hampshire where the method originated, and in Kent, Sussex, Surrey, Somerset, Dorset, Devon and Cornwall. Smaller areas will be seen in the Vale of Evesham and Essex and even further north wherever a sheltered site and local knowledge indicate that wrapping up the plant in a plastic overcoat against the spring winds profitably forwards the crop.

Originally this method of protection was developed as an alternative to the expensive and difficult-to-handle glass cloches. It enables the smaller grower, on sheltered favourable sites, to produce profitable early crops. Plastic was first used in the early nineteen-sixties but a few years later some of the larger scale producers decided also to cover plants with plastic. Some of these growers are covering as much as 10 to 20 acres each year and have been forced to develop machine methods of laying the plastic over the plants. On a small scale the grower normally inserts the simple wire hoops (Figs. 41, 42) by hand and lays out the polythene to protect the plants, usually in January to March, also by hand or with the use of a simple trolley. This method is satisfactory for up to 2 or 3 acres and enables a single-handed grower to cover his plants during the winter months. It will be appreciated that the use of herbicides is absolutely essential to the production of protected strawberries and it is interesting that the development of both plastics and herbicides came along at the same time to enable their complementary use on this crop.

Unless this labour requirement could be reduced for the large scale producer of early strawberries, the crop was not profitable. These growers developed, therefore, jigs to go on tractors for laying hoops and tunnels. The runners are planted by machine, two rows at a time. The machines for laying polythene are also worked over two rows so that slight variations in the original planting can be followed by the subsequent machine. The wire hoops can be inserted by workers riding on the rig with piles of hoops to hand, while the tractor moves slowly over the rows. A stone-free soil is necessary; stony soils present problems as the hoops cannot be forced into the ground quickly enough. The rolls of polythene are carried on spindles and the end of the polythene is either attached to a stake or, more usually, buried in the soil at the end of each row. As the tractor travels down the rows the hoops are inserted and the polythene unravelled and pulled out over the hoops. Originally wire ties were used to secure the polythene to the hoops but polypropylene baling twine is now used. There are two methods of using this twine to secure the polythene to the hoops. Some growers attach the polypropylene so that it criss-crosses over the tunnel, is looped over the hoop on each side and criss-crossed back. Thus a continuous twine is used and two workers can hand the twine over to each other as they slip it under the hoop loops. The tractor machine tensions the twine, and every so often an extra loop of the twine is made round the hoop to prevent unravelling should the twine break. Other growers continue to use the older method of a single short piece of twine, preknotted to the required length to give two end loops that are hooked over the wire hoops thus securing the polythene firmly to the hoop. The great secret, whether the tunnels are set by hand or by machine, is to ensure that the polythene is pulled tight to the hoops and ground. This ensures a reliable tunnel tight to the ground to prevent draughts and able to withstand moderate gales.

The smaller specialist producer makes some attempt to ventilate the plants on hot days during April and May. At the A.D.A.S. Experimental Horticulture Station, Efford, many experiments on strawberries under tunnels have shown the value of the correct planting date, use of herbicide, type of runner, and more recently best methods of ventilation. In one trial it was found that if the tunnels were ventilated when the temperatures inside reached 70°F, the very high temperatures that can be experienced on sunny days when the tunnels are kept closed, can be avoided, and resulted in the heaviest yield and the best quality and size of berry. The tunnels which were kept closed produced the earliest crop, but the fruit was often small and sometimes had a "baked" appearance. This opening and closing of the tunnels is, however, laborious and the growers of larger acreages generally do only a certain amount of ventilation on hot days. In Hampshire on sheltered sites where conditions are very favourable in the spring, many growers completely or partially open the tunnels during the whole flowering period. That area is not likely to have frost, or indeed cold weather during this April period, and the plants seem to benefit from the free air movement. Experienced growers are certain that this opening of the tunnels assists in the setting of the flowers and avoids mis-shapen fruit which is often produced under tunnels. This ventilation, as was shown in the Efford experiments, does delay ripening by a few days and would not be recommended for less favoured areas.

Where a large acreage is being grown the Efford results suggest the use of different ventilating methods in order to spread the peak pick of the tunnel-protected strawberries. A small area could be kept closed to ensure the earliest crops; the main area might be manually ventilated as much as possible and another smaller area, assuming the locality was suitable, could be opened during part of the flowering period. Such a programme would ensure three peaks of high quality fruit throughout the picking period and some levelling out of the labour demand over the whole crop period. On a garden scale, in addition to the use of early and mid season varieties to spread the season, the use of tunnels treated in different ways could help to spread the ripening period.

Because of the increasing acreages covered by tunnels there has been a tendency for the price per pound to decrease through the natural laws of supply and demand. However in 1972 with a cold late spring, tunnel-protected plants were particularly useful and although late to yield, met ready demand because the unprotected maincrop plants were so slow to ripen. In 1971 the opposite occurred and there was considerable overlap between the last of the protected strawberries and the first of the earlier-than-average-outdoor-strawberries, due to the warm May. This illustrates the unpredictable nature of this crop when grown commercially. Growers should not be encouraged to attempt to grow this crop unless they have a favourable site and are prepared to grow it over several years. The capital costs involved in growing strawberries under plastic tunnels are considerably lower than with expensive glass cloches.

A more recent innovation has been the use of the simple plastic walk-through house for protecting and forwarding early strawberries. Trials at Ellbridge Experimental Horticulture Station and commercial experience at Plant Protection Ltd., Fernhurst, and by growers, has shown that the 14-feet wide house produces earlier strawberries than low continuous tunnels. Originally these plastic houses were developed as a cheap alternative for the production of glasshouse crops. Various types and sizes are available. One value of the plastic house is that work can continue during inclement conditions. On the other hand the capital costs are far higher than for the continuous polythene tunnel and, owing to construction and ventilation problems, it is unlikely that large areas will be used to forward strawberries. The plastic house, provided the ends are made so that they can be taken away, has the advantage of permitting the passage of a tractor enabling spraying to be done more easily than by opening the tunnels. Ventilation can be a problem and very high temperatures can be experienced particularly during picking once the fruit has ripened. In contrast to the tunnels which can be left open, the plastic houses cannot be removed until picking is finished. Some growers cut large holes in the plastic to obviate this problem but this means that the thicker, and more expensive 500 gauge plastic is only used once.

It is likely that we shall see an extension of plastic houses over part of the early protected crop on the specialist holdings, but only if the price is such that the early fruit still retains a premium. Both techniques, low tunnels or plastic walk-through houses, are ideal for gardeners to enable early strawberries to be grown in most gardens.

Glass cloches

The use of glass cloches is still one of the best ways to obtain early strawberries, some two weeks ahead of those ripening under low continuous polythene tunnels. Because of the difficulties in handling cloches their use on commercial holdings is limited but they are extremely valuable for private gardens.

Recent experiments at Efford E.H.S. have shown that there is no advantage in covering the plants in the autumn and that the best time is to put the cloches over the plants in mid-February or thereabouts. If covering is delayed until April then crop ripening is also delayed. Many cultivar trials show that cultivars that succeed under polythene tunnels or plastic houses also do well under glass cloches.

It is important to ventilate glass cloches adequately—as it is polythene tunnels—to ensure the warm buoyant atmosphere ideal for pollination during flowering, and growth of the berries. Glass cloched strawberries tend to become much drier than those forwarded under plastic so irrigation, either overhead or through layflat or trickle lines, is generally essential to ensure full crop and improve berry size, particularly after the first berries have been harvested.

Looking back over 30 years of association with strawberry growing I see the forties as being the time of improvements in the health of the planting stocks, the Ministry certification schemes and the start of the availability of modern fungicides and pesticides. The fifties saw even better chemicals, for those that needed to use them, and the start of the herbicide story. In the sixties the herbicides were well tested and that decade also saw the dramatic expansion of tunnel-protected straw-berries. In the seventies we will hope to see the production of new cultivars to spread the season of this fruit over the summer and into the autumn and perhaps also improvements in quality.

One problem still remains and is not likely to be solved. This is the control of runners. The strawberry plant propagator needs runners but the fruit grower needs few or none. Will the seventies or even the eighties lead to the discovery of a growth regulator chemical that can be sprayed on to strawberry plants to control runner production? Most research workers in this field seem to think this unlikely, but the subject remains an interesting challenge for them.

Diseases of Currants and Gooseberries

A. T. K. CORKE

University of Bristol, Long Ashton Research Station

THE yield of fruit from currant and gooseberry bushes is closely related to the weather and to the health of the bushes in the cropping year as well as in the preceding year. The production of these bush fruits in the United Kingdom is almost confined to plantations in England and Wales, where the area has steadily declined during the past eight years to less than 14,000 acres (Ministry of Agriculture). The average yield of black currants has seldom risen above 30 cwt per acre since 1958, the yield of gooseberries has been less than 60 cwt and of other currants less than 43 cwt, all reaching a peak of production in 1966.

In recent years, spring frosts have often reduced the crop to a much greater extent than would have been the case if fungal diseases alone had been the cause. The extent of loss due to disease is always difficult to assess, since one can only guess at the true potential of a completely healthy plant growing under optimum conditions. Nevertheless, some indication of the loss due to fungal infection can be deduced from the cropping of bushes used in trials for the chemical control of a single disease, since care can be taken in such cases to account for the effects of all the other known factors which influence yield. For example, summer spray trials carried out at the Efford Experimental Horticulture Station from 1959 to 1964 showed that a reduction in leaf spot infection of black currants by about one half during one season led to an increase in crop of 30 cwt per acre in the next. When infection was reduced by spraying for three successive years, the benefit was cumulative, 'Baldwin' bushes yielding 124 cwt and 'Mendip Cross' 132 cwt per acre, increases of 48 and 66 cwt respectively over the crops carried by the same bushes before the trial. At that time, the 'Baldwin' bushes had carried about 75 cwt and the 'Mendip Cross' 79 cwt per acre, i.e. twice the national average yield (Corke, 1962, 1963, 1966). Elsewhere it was found that black currant bushes heavily infected by American gooseberry mildew carried 84% fewer flowers the following spring than bushes showing little or no infection, and 87% less crop in the summer (Corke, 1965b).

It is clear that, given freedom from frost damage, the yield of bush fruits can be raised considerably by achieving a good control of fungal diseases. In commercial plantations the size of the area under cultivation with a single plant species is one of the major factors acting against effective disease control. A shortage of labour and the introduction of machines to perform almost every task from pruning to picking have

153

done nothing to help to reduce the reservoir of infection which survives, often unnoticed, from one season to the next. In fact, during the last 20 years, leaf spot has begun to appear at least six weeks earlier on black currant bushes, American gooseberry mildew has become sufficiently widespread and severe to warrant the introduction of special control measures, and *Botrytis* (grey mould) infection of the shoots and the fruit has become a matter for concern.

While the commercial grower is bedevilled by the problems associated with the size of his undertaking, the small grower who is prepared to emulate his ancestors in the fruit garden can derive pleasure and satisfaction from the appearance of his bushes as well as from the crop resulting from his labours. An understanding of the life cycles of the important diseases, and of their relationship with the plants which they attack, is essential if the best use is to be made of the methods available for disease control. Much can be achieved, as in the past, without recourse to chemicals, and it is mainly for the fruit gardener that this is written.

Although black, red or white currant or gooseberry bushes are attacked by a wide range of fungi, most occur relatively rarely and locally. The commonest, and therefore the most important economically, are leaf spot, caused by *Pseudopeziza ribis*, American gooseberry mildew (*Sphaerotheca mors-uvae*) and grey mould (*Botrytis cinerea*). Since black currants are the major crop under consideration here, the biology and control of these diseases on currants will be discussed first, but it must be borne in mind that differences which appear between currant and gooseberry bushes infected with the same fungus are due to the reaction of the host to infection more than to any other cause. The principles of control, based on the life-cycle of the fungus, are similar whatever the host.

Leaf spot

The leaf spot fungus attacks many *Ribes* species, both wild and cultivated, throughout the world. Although it attacks the fruit and other parts of the host plant, it is the infection of the leaves, repeated again and again whenever enough rain falls to disperse the spores, which causes early defoliation. The premature loss of leaves reduces the quality of the fruit by exposing it to sun and rain and affects the formation of the new shoots and buds, thereby reducing the following year's crop.

Infected dead leaves overwintering on the ground carry the resting stage of the fungus from one season to the next, and the initial infection of new leaves in the spring is almost exclusively dependent on this method of survival. It has been shown experimentally that the removal of dead leaves from currant plantations is much the most effective single method of reducing the inoculum (Corke, 1954), and the fruit gardener can do this by raking up the leaves and burning them. Leaves break down to small fragments during the winter months, so the earlier after leaf fall that this cleaning up is completed the easier it is and the better the result.

Because of the problem of removing the leaves on a large scale, the commercial grower must resort to chemical treatment to destroy the fungal inoculum. Many chemicals have been tested and found to be effective for this purpose when dead leaves were immersed individually under laboratory conditions (Corke, 1960). In the field, however, the difficulty of getting a good cover of chemical on all dead leaves once they have begun to form a mat on the soil has led to far from adequate results. To overcome this, the leaves can be treated with appropriate chemicals at or immediately after leaf fall. Since trials have shown that some chemicals are less effective when applied in the autumn than when used in the spring, some care in the selection of a chemical is necessary.

The differences in the effect obtained by applying chemicals to dead leaves at different times of the year reflect the stages of development of the fungus before and after the winter. At the end of the summer the production of conidia, the spores by which the fungus spreads by rain-splash throughout the growing season, gradually declines on both the upper and lower surfaces of the leaves. On the lower surface, very small spores are formed in their place, and the evidence available suggests that the development of the sexual phase of the fungus life cycle is dependent on the presence of these spores. Certainly the apothecium, the fruit-body which overwinters and becomes active in the spring, forms only on the underside of fallen leaves and on those on which active lesions were present in the autumn. The spores (ascospores) contained within the fruit-body mature at about 54–61°F (12·4–16·6°C) and are released at temperatures above 60°F (16°C). The most suitable conditions for spore discharge are when leaves wetted overnight dry out in the morning; the spores, which are released into the air, are then readily carried upwards in convection currents to the leaves near the base of the bush.

Treatment of leaves with a chemical in the autumn may upset spore production or some other process on which the development of the overwintering stage depends, or it may affect the tissues of the leaf in such a way that they are no longer a suitable source of nutrient for the fungus. Several defoliant chemicals have been found to be effective in reducing spore production in the spring following treatment in the autumn: herbicides such as simazine (0·2%) and dalapon (0·4%) have also proved very effective. In practice, it has been found that fungitoxic chemicals are most effective when used in late winter, dinitro-*ortho*-cresol (DNOC at 0·0125%) in 3% diesel oil, for example, being particularly useful in reducing spore production.

Over a period of about 15 years the release of mature ascospores has occurred in the south-west between mid-March and the end of May, depending on rainfall and temperature. The bushes normally develop during this time from the stage when the first leaves are visible to the end of flowering (green fruit) and the start of shoot extension. In most years the majority of the ascospores are dispersed in no more than 3 weeks, at a time when the grape stage in the development of the flowers is reached. Easy recognition of this stage of development forms the basis of the timing adopted for the control of this disease by chemical sprays.

Leaves become infected by the leaf spot fungus only through the lower surface, where conditions are better suited to germination of the spores and penetration into the tissues. In spring, when temperatures are often rather low, lesions may not develop for 3 to 4 weeks, whereas later in the summer they become visible after 7 to 10 days. They appear as minute, deep brown spots on the upper surface, and a paler brown below, which expand slowly to about 2 mm in diameter: further expansion is restricted by the venation of the leaf. On both surfaces the summer spores, the conidia, are produced in a mucilaginous matrix which forms a hard crust in hot, dry weather, protecting the lesion from desiccation. In the wet, however, the conidia readily separate and are dispersed in run-off and rain-splash droplets to the undersides of other leaves. This process gives rise to the generally characteristic appearance of infected bushes: the infection of the lower leaves, especially those around the flower trusses, by the airborne ascospores is followed by infections by the water-borne conidia in an upwards and outwards direction. Repeated infection of a leaf leads to eventual death, and the process of defoliation thus also begins at the base of the bush and extends upwards.

A realization of the importance of the early spring as the time when the initiation of the summer epidemic occurs is essential if an effective control of the disease is wanted. It has been shown experimentally that, as an alternative to the destruction of the inoculum on the fallen leaves, a spray applied to the bushes just before the start of ascospore discharge can delay the build-up of the disease for many weeks. Some 20 years ago, when tar oil winter washes and lime sulphur in the spring were applied regularly for the control of insect pests, leaf spot infection was seldom noticeable before mid-June. Nowadays, the infections are frequently visible at least six weeks earlier, and although neither tar oil nor lime sulphur on its own was sufficient to control leaf spot, the combined effect of the two sprays on the overwintering inoculum and the early spring leaf infections was considerable. One of the major criticisms levelled at the use of lime sulphur was the damage done to young leaves, often causing them to fall. At the time when the sprays were applied, the majority of the leaves affected were those around the flower trusses (Fig. 44); it is these same leaves which act as sites for the primary ascospore infections, and from which the subsequent infections spread. The use of lime sulphur against big bud mite (*Cecidophyopsis*

Diseases of Currants, pp. 153–162

Photos: Long Ashton Research Station

FIG. 44—*above left*: primary lesions of leaf spot on a young black currant leaf associated with a flower truss. The lack of fruit and infection of a flower stem by *Botrytis* can be seen. FIG. 45—*above right*: new shoots arising from the tip of a black currant shoot killed in the previous season by American gooseberry mildew. FIG. 46—*below*: infections of open black currant flowers and stems by *Botrytis*

Highbush Blueberries, pp. 163–166
Photo: Kinsealy Research Centre
FIG. 47—a nine-year-old bush of blueberry 'Coville'.

RUBEL — Found wild

RANCOCAS — 1926

BLUECROP — 1952

DARROW — 1965

Highbush Blueberries, pp. 163–166

Photos: Kinsealy Research Centre

FIG. 48—*left*: the development of the blueberry from the wild fruit (scale in cm). FIG. 49—*below*: the blueberry carries its fruit in many flowered clusters.

Dessert Grapes for the Amateur, pp. 167–173

Photos: H. R. Youngman

FIG. 50—*above*: Dutch light cloches for vines. FIG. 51—*below*: vine in a cloche in June

ribis Nal.) may thus have been advantageous in reducing leaf spot infection by causing limited defoliation.

Once again, the fruit gardener has an advantage over the commercial grower. Since the first infections occur at about the grape stage, leaves showing infection can be removed without detriment to the bush, provided that the infection is not exceptionally severe. Alternatively, with a small number of bushes, spray applications can be timed very accurately and care taken to obtain a good cover of both surfaces of the leaves. Once the disease spreads to the foliage on the new shoots, spraying is the only practical method of control.

The number of sprays needed to keep the level of infection within acceptable limits depends on the persistence and effectiveness of the chemical used and on the frequency with which weather conditions suitable for spore dispersal and infection occur. To provide protection for the leaves from the start of ascospore release it is sufficient in most parts of this country to apply the first spray at the start of the grape stage: a second spray can then generally be applied before the flowers are fully open. A further spray applied immediately after flowering followed by another after no more than 14 days may be needed to give adequate control of leaf spot infection in most years, but in particularly adverse seasons extra applications may be needed to maintain the level of control required.

Chemicals which are used before harvest must be safe to use on leaves and young fruits and must leave no harmful residue on the fruit at harvest. A wide range of organic fungicides has been tested to replace the post-harvest copper sprays of 20 years ago, and suitable spray materials are shown in the List of Approved Products published annually by the Ministry of Agriculture, Fisheries and Food. Experience has shown that the effectiveness of spraying is generally more dependent on the efficiency of the application and the accuracy of the timing than on the choice of chemical. However, the recent introduction of fungitoxic chemicals with systemic activity has shown that infection by several fungi can be simultaneously reduced by the use of a single chemical, perhaps promising easier disease control after further development (Gilchrist and Cole).

It has long been considered that the maximum amount of leaf should be retained for as long as possible in order to build up reserves for the following year's crop but, at the same time, it has been found that some defoliation can occur without detriment to the next crop. The question of whether it might not be an advantage, under certain circumstances, to rid the bush of its leaves at a time governed by the amount of leaf retained is at present under investigation. There would clearly be much to commend such treatment if the cycle of fungal development could be upset at the same time.

The natural susceptibility of black currant bushes to leaf spot infection can be influenced to some extent by local conditions of soil and climate and also by the manuring and pruning treatments which they receive since, for example, lack of nitrogen or loss of vigour renders the bushes liable to heavy infection and defoliation. New cultivars of black currant with very much lower susceptibilities to leaf spot will no doubt be available in the future, following the introduction of suitable genetic material from other species within the genus *Ribes*, as described by Dr R. L. Knight and Dr Elizabeth Keep in the first volume of this book.

Nevertheless, evidence is available which suggests that considerable variation can be found among the existing cultivars. Of those widely grown, 'Baldwin' and 'Wellington XXX' are susceptible to leaf spot, and 'Westwick Choice' is very susceptible. 'Amos Black', 'Daniel's September Black' and 'Boskoop Giant' are only moderately susceptible, while 'Mendip Cross', the newly introduced 'Tor Cross', 'Blacksmith' and the less common 'Laxton's Grape' and 'Silvergieter' have low levels of susceptibility. Among these are early, middle and late season cultivars, so the gardener may find it worthwhile to examine the value of some of those less widely grown, bearing in mind that there appears to be generally a greater likelihood of late cultivars being more susceptible to leaf spot than early ones.

Considerable variation in the susceptibility of cultivars to mildew is also evident and Bauer stated that, of the many that he had tested, none had been resistant.

American gooseberry mildew

As its name implies, the gooseberry bush has traditionally been the host of this fungus in this country. Although seen on black currant bushes since 1908 (Salmon), mildew attacks were still of minor importance and infection was, at the worst, only moderate on seedlings tested for susceptibility to leaf spot and mildew in 1962/63 (Wilson *et al.*). In 1964, however, mildew became such a widespread and serious disease of black currant plantations that detailed information on infection and on methods of prevention and control was urgently needed. An intensive study of the problems was carried out during the next few years (Jordan, 1967).

As is the case with other diseases common to the different *Ribes* species, the behaviour of mildew varies according to the species infected. On black currant bushes it is mainly the leaves and shoots at the top of the extension growth which become infected: the leaves become distorted, remain small, shoot extension is restricted and fruit bud formation is drastically curtailed (Fig. 45). Direct infection of black currant fruit by the fungus is not a major cause of loss of crop.

The amount of damage done to leaves and shoots by mildew depends on the time of year when conditions are right for rapid colonization of the young tissues. The fine, colourless threads (hyphae) spread over the surface putting down "roots" in the form of microscopic pegs, which penetrate into the epidermal layer and supply the fungus with nutrients. For some days there is no sign of new infection to the untrained eye, but the spore-bearing branches soon develop, giving rise to chains of colourless spores (conidia) which reflect the light and give the surface a powdery appearance. At this stage the pegs formed during the development of the infection have already caused considerable and irreparable damage to the surface of the plant.

The conidia are dispersed by wind to new infection sites. In laboratory conditions, conidia require a temperature of about 64°F (18°C) and almost 100% relative humidity for 12 hours or more for good germination to occur on glass. On black currant leaves, however, infection can occur at 60% relative humidity, the infection being more severe on plants growing in dry soil. Such conditions, liable to result in a rapid increase in infection, generally occur during spells of warm weather when, during daylight hours, spore dispersal is assisted by convection currents and light winds, whereas germination can take place readily in the cooler, moist conditions which prevail during the hours of darkness.

As the lesions become old or as autumn approaches, the mass of hyphae becomes brown and perithecia develop, firmly embedded in the felt of hyphae. The perithecia, containing a single ascus from which the eight ascospores are discharged in the spring, are formed mainly at the base of the lamina, or on the petiole of a leaf, and on the terminal internodes of the shoot itself. Jordan (1967) found that on black currant shoots the maturation of ascospores reached a maximum by about the middle of May, at about the time of full blossom and that, under normal spring weather conditions, primary infections were closely related to the strength and direction of the wind.

From the evidence available, it is almost certain that the only way in which new infections can arise in the spring is by the discharge of ascospores from perithecia embedded in the hyphal felt overwintering on the shoots and fallen leaves. It is clearly prudent, therefore, as with leaves infected with leaf spot, to remove all dead leaves from the soil beneath the bushes. Here again, chemical treatment of the leaves and bushes can reduce the overwintering inoculum by as much as 75%. Tipping of shoots during the growing season may be beneficial but will not control the disease completely, and since heavily-infected shoots bear little or no crop in the following year the complete removal of such shoots will make little difference to the crop and will keep the bush more open.

Mildew on gooseberry bushes of most cultivars has traditionally been controlled by sprays of sulphur in some form, in spite of the damage done to some. As mentioned above, black currant bushes were, until quite recently, sprayed with lime sulphur to control the big bud mite, and the continued use of sulphur on non-fruiting bushes seems rational. On fruiting bushes, on the other hand, one of a number of approved chemicals may be used, and again the essential ingredient for an effective programme of spraying is the timing of the applications. Recent experience has suggested that the first spray should be applied not later than first green fruit if the primary infections are to be reduced. (Corke and Jordan; Jordan, 1969). This must be followed by further sprays at intervals of 10 to 14 days, the number depending on the reduction in infection obtained.

In contrast to its effect on leaf spot infection, increased vigour renders currant shoots more liable to severe mildew infection. High levels o phosphorus and potassium also favour the disease, and the increases in the severity of infection seen with high dosage rates of simazine may be due to the presence of more readily available nutrients.

Although, as already mentioned, no cultivar is known to be resistant to mildew infection, 'Tor Cross' and 'Mendip Cross' show some resistance.

Grey mould

Although *Botrytis* grows saprophytically on almost all moribund tissue and is the cause of stem die-back, root rot or leaf spotting on a wide variety of host plants, it is only comparatively recently that losses due to *Botrytis* infection have become substantial in black currant plantations. Inoculum from a wide range of host plants has been found to be equally capable of infecting ripe currants (Corke, 1965a) so that sources of inoculum have always been present in plantations. The most likely cause of the increase in infection is an increase in the inoculum level within currant plantations, particularly early in the season. One contributory factor was almost certainly the abandonment of insecticidal winter washes, many of which have subsequently been shown to be very effective against *Botrytis* infections of currant wood (Corke, 1965a). Another factor has been the susceptibility to *Botrytis* infection of shoots weakened by mildew infection and lastly, the tendency to leave prunings in the plantation, macerated or not, has added to the sources of inoculum. The removal of all dead and dying plant material from the vicinity of the bushes will go a long way towards reducing the amount of *Botrytis* infection to the low level at which it once was.

The open blossom has been shown to be readily infected by *Botrytis*, leading to loss of the flower and invasion of the stem (Fig. 46). Although undamaged and unripe fruit is not susceptible to infection, entry of the fungus into green fruit frequently follows invasion of the stem elsewhere, causing the berry to colour prematurely. Once the fungus is established, the infected berry serves as a source of inoculum for the infection of any damaged fruit, which becomes more susceptible as it ripens. Shoots which become infected by *Botrytis* carry the fungus through the winter in a resistant form, a small black body (sclerotium), which breaks through the surface of the bark. In the spring, conidiophores develop from the surface of the sclerotium and the familiar brownish grey conidia are formed.

As with the previous two diseases, lime sulphur is very effective in reducing berry infection (Corke, 1965a), but there are many other fungicides which can safely be used to protect the fruit. Nevertheless, the difficulties involved in providing adequate protection for the fruit, from the appearance of the first open flower to harvest, are unreasonably numerous compared with those involved in adopting a strict hygiene aimed at reducing the inoculum in the plantation between seasons.

The changes in horticultural methods adopted in recent years on grounds of economic necessity and advancement, the abandonment of winter washes and lime sulphur for insect control, the widespread use of herbicides for weed control, the introduction of machines to harvest the fruit or to macerate prunings *in situ* and the production of numerous spray chemicals to protect the bushes against infection (but often limited in the number of diseases which they will control), have together made the control of black currant diseases today a complicated and costly business. The situation pertaining now is in marked contrast to that in the early 1950's, when leaf spot was controlled by post-harvest copper sprays and losses due to mildew and *Botrytis* were negligible. The difference lies in the reliance now placed, not on prevention, but on cure. To place the greatest possible emphasis on the removal of as many sources of inoculum between one season and the next is unquestionably the most rational approach to the problems of disease control. Much can be achieved in this direction by the commercial grower by the use of sprays and by avoiding procedures which increase the likelihood of adding to the overwintering inoculum, but the gardener can obtain considerable benefit from the use of secateurs and a rake. In addition, by preventing bushes from becoming thick with excessively vigorous growth, and by a careful selection of more resistant cultivars, the fruit grower can expect to obtain further benefits.

The biology and control of leaf spot, mildew and *Botrytis* on gooseberry and red and white currant bushes need only a brief mention. The effect of infection by all three fungi is generally more severe on gooseberry than on currant bushes. Leaf spot causes gooseberry leaves to turn yellow and fall much more readily than is the case with currants; mildew infects the fruit, causing blemishes which lower the quality of the berries and *Botrytis* frequently invades the shoots and branches, causing a die-back and the death of the bush. In other respects, the life histories of the fungi are so little different from those described above that the same principles can be applied for their control.

REFERENCES

BAUER, R. 1955. Resistance problems in the genus *Ribes* and possibilities of their solution by making intra- and inter-specific crosses. *Proc. 14th Int. hort. Congr., Scheveningen*, Vol. 1, pp. 685–696.

CORKE, A. T. K. 1954. Black currant leaf spot: I. Studies of perennation and infection. *Rep. Long Ashton Res. Stn 1953*, pp. 154–158.

CORKE, A. T. K. 1960. Black currant leaf spot: treatment of overwintered leaves with fungicides: summary of experiments 1953–59. *Rep. Long Ashton Res. Stn 1959*, pp. 118–122.

CORKE, A. T. K. 1962. Black currant leaf spot: spray trial 1959–1961. *Rep. Long Ashton Res. Stn 1961*, pp. 144–153.

CORKE, A. T. K. 1963. Black currant leaf spot: supplementary note on 1959–61 spray trial. *Rep. Long Ashton Res. Stn 1962*, pp. 103–105.

CORKE, A. T. K. 1965a. Experiments on the control of *Botrytis* on black currants. *Proc. 3rd Brit. Insectic. Fungic. Conf., Brighton*, pp. 150–153.

CORKE, A. T. K. 1965b. American gooseberry mildew on black currants. *Proc. 3rd Brit. Insectic. Fungic. Conf., Brighton*, pp. 336–339.

CORKE, A. T. K. 1966. Black currant leaf spot: summer spray trials, 1959–1964. *Expl Hort.*, Vol. 15, pp. 71–76.

CORKE, A. T. K. and JORDAN, V. W. L. 1966. Observations on American gooseberry mildew on black currants. III. Preliminary experiments on control by spraying. *Rep. Long Ashton Res. Stn 1965*, pp. 184–192.

GILCHRIST, A. J. and COLE, R. J. 1971. Control of diseases of soft fruit and other crops in the United Kingdom with thiophanate methyl. *Proc. 6th Brit. Insectic. Fungic. Conf., Brighton*, pp. 332–340.

JORDAN, V. W. L. 1967. A study of the American gooseberry mildew on the black currant. *M.Sc. Thesis, University of London.*

JORDAN, V. W. L. 1969. The control of American gooseberry mildew on black currants. *Proc. 5th Brit. Insectic. Fungic. Conf., Brighton*, pp. 127–129.

MINISTRY OF AGRICULTURE, LONDON. 1971. Agricultural Statistics 1968/69. HMSO, London.

MINISTRY OF AGRICULTURE, LONDON. Horticultural Crop Intelligence Reports.

SALMON, E. S. 1908. The American gooseberry mildew attacking red and black currants. *Gdners' Chron.*, Vol. 44, p. 203.

WILSON, D., CORKE, A. T. K. and JORDAN, V. W. L. 1964. The incidence of leaf spot and mildew on black currant seedlings. *Rep. Long Ashton Res. Stn 1963*, pp. 74–78.

Highbush Blueberries—A New Fruit for Europe

J. G. D. LAMB

Kinsealy Research Centre, Dublin

THE blueberry belongs to the same botanical family as the heathers and rhododendrons (Ericaceae) and to the same genus (*Vaccinium*) as the bilberry. In north America several species grow wild, and two groups of these are important commercially. The low-bush group, as the name implies, are of low growing habit, resembling in stature the bilberry, but are more productive as the fruits are borne in clusters. No named cultivars have been propagated for commercial planting, but the wild stands are very valuable, especially as a source of fruit for processing. These lowbush fields are carefully managed by a system of rotational burning over to renew the growth and to kill back invading weeds and scrub. Some 100,000 acres of lowbush blueberry land is managed in this way in U.S.A., the lowbush species growing within a wide area from Maine to Minnesota, south to West Virginia, with a substantial acreage in Canada.

It is highbush types, however, that have responded to cultivation and improvement to a spectacular degree. These are derived from two main species, *V. australe* and *V. corymbosum*. These wild progenitors of the modern highbush cultivars grow further south, in southern Michigan and along the eastern seaboard from Maine to the borders of Florida. The bushes grow from four to twelve feet high, carrying the berries in large clusters (Fig. 49). Initially, selected wild bushes were brought into cultivation at the beginning of the century, and in 1909 Dr F. V. Colville of the U.S. Department of Agriculture initiated a breeding programme. So responsive was the blueberry that by the time of his death in 1937 fifteen improved cultivars had been introduced and named. These efforts have been continued by his successors, so that today leading cultivars bear fruit far larger and better than the wild types (Fig. 48). This is very rapid progress compared with the centuries of cultivation of our more familiar soft fruits.

Today blueberry growing is a multi-million dollar industry in America, there being upwards of 23,500 acres of the cultivated high-bush types alone. It might have been expected that blueberries would be popular in Europe too, but only in recent years has an interest been taken in this crop, with pioneer growers in West Germany, Holland and Britain. Experimental stations in several countries are conducting trials and it is likely that this fruit will be increasingly cultivated on this side of the Atlantic.

There are, however, a number of restraints which prevent its success in many districts. The blueberry is demanding in its soil requirements.

Unless the soil is acid, with a pH of below 6, the bushes will not thrive. Planting stock is still scarce and expensive in Europe. Rabbits and hares will devour the young bushes unless the field is fenced in. Birds will eat the ripening berries, and a small planting must be netted if any fruits are to be harvested, just as with a small strawberry plantation. On the positive side the crop ripens in August and September when the other soft fruits are over; the berries are easy to pick, no topping and tailing is required as for gooseberries, nor strigging as for currants. A skilled picker can pick straight into the punnets in which the fruit will be marketed, leaving the stems behind. The berries have a long shelf life, about five days without refrigeration, and their resemblance to bilberries makes an intensive promotional campaign unnecessary for their acceptance by consumers. The high cost of establishment can be offset by the long life of a plantation, thirty years or more.

In Ireland a trial on blueberry culture has been cropping since 1963 (Table 1). This plantation was established on a heavy loam soil (pH 4·5)

TABLE 1. Crop yields of nine blueberry cultivars (lb per bush, average of 12–15 bushes)

Cultivar	1963	1964	1965	1966	1967	1969	1970	1971	1972
Bluecrop	<0·5	2·9	6·4	5·1	6·9	9·6	10·7	13·9	18·5
Berkeley	0·5	2·2	4·4	5·6	6·3	8·7	13·6	9·2	18·5
Dixi	0·5	1·6	3·2	5·0	6·3	7·9	7·7	8·1	11·6
Coville	0·5	1·5	2·4	4·3	4·7	6·2	6·9	8·2	12·2
Blueray	<0·5	0·5	1·4	0·6	1·6	4·5	3·2	3·8	9·9
Jersey	0·5	1·7	2·8	2·8	1·6	4·2	eliminated from trial		
Herbert	<0·5	0·9	2·1	2·2	3·7	3·9	4·7	3·3	6·9
Earliblue	0	0·5	1·1	0·5	1·6	2·7	3·2	3·3	6·6
Weymouth	0	0·5	1·2	0·5	0·5	1·0	eliminated from trial		

at Johnstown Castle, Wexford, not a soil that might have been thought suitable in view of the high organic matter in the sandy loams associated with good blueberry plantations in such areas as New Jersey. Undoubtedly, success has been aided by mulching with sawdust, a common practice in U.S.A. From the yields obtained it is evident that the cultivars 'Bluecrop', 'Berkeley' and 'Dixi' are the most productive of those in the trial. The first two of these ripen from the first days of August to mid September. 'Dixi' extends the season, usually being in full pick a fortnight later than the others (i.e. at the beginning of September). Though the picking season extends over some weeks, the berries hang well on the bush and it is usually sufficient to pick once or twice a week to harvest the full crop.

Twelve to eighteen pounds per bush is indeed a remarkable yield, but it must be emphasized that the plantation is netted in to exclude birds. The yields on a field scale remain to be determined, but if they were half the experimental yield they would still be well above the average American yield of 3 to 3½ tons per acre.

In taste panel assessments carried out at Kinsealy over three seasons 'Bluecrop' and 'Herbert' received a high flavour rating whether in fresh, canned or frozen form. It is fortunate that the well flavoured 'Bluecrop' has also been the highest yielding cultivar. Meanwhile development of new cultivars continues energetically in U.S.A. Observation of some of these in our conditions indicates even better blueberries in the future. 'Darrow', for example, is remarkable for the size of the fruit and promises to be productive.

The growth and cropping habit of the blueberry is to produce very vigorous shoots from near the base of the bush or from ground level. These fruit on side shoots in the second and succeeding years, but gradually become more twiggy in character, with smaller fruits more irregular in ripening. Hence good cropping depends on the production of vigorous replacement shoots through good manuring and pruning practices.

Work in America indicates that nitrogen is the principal nutrient required. As the soil in the experimental plot at Johnstown Castle has medium to high levels of available potassium and phosphorus, the annual routine has been to apply 1 to 2 oz of sulphate of ammonia each year when the bushes are in bloom, since extension growth does not start until after flowering. The sawdust mulch has been topped up as required to maintain a depth of about one inch. When sawdust is applied care is given to ensure that the higher rate of nitrogen fertilizer is recommended. Our pruning practice has been to leave the bushes alone for the first two years after planting, then to cut out from one to three or four of the oldest shoots with their twiggy side branches in winter, cutting back to where a vigorous shoot springs or else to ground level. Branches too close to ground level are also removed.

The only disease that has been troublesome so far is die-back of shoot tips during winter, often associated with *Botrytis* infection. This disease also is seen on growing shoot tips and flowers during cool damp spells. However, the yields shown in Table 1 have been obtained despite this infection. The bushes have been less prone to the conditions as the plantation gets older. More recently trials have indicated that spraying with benomyl early in the season could be an effective control should *Botrytis* become severe. It is important, however, to space the bushes widely to admit sun and air. American recommendations are for a spacing of 10 by 5 feet. Growth in our trial has been such that at least an extra two feet between the rows would be necessary.

Propagation of the blueberry is by cuttings. Our experience has been that hardwood cuttings, the usual American method, are slow to root and slow to get away afterwards. Better results have been obtained from using soft cuttings of the side shoots, taken as soon as they can be handled in April or May. Cuttings rooted early have time to make growth before winter, whereas late struck cuttings may fail to over-winter. Mist propagation is successful, though the cuttings deteriorate if not rooted quickly and removed as soon as possible. Rooted cuttings in a more satisfactory condition are obtained when a sheet of light gauge plastic is substituted for the mist spray as the means of main-taining turgor in the plant material. It is important to give the young plants good growing on conditions, e.g. in a frame of fertilized peat.

Production on a commercial scale will be a job for the specialist, willing to invest relatively heavily in the necessary fencing and planting costs and prepared to cope with the bird problem. Further developments may well be largely on acid peat soils. Very recent plantings have made a good start on such peats in Ireland. Experience has shown that weeds can be controlled with simazine and chlorthiamid. In U.S.A. harvesting machines are already in use, though in their present form they are only economic on substantial acreages. In the meantime the interested amateur may well experiment, if necessary making up a bed of suitable soil, and protecting the bushes against birds with netting. We have obtained good results from bushes planted in peat to which John Innes base fertilizer has been added at 5 lb per cubic yard. On the other hand, if rhododendrons flourish in the garden, this is an indication that the blueberries will succeed in a sunny spot. It should be clear that like any cultivated fruit they need pruning and feeding if they are to yield good crops of acceptable fruit.

Dessert Grapes for the Amateur

H. R. YOUNGMAN
Cambridge

T HE vines in our small garden (Youngman, 1960; 1970) have increased from one in 1951 to thirty-one now. We moved house, taking rooted cuttings with us, in 1965. At present we have twenty-two cultivars, so in most cases there is only one of a kind.

SITE

The ground is level and occasionally becomes waterlogged. The open-air and cloched vines are in an area that has been raised nine inches above the general level; enough to make a big difference, as we have observed with other plants that hate bad drainage, such as lilies. The vine beds in the greenhouse are 3 feet above ground level.

At English latitudes summer warmth and maximum exposure to the sun are of the first importance for vines. All the plants are now on or near our south boundary which runs due east and west. They face an open field and get all the sun there is. Buildings and hedges shelter them from the north and east. The ones in open air have no protection from the prevailing south-west wind, which is often violent but seldom cold in the growing season. Sixteen vines are in the open, eight in cloches, six in a cool and one in a warm greenhouse.

Three experiences illustrate the importance of site:

1. A 'Siegerrebe' vine was planted near our north, solid fence, receiving sunshine all the morning but after midday in the shadow of trees. Soil and drainage conditions were good, but it grew poorly and bore no fruit in its fourth or fifth year. A cutting from it, planted under the south wall of a friend's house which was in sunshine most of the day, grew vigorously and in its fourth year ripened several good bunches of fruit at the end of August.

2. A 'Cambridge' vine, trained espalier fashion on the south wall of our former house, in 12 years developed a permanent framework with 140 feet of bearing wood which was allowed to carry over 200 bunches each year. A cutting from this vine was rooted in 1963 to grow on to a pergola, part of the new house. Unavoidably it had first to be trained to the top of a 9-foot wall in the shade. Growth has been very slow; only in the winter of 1971–72 had a good woody trunk been built up to the beams and the sunshine. The green growth of 1972 bore the first bunch of fruit after nine years.

3. 'Russell Street' is a white grape which we found in a cottage garden in a hot, sunny site surrounded by brick walls. It was

producing in total neglect the largest berries and bunches we have seen growing outdoors, fully ripe in October. We planted a cutting here, still in full sun but in a more exposed site, to be trained up the south side of the pergola. It has grown and fruited with the same vigour as before, but the splendid bunches hanging from the beams are too late to ripen.

SOIL AND FEEDING

The soil is heavy, pH 8·0, with pure clay as subsoil. At the start we were advised that vines do best on a poor soil—for example, on stony hillsides—because their vegetative growth always has to be restricted to divert their vigour to development of fruit. Shortly after this we watched terraced vineyards in Switzerland being irrigated with floods of liquid manure from the winter quarters of dairy cattle. We have taken more and more to generous feeding. The leaves are large in consequence, and the growth of stems and laterals (only to be pinched back repeatedly) more lush, but the fruit also is larger and better. The past year is representative: in November a layer of farmyard manure was spread to 4 feet distance around the outdoor and the cloched vines. In January each vine received 5 oz of Growmore fertilizer with an extra two ounces of potassium sulphate, spread over the same area. One or two which had not seemed as vigorous as the rest in 1971 were also given 5 oz of ammonium sulphate. In late spring a mulch of garden compost was spread. Throughout the growing season the plants are sprayed fortnightly with Maxicrop. Some occasionally show signs of chlorosis, which is corrected by adding 2% of magnesium sulphate to the spray.

The vine beds in the greenhouse were made with a mixture of two parts garden topsoil, one part peat and one part gravel up to 1 inch in size. To this was added John Innes Base, ½ lb per bushel. The beds are periodically top-dressed with the same mixture. The same foliar feeds are given as to the outside vines.

WATERING

The vines give no visible sign of water-shortage in drought periods. All the same when other plants in the garden look thirsty and the soil is dry 2 or 3 inches down we do water the vines with a Supplex hose. A rough experiment using metered water indicates that this year the ground for 4 feet each side of the vines has received 8 inches of extra water in this way.

TRAINING AND GENERAL MANAGEMENT

Open air. Our south boundary is a fence of steel posts and strained wires; we are fortunate in being allowed to trespass on the field outside it. Of the vines in the open, five are trained on the fence, using the Double Guyot method of replacement pruning (Brock 1961; Pearkes, 1969), each plant having a span of 5 feet. Two stand in a flower-bed and have 2-foot trunks carrying six fruiting canes at the top. These droop in the shape of an umbrella frame and are stopped at 3 feet. In winter they are pruned to short spurs. Five more vines are grown with a permanent framework in the shape of a T, the trunk being kept bare and the horizontal part, 12 feet long, spur-pruned. These five overlap each other to form a living trellis filling a reactangular arch. Finally the remaining four open-air vines are growing on to a pergola 14 feet square; one cane will be carried along each beam and spur-pruned.

The cloches (Fig. 50). Eight vines grow in a row of cloches made from standard Dutch lights. In the illustration the lights can be seen to rest on retaining brackets fixed to a wooden frame 6 inches high and 18 inches wide. Each pair is held against the fence-posts by a spring and hook, leaving a 2-inch gap at the top. Any light can be lifted off after releasing one spring hook. Note the bottom ventilation slot on the south side of the frame.

Experience suggests it would be an improvement to make the box 12 inches high and 24 inches wide.

Each double-Guyot-pruned vine, like those in the open, has a 5-foot span (Fig. 51). The bearing canes are tied to a wire 12 inches from the ground. The fruiting laterals and the replacement shoots for next year grow up and through the gap at the top of the cloche. Their tips are pinched out when they have grown another eighteen inches. A certain amount of tying-in is done to keep them in an orderly row. All sublaterals inside the cloche are rubbed out. Outside, sublaterals and sub-sublaterals are stopped at one leaf. The fruit hangs warm in the cloche, protected from bad weather and not overcrowded by foliage.

The lights remain in position all the year. The bottom ventilation slots are closed only from March until the danger of frost is past. In summer the temperature in the cloches can rise to well over 100°F even with shading. Both cloches and greenhouse have to be shaded on the south side to prevent scorching of the grapes. For this we use washable distemper of the off-white tint called 'haze', four heaped tablespoons to a pint of water. It sticks well until the autumn and then is easy to wash off.

The greenhouse. No detail will be given here as there are many authoritative accounts of greenhouse vine management (Parsons, 1955). Like most amateurs we have to depart from the ideal, in that the greenhouse is packed with miscellaneous half-hardy and tender plants in winter. Because of this a minimum temperature of 35°F is maintained in the cooler part of the house and 50°F in the warmer. This does not seem to prevent the vines going sufficiently dormant to be pruned at the turn of the year. We lengthen the grape season at both ends by having in the greenhouse an early variety, 'Pearl of Czaba' and one, 'Mrs Pince' which can usually hang safely until Christmas.

The grapes of all our vines, except 'Slade Blue' and 'Riesling Sylvaner' when it is to be kept for wine, are thinned drastically when they are the size of peas, and again later if any threaten to press tightly together (Baker and Gilbert 1972). This allows the remaining fruit to develop to a good dessert size and the free circulation of air through the bunch as its ripens discourages *Botrytis* infection and allows penetration of fungicides.

We have learnt to vary the number of bunches per plant according to variety; for example the prolific hybrid 'Schuyler' does best when allowed to retain two or three bunches per shoot, a total of 25 or 30 small bunches being usual. 'Muscat Queen' is at the other extreme; as the bunches develop it is best to remove all but four or five of the largest. 'Muscat Hambro' has borne as many as 14 bunches, 12½ lb of fruit, on its 5 feet of cane without suffering any harm.

PESTS AND DISEASES

Mildews, powdery and downy. Briefly: assuming that mildew can be prevented but not cured, we give one treatment when the buds have burst and three or four more during the season. Whenever karathane is prepared for the apples and pears we spray the vines with it too. Alternatively we powder with a mixture of two parts bordeaux, one part flowers of sulphur—best done when the leaves are damp. We have seen mildew only when this programme has been neglected.

Botrytis has appeared in some of the bunches in greenhouse or cloches, especially if inadequately thinned, every year. A small fan continuously running in the greenhouse has probably reduced the amount of infection; so have bottom ventilation of the cloches and powdering the bunches with captan, but it still occurs.

The new fungicide benomyl has been shown to control *Botrytis* on a wide range of crops. It becomes systemic only in soft plant tissues such as young shoots. Used early in the season it may have an adverse effect on growth. It has no influence on downy mildews. (Statements at Long Ashton and Fison's Levington Research Stations.) On July 31, 1972, at the first sign of *Botrytis*, our vines were sprayed with benomyl. This was repeated on September 14. Up to the time of writing, September 27, no more *Botrytis* has been seen. We shall try it again next year. It will be necessary at the same time to use a copper compound or some other fungicide against downy mildew. We hope to find one which can be mixed with Benlate.

Phylloxera. Our vines are on their own roots. The opinion is gaining ground that ungrafted *vinifera* vines in Britain cannot long escape the fate that overtook them abroad. The method of grafting vines on a phylloxera-tolerant stock is called by the French "la greffe anglaise";

it is pleasant to hear that at least one English nurseryman has begun to apply the technique in its country of origin. Meanwhile imported grafted vines are available, retail and wholesale.

Birds, wasps and flies devour grapes with such enthusiasm that in a year when we gave the fruit no protection not one berry was left in the garden. The bottom ventilators of the cloches and greenhouse are netted and so far the birds have not ventured through the top openings. We do our best to find and destroy wasp nests, and have had some success with poisoned baits, designed not to trap or kill at once but to be carried back to the nest. The best is the syrup in which ginger has been preserved, mixed with BHC powder. But in most seasons we have to use the only method of total control: bags made from nylon stockings are drawn over the bunch and each side of the shoot from which it hangs, twisted at the top and secured with a clothes-peg. This material has the great advantage over muslin that it dries rapidly and does not cling.

CULTIVARS

The following list contains the cultivars we are now growing. Some are quite young plants. Several kinds which were recommended for open-air cultivation have been given up because they proved too late to be reliable in our conditions, or because of poor flavour. Those marked ● constitute a short-list of the ones we have had for several years and found to be the best for flavour, size of fruit, reliable ripening and regular cropping.

In the open
'Cambridge': see also page 167. In our present garden we have no sunny wall for a vine. It remains to be seen whether this variety will ripen regularly without that advantage.
● 'Chasselas Rose Royale': a pretty, pink grape, berries ¾ inch, round, with a good non-muscat flavour, ripening here every year during October.
'Marshal Joffre': small black non-muscat. Said to be very vigorous. Young plant, no fruit yet.
'Noir Hâtif de Marseille': this would have been starred but for the fact that this year and last, the weather being cold and dull when it was in flower, the set was extremely poor. In 1970 it produced good bunches of ⅝-inch, round grapes with an outstanding, slightly muscat flavour, ripe at the end of September. It would probably set better with cloche protection.
'Oliver Irsay': white muscat; young plant, no fruit yet.
● 'Pink Strawberry'; without the leaves, almost indistinguishable from 'Chasselas Rose'; but has a refined form of the American "strawberry" flavour which we and most of our visitors enjoy.

Ripens October or early November and stands up well to deteriorating weather. We have seen this cultivar standing with clean leaves and fruit among other neglected vines which were grey with mildew. (The *black* grape usually supplied under the name 'Strawberry' proved too late to ripen in the open here.)

'Pirovano XIV': black, non-muscat but rich flavour; but is another example of a kind which flourished on a hot wall; in a more exposed position, though still in full sun, has grown and cropped poorly.

'Précoce de Malingre': white, good non-muscat flavour; highly recommended as prolific and early when we planted it six years ago, but has produced only a few ounces of grapes so far.

'Russell Street': see also page 167. Having seen this variety doing so well elsewhere we shall try it again nearer the ground or in a cloche.

'Siegerrebe': see also page 167. A deep golden grape with excellent muscat flavour; berries $\frac{3}{4}$ inch long. The earliest variety we have grown. Fruit on the favourably sited specimen already mentioned was picked for wine-making on September 17, 1972; fruit sugar-sweet, S.G. of juice 1,085.

'Stapleford': another white grape from a local garden, similar to 'Russell Street' but not so large. Heavy crops, ripe late October.

'Seyve-Villard 5.276': primarily a wine grape; white, fair dessert flavour, ripe late October.

Under cloches

'Muscat de St Vallier': white. Young plant, no fruit yet.

● 'Muscat Hambro': see also page 173. Not to be confused with 'Black Hamburgh'. A classical black muscat which takes well to the cloche environment, crops heavily there and ripens within the month of October. Berries $\frac{7}{8}$ to 1 inch long. Every amateur should plant this variety, and harvest grapes more delicious than money can buy.

'Muscat Queen': see also page 173. Yellow grape, 1 inch, excellent flavour. Rather prone to "shanking"—shrivelling of the stems of individual berries preventing them from ripening.

'Riesling Sylvaner': three plants of this white grape are grown in cloches, mainly for a wine-making friend. They produced 19 lb of fruit in 1970 and 9 lb in 1971; and in 1972 there were 25 lb. Pleasant to eat early in October. In 1970, when left to hang in the cloches, warm and protected, until October 31, the fruit became wrinkled, dull-coloured and sugary—the Noble Rot that delights the maker of wine.

'Schuyler': see also page 170. An American hybrid, rich but with only a trace of "strawberry" taste. Black round $\frac{1}{2}$-inch berries, ripe early September. Like 'Noir Hâtif' it sometimes sets poorly; this is probably helped by cross-pollination from other cultivars—stroking the flower-bunches with the cupped hand. Formerly grown in open air without much success.

Cool section of greenhouse
'Black Strawberry': moved from open air to greenhouse for further trial; no fruit yet.

● 'Mrs Pince': black muscat, ripe in October, which will hang in good condition for several weeks.

● 'Muscat Hambro' and 'Muscat Queen': ripe two to three weeks earlier than in the cloches.

'Pearl of Czaba': an early white muscat, grown outdoors south of London. Crop often poor, but we keep it because it gives our first grapes, in July or August, and for the sake of of its particularly delicate flavour.

'Slade Blue': large bunches of small, black seedless grapes, sweet in September. Usually dismissed as a useless variety. We leave it unthinned and find it pleasant to eat straight from the bunch like sweet-corn. The lazy man's grape.

Warm section of greenhouse
● 'Muscat of Alexandria': delicious, translucent and yellow when fully ripe. Demands luxury treatment; best when only 5 bunches left on its 9 feet of bearing cane. Drastic thinning, allowing for berries to grow to $1\frac{1}{4}$ inches.

REFERENCES

BROCK, R. B. 1961, 1964. *Rep. Vitic. Res. Stn, Oxted*, Nos 3, 4.
BAKER, H. and GILBERT, E. G. 1972. Apricots, Peaches, Nectarines, Figs and Grapes. *Wisley Handbook 8, R.H.S.*, London.
PARSONS, H. 1955. *Grapes under Glass*. Collingridge.
PEARKES, G. 1969. Growing Grapes in Britain. Amateur Winemaker Publications, Andover, Hants.
YOUNGMAN, H. R. 1960. Vines in the Open Air. *J. Roy. hort. Soc.*, Vol. 85, p. 186.
YOUNGMAN, H. R. 1970. Fruit Growing in a Small Garden. *J. Roy. hort. Soc.*, Vol. 95, p. 171.

The Fruit Section of the International Society for Horticultural Science

F. R. TUBBS

Chairman I.S.H.S. Fruit Section

THE *Sections* of the Society are those devoted to broad groups of horticultural plants, i.e. fruit, vegetables, and ornamentals; the *Commissions* of the Society deal with specialized scientific or technical aspects of horticulture in general of wide interest irrespective of groupings of horticultural crops appropriate to the Sections. Thus initiative and study of any particular aspect can be undertaken by Section or Commission as appropriate, joint membership and liaison ensuring fruitful collaboration.

In any international body of expertise with widely distributed membership, successful collaboration depends on an informal and flexible organization and, equally, upon ready co-operation and mutual assistance. Such qualities enable wide delegation, again on an international basis. Within the Sections, *Working Groups* with defined subjects or objectives are set up by recommendation of the Section and approval of the ISHS Council. The method of working is as varied as are the Working Groups. It is normally based upon the organization of one or more international symposia and the publication of proceedings, collected information, lists of research workers etc. Recently parallel symposia organized jointly in America and in Europe, with exchange of observers, have been used to avoid difficulties of finance and of travel inseparable from large international events. Working Groups are normally set up for the four-year interval between major International Congresses of Horticulture, the function of each being reviewed afresh at each Congress and at meetings of the Section between Congresses. Working Groups such as those on raspberries and cherries have, after successful functioning, been dissolved but can always be reformed. Others extend their field of responsibility while a few, e.g. the Working Group for Nomenclature and Registration of Fruit Cultivars, under J. M. S. Potter, O.B.E., V.M.H., have a continuing task.

The Working Groups of the Fruit Section at present are as follows: apricots and apricot culture: nomenclature and registration of fruit cultivars: plum genetics and plum breeding: blueberry and cranberry culture in Europe: mango and mango culture: pears and pear culture: viticulture in south-east Asia: growth regulators in fruit crops: high density planting. The width of outlook and effectiveness of these Working Groups is steadily being enhanced, not only by the participation of an ever-increasing list of member countries, e.g. from south

America but also by the operations of the Commission for Tropical and Sub-tropical Horticulture.

Membership of the ISHS embraces research workers, advisory officers, teachers and practical men. The fruits of their co-operation and interchange of experience are in augmenting the continuous flow of improvements and adaptations of horticultural practice to meet man's developing knowledge of the fruit plant and of methods of controlling its cultural environment. One pertinent example springs at once to mind in the identity of the Chairman of our Fruit Group with that of the Chairman of the ISHS Working Group for Nomenclature and Registration of Fruit Cultivars—need more be added?

INDEX

(compiled by Patricia Rowe-Dutton)